Eccentric California

THE BRADT GUIDE

PUBLISHER'S FOREWORD

The first Bradt travel guide was written in 1974 by George and Hilary Bradt on a river barge floating down a tributary of the Amazon. In the 1980s and '90s the focus shifted away from hiking to broader-based guides covering new destinations – usually the first to be published about these places. In the 21st century Bradt continues to publish such ground-breaking guides, as well as others to established holiday destinations, incorporating in-depth information on culture and natural history with the nuts and bolts of where to stay and what to see.

* * *

I lived in San Francisco between 1967 and 1969. In those heady days of 'flower power', we thought our city was entirely normal – in a trend-setting sort of way – but looked across the bay for the truly weird. 'Beserkeley', we called it. Residents sported bumper stickers proudly proclaiming 'Berkeley, the open ward'. I remember watching a girl hitchhiking on one of the leafy roads near the University of California campus. A car stopped, she spoke briefly to the driver to check where he was going, untied a goat which was hidden in the bushes, popped it in the back seat and climbed in after it. Wonderful!

Berkeley students may be a little more conventional these days, but California is still gloriously off-beat and still, of course, considers itself perfectly normal. Who better to chronicle its oddities than Jan Friedman, a Californian whose *Eccentric America* has won just about all the guidebook awards going, as well as catching the attention of the US media? Jan has such an eye for eccentricities she even thinks England is pretty weird. Now that is peculiar.

Hilary Bradt

23 High Street, Chalfont St Peter, Bucks SL9 9QE, England
Tel: 01753 893444 Fax: 01753 892333
Email: info@bradtguides.com
www.bradtguides.com

Eccentric California

Jan Friedman

Bradt Travel Guides Ltd, UK
The Globe Pequot Press Inc, USA

First published August 2005

Bradt Travel Guides Ltd
23 High Street, Chalfont St Peter, Bucks SL9 9QE, England
www.bradtguides.com
Published in the USA by The Globe Pequot Press Inc,
246 Goose Lane, PO Box 480, Guilford, Connecticut 06437-0480

British Library Cataloguing in Publication Data
A catalogue record for this book is available from the British Library

ISBN-10: 1 84162 126 9
ISBN-13: 978 1 84162 126 5

Photographs
Front cover Harrod Blank, www.artcaragency.com (MondrianMobile © Emily Duffy,
www.braball.com)
Back cover Harrod Blank, www.artcaragency.com (Pico De Gallo, photo by Hunter Mann)
Text Harrod Blank/www.artcaragency.com (HB), Gregory Cox (GC), Margot
Duane/www.planetmargot.com (MD), Brandi Easter (BE), Jan Friedman (JF), Bob Hale
(BH), Larry Harris (LH), Mark Hundley (MH), Paradiseranch.com (PR), Keith Sutter
(KS), Dr Wilkinson's Hot Spring Resort/www.drwilkinson.com (DW)

Illustrations Dave Colton, www.cartoonist.net
Maps Alan Whitaker

Typeset from the author's disc by Wakewing, High Wycombe
Printed and bound in Spain by Grafo S.A., Bilbao

Author

Jan Friedman has spent most of her life in the San Francisco Bay Area where, she says, 'they take their eccentricity very seriously'. A travel writer, photographer and former tour guide, she explored 56 countries before discovering that her very own could offer as much adventure as the most exotic foreign locale. She is the author of the national edition of *Eccentric America*, winner of three book awards including the prestigious Lowell Thomas award for travel journalism.

DEDICATION

This book is dedicated to delightful deviates everywhere who make the world a saner and more interesting place.

Contents

Acknowledgements

I can't imagine how I would have completed this book without the help of my tireless assistant Katherine Meusey, who put in months of work chasing down new oddities and fact-checking all the entries. It certainly helps that she's a great fan of weirdness and can sniff out a potential entry anywhere it might be lurking.

Initially, dozens of tourism bureaux were involved in this project, suggesting sites, confirming details, obtaining photos, marking maps, and providing travel assistance during research trips. Barbara Steinberg from the California Travel and Tourism Commission was especially helpful as was the Travel Industry Association of America (TIA). Once word got out, however, it was an ever-evolving network of informants, many alerted to my quest by the *Eccentric America* website, which provided the leads that resulted in so many of this edition's entries. I'm so grateful for their interest and participation.

Naturally, there are many others I'd like to thank: Amy Rennert, my agent; Hilary Bradt, Tricia Hayne, Adrian Phillips, Debbie Everson and the rest of the staff at Bradt Travel Guides in the UK; Theresa Eldridge and the staff at Globe Pequot in Connecticut; Alan Whitaker for creating the maps; Elaine Petrocelli and all the mentors at the Book Passage Travel Writers' Conference who so willingly share their skills and encouraging words with aspiring writers; Bill Bryson, Dave Barry, Jill Conner Browne, Carl Hiaasen, P J O'Rourke, Doug Lansky, Tim Cahill and David Sedaris, famous writers who, unbeknownst to them, inspire me to ever quirkier heights; and, finally, to my dear friends and family who by now are used to my breathless requests, 'Ya gotta read this, you won't believe it!'

Special thanks to:
Enterprise Rental Car for their continued support of *Eccentric America* and *Eccentric California*

and

The Red Lion Hotel in Eureka for their kind and convenient accommodations during the Kinetic Sculpture Race

and

The Foghorn Harbor Inn in Marina Del Rey for their hospitality during my Venice Beach explorations

Preface

ECCENTRIC CALIFORNIA: THE AUTHOR'S VIEW

I've lived in Northern California most of my life. While I accept that we're 'different', I never really understood why the rest of the country thinks we're so weird. Until now, that is. Darting up and down the state, looking at us through tourist eyes, I've come to see what is obvious to non-Californians: we're one strange bunch. Not that that's a bad thing, mind you. Every society needs a fringe and we serve the country admirably in that regard.

I used to think of us as a fairly homogenous group, united in our well-meaning, if naïve, political interests and in our relentless pursuit of the perfect latte. But once I got beyond this stereotype, venturing into regions new to me and meeting people that don't live within a short drive of some sparkling body of water, I found a surprising range of viewpoints and lifestyles that run the gamut from beyond-belief-bizarre to red-state conservative. No wonder our politics are ridiculed, our self-centeredness mocked, our legislature mired in conflicting interests. This place is simply too huge and too varied to ever be effectively represented by a single point of view.

Prior to writing this book, my perspective was that of most San Franciscans: 'We're perfectly normal. It's those self-centered, shallow, roller-blading, star-worshiping, surgically enhanced nut cases down south that give the state a bad name.' Ask Angelinos, though, and they'll snort that we Northerners are a bunch of tree-hugging, hybrid-driving, Birkenstock-wearing, liberal, elitist intellectuals who take ourselves way too seriously.

Still, we're of one mind, one soul, when it comes to our unshakable belief in the future. We're endlessly optimistic, certain we're leading the way to a better life for all humanity. And you can be sure of one thing: we won't be shy when it comes to sharing our quirky opinions.

Jan Friedman
June 2005

ECCENTRIC CALIFORNIA: A RESEARCHER'S VIEW

When I announced that I was moving to San Francisco, my mother was appalled. To this Midwestern woman, who thought Haight Ashbury was a park, nothing could be more improbable short of relocating to Sweden. At least in California, I pointed out, they spoke the language.

Little did I know that thousands of miles away a similar conversation was taking place in the UK between the woman who would become my mother-in-law and the man who would become my husband. She could not see the point of leaving London to move halfway across the world to California. I mean, *California*.

Never mind that both my husband-to-be and I had lived in various locations in our respective countries and were both well traveled. The point was that we were moving to California where, as my mother-in-law Sheila pointed out, 'they're all a bit...weird'.

But you see, that is the point. California is weird, and so are many of the people who live here. You'd think that would make researching *Eccentric California* easy, but that's what made it a challenge. Just being weird isn't enough.

The one thing the people in this book share is a unique way of expressing their love of something strange. Whether it's showing visitors San Francisco in a fire engine, decorating their car with Pez dispensers, or mooning Amtrak trains en masse, they're having fun doing it and they want to share it. There's a sense of irreverent fun that permeates a lot of the state, and in many ways, a sense of pride in their ability to do so.

So I hope you enjoy discovering eccentric California as much as I have. I think you'll find that it's a deeply quirky place steeped in weirdness, just as my mother feared. And I wouldn't have it any other way.

Katherine Meusey lives in northern California with her husband, a French Bulldog called Fester, and an ever-changing collection of permanent and foster cats. She's an aspiring librarian and bibliophile with a nose for the off-kilter. Her mother has since seen Haight Ashbury and thinks it would do better as a park.

Introduction

THE NATURE OF CALIFORNIA ECCENTRICITY

Defining eccentricity is like defining beauty – it all depends on who's doing the judging. But for the one-in-eight Americans who live in California, the strange and the weird is just business as usual, so defining it here becomes somewhat problematic. By definition an eccentric is someone whose behavior varies wildly from the norm and, in most cases, society is a pretty good judge of who earns such a title and who doesn't quite make the grade. But in a state where eccentricity hardly registers on anyone's consciousness, in a state where it could be said that most everyone's behavior varies widely from some norm or another, it's hard to know whom to trust with the gavel.

California is a place where much of the population is considered off-kilter by many Americans not living there. Not that this bothers them much as they revel in the uniqueness of their collective eccentricity. Indeed, they consider themselves to be the envy of eccentrics the world over. They're just following their bliss, allowing themselves the freedom to behave in ways that most of us would find odd or scary. They're quite blessed, really, since they don't care what others think, only needing to live up to their own expectations to be happy. They have absolute faith that their way is the right one and if you can't see the light, well … it's your loss.

In order for eccentricity to flourish, people need the right set of circumstances, most importantly, freedom of speech and a culture that encourages individual expression without fear of negative consequence. California is such a place, a healthy society that thrives on a variety of ideas, including the far-fetched and extreme. And no wonder. America itself was founded by malcontents who resisted authority and social constraints. Anxious to seize their own futures, our founders embarked on a quest for a better life, one of self-determination and self-actualization. When the societies they'd formed became too structured, the most adventurous among them again headed west, and the cycle was repeated over and over until such rugged individualists could go no further. California became the promised land, and it remains so to this day, filled with a never-ending flow of dreamers and achievers. Former President Ronald Reagan accurately dubbed it, 'the land that never became, but is always in the act of becoming'.

California likes to think of itself as the 'I told you so' state, always first to think up unconventional ideas like Frisbees, Barbies, motels, skateboards, hula hoops, ant farms, drive-in churches, popsicles, Levi's, McDonald's, fortune cookies, and the Jacuzzi. By the time the rest of the country enthusiastically embraces their cutting-edge concepts, the trend is already over in California, even if it just surfaced yesterday. They're also first with more serious concerns, incubators of environmental and political issues that often seem absurd at first (and sometimes for decades) until the time is ripe and some Washington politician adopts a previously ridiculed crusade as his own.

It's no surprise that eccentricity flourishes in such an environment of individualism and creativity as California enjoys. Eccentrics are non-conformists, rejoicing in being different. They're highly creative, motivated by curiosity, and often idealistic, just wanting to make the world a better place through their contributions. By choosing to behave unconventionally, and by not needing reinforcement from others, they enjoy a freedom that eludes most of us. Happily indulging their obsessions, they'll persist at whatever makes them happy regardless of what society may think. Opinionated and outspoken, eccentrics think that if you'd just come around to their way of thinking, you'd be as happy as they are. They'll bend your ear for hours if you'll let them, going on and on about the virtues of their passion, be it collecting hubcaps, protecting some disadvantaged species, or building a three-story mountain in God's honor out of hay, adobe, window putty and old paint. By filtering out what is inconsequential to them, they're free to focus, usually obsessively, on their peculiar pursuit. For them, happiness is the light at the end of a funnel.

THE NORTH VS THE SOUTH

You'll undoubtedly notice major differences – other than the weather – between northern and southern California. The Bay Area is known for its politically active and self-styled cultural elite while Los Angeles is famous for its style-setting and pop-culture divas. For years there have been proposals floating around, some serious, some tongue-in-cheek, to divide the state in half, the reasoning being that the two regions are just so far apart politically that the government's infamous legislative gridlocks will never be resolved as long there's only one governor. The liberal Bay Area, politically marginalized, idealistic, and stubborn, is so out of step with the rest of the state that the most progressive among them apologize to foreigners for being American. They're like a nation unto themselves, a city-state with their own radical-chic culture and eccentricities.

Meanwhile, primarily conservative southern California is on a very short cultural fuse, reinventing itself almost daily. They have a 'look at me, aren't we quirky' mentality that both shocks and delights tourists. The eccentricities you'll find there are obvious and meant to be observed, purple hair, nose rings and the like. Northern Californians, on the other hand, practice a quieter, gentler eccentricity by simply going about their business, not caring much whether you notice how strangely they're behaving. Their weirdness is much less 'in your face' than that of their southern neighbors whom they basically consider plastic and shallow anyhow. Says one Berkeley man with contempt, 'You can always tell if a woman's from southern California – she's shaves her legs.'

Beyond the entries in this book, finding the eccentricity *du jour* is a matter of positioning yourself so as to watch weirdness unfold before your eyes. Experiencing eccentric California is much more than a guidebook and a map. It takes conscious awareness of what is going on around you, eavesdropping on snippets of conversation and paying attention to the kinds of businesses, décor, clothing and hairstyles you find in any particular neighborhood. Above all, it takes an open mind, one willing to explore the endless possibilities that this most welcoming and addictive of states has to offer.

Guide to the Guide

THE ECCENTRIC YEAR
Here you'll find a month-by-month summary of all the festivals and events covered in the guide along with the page on which you can find the entry itself.

THE REGIONS
Geographically speaking, the state is divided into seven regions. Touristically speaking, however, fully half of the book originates in the San Francisco and Los Angeles areas, with a total of 85% taking place in the coastal regions. This explains why you've probably never heard of weird goings-on in Fresno or Visalia.

CATEGORIES
Deciding where to put all 475 entries in *Eccentric California* wasn't easy, especially since many of them could fit into multiple categories. Nonetheless, here's a brief description of the type of eccentricities you can expect to find in each category:

Festivals and events
With almost 100 events celebrated annually in the state, there's hardly a dull moment, festivally speaking. Most of the festivals, celebrations, and events are based on politics, pop culture, eccentric lifestyles, or on themes created simply as a reason to have fun. In this category you'll discover where (and, perhaps, why) folks gather to moon Amtrak trains, race worms and banana slugs, compete for pillow fighting or faux drag queen titles, hold an Urban Iditarod, or honor weeds and tarantulas with festivals of their own.

Peculiar pursuits
These are strange activities pursued by others, or activities that you can pursue yourself, should you be so inclined. For example, this is where you can indulge your desire to perform on the high wire or the flying trapeze, attend a cowgirl boot camp with your mother, or join the rock/paper/scissors movement. You'll also learn about the artist in residence at the San Francisco dump and a church that worships John Coltrane.

Museums and collections
Throughout California you'll find quirky museums and halls of fame proudly displaying the odd and curious, the result of years spent amassing some mighty strange and bewildering collections that have usually been the focus of their founders' lives. The range of California collectibles includes asphalt, celebrity lingerie, Pez containers, hand fans, yo-yos and 'proof' of Bigfoot. Americans are among the world's most skilled and prolific collectors, sometimes creating objects just for the sheer joy of collecting them.

Eccentric environments

'Outsider artists', those with no formal art training who become obsessed with creating one specific kind of art, are responsible for the eccentric environments described here and California is home to more such environments than any other state. In this category you'll find things like a colorful, three-story mountain made of hay, adobe and old paint, a house made of bottles, an underground garden, and an opera house so remote that the owner had to paint an audience on the walls.

Often these creations are the result of a syndrome dubbed concretia dementia, an excessive compulsion to build using whatever materials are readily available, usually concrete, bottles, cans, scrap metal, and other industrial and household junk. This dementia most often strikes people in their later years. The majority of eccentric environments you can visit here were built in the early and mid 1900s, before the advent of drugs to control compulsive behavior. Today, if one of your relatives started building a concrete and scrap-iron tower in your backyard, you'd have them on Prozac – and in a Lazy-Boy – in no time, squelching their propensity to turn your home into a tourist attraction.

Quirkyvilles

Quirkyvilles are towns with a twist, places with some strange claim to fame that sets them apart from the mundane. Whether it's a town that speaks its own language, a living ghost town, or one that passes absurd laws in the hopes of changing American culture, these hotbeds of quirk are worth a detour, if only to find out what on earth their citizens are thinking.

Tours

Big cities like Los Angeles and San Francisco can best be appreciated by taking tours, especially of – and by – the offbeat. Listed are dozens of tours led by knowledgeable guides who are themselves interesting characters or are leading a tour that fits the eccentric theme. You can ride an antique fire engine across the Golden Gate Bridge, tour Muir Woods with a comic political activist, ride the dunes in a Humvee, or walk the streets with a certified ghost hunter.

Odd shopping

Californians rank among America's best when it comes to shopping and our gift shops are famous for catering to tourist whims as well as to whims you never knew you had. Among the bizarre offerings you'll find is Skeletons in the Closet, the Los Angeles Coroner's Office gift shop; a place manufacturing the 'paraphernalia of conjure' for all your spell-casting needs, and shops selling everything from new clothes for dogs to used clothes for humans that have been previously worn by movie stars.

Quirky cuisine

Memorable for their quirky character, these restaurants are included not for the quality or price of their food, but rather because they provide an entertaining eating experience. They also give you an alternative to the utter predictability of America's chain restaurants. Most of these establishments are run by highly individualistic people or by corporations who know how to make eccentricity pay. You can dine surrounded by 105 aquariums or by 9,000 neckties, eat Manchurian ants sprinkled on potato strings, order take-out barbeque at an auto repair shop, or watch artists do their work while you're eating.

Rooms with a skew

Entries for these four-dozen quirky quarters include a faux safari, converted rail cars, over-the-top fantasy theme rooms, a former hospital B & B, and entire ghost towns. Like the eating establishments above, you can expect to find some very out-of-the-ordinary individuals behind those front desks as well as some very out-of-the-ordinary experiences.

Attractions

Kitschy, kitschy koo. Here you'll find offbeat and wacky attractions like weird buildings, strange amusements, and the kind of kitsch roadside for which California is famous. While some are professionally designed and managed, others are homemade and funky. Among them you can feel music as it moves over, under, and right through you or enjoy one man's idea of a Playland-Not-at-the-Beach.

Just plain weird

This catch-all category describes people or places that defy labeling, although it could be said that most of the entries in this book could fit in this category. So, if a listing doesn't fit naturally into one of the other categories, or, if it has a multiple personality, it ends up here.

Quirk alerts

These are entries worthy of extra attention, either because the story is just too weirdly wonderful to be missed or because it's a not-to-be-forgotten eccentricity that no longer exists. Most of them are of the 'You just won't believe this' variety.

Statewide quirks

This chapter covers activities taking place throughout the state, put on by varied groups devoted to peculiar pursuits such as canine freestyle dog dancing, competitive eating, art car caravans, historical re-enactments, and earth-bound explorations of Mars.

KEEPING CURRENT

Keeping up with eccentric Californians can sometimes be problematic. The weather, politics, or the news can affect their moods and they may change their hours abruptly. Festival organizers may be overly optimistic about their chances of remaining 'annual'. From time to time, eccentric attractions just up and vanish, their quirky legacies left to languish from inattention. That said, it's worth putting up with some unpredictability to experience the unique and entertaining qualities these oddballs have to offer.

While travel and contact details were current at press time (spring 2005), inevitably some of it will become out of date. That doesn't mean the activity or attraction no longer exists, though. It may have moved, changed contact numbers or websites, been renamed, or been taken over by someone new. An online search or a conversation with neighbors often turns up current information. It may take a bit of sleuthing on your part to find these wayward entries, but you'll usually be rewarded for your efforts. If nothing else, you might meet some budding eccentrics along the way.

Check out **www.eccentricamerica.net** for regular updates to this guide.

MAPS AND ADMISSION CHARGES

You may need supplemental road **maps**, as those in this book won't always provide the detail you need to find out-of-the-way places. When you get near your destination, especially to those way off the beaten path, ask a local to direct you the rest of the way. Most of the entries in this guide are well known to those who live in the area although, occasionally, you may need to ask several people along the way.

Unless otherwise noted as 'Free', you can expect an **admission charge** that varies according to age and season.

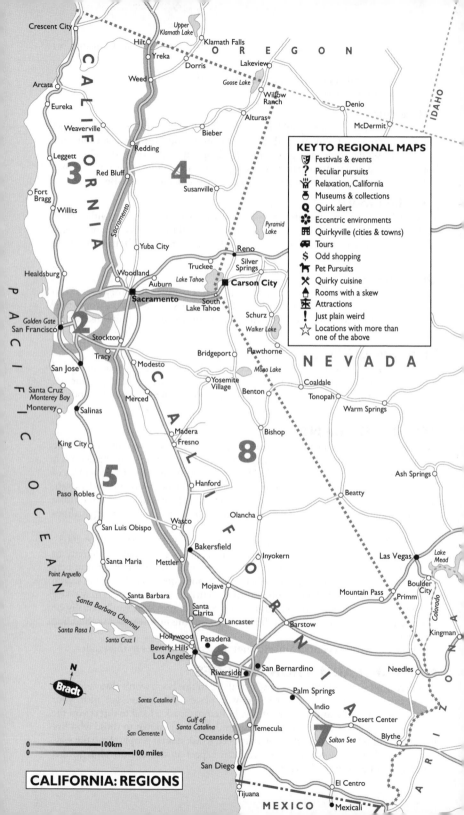

KEY TO REGIONAL MAPS

- 🏰 Festivals & events
- ❓ Peculiar pursuits
- 💆 Relaxation, California
- 🏺 Museums & collections
- Q Quirk alert
- ❋ Eccentric environments
- 🏢 Quirkyville (cities & towns)
- 🚌 Tours
- $ Odd shopping
- 🐾 Pet Pursuits
- ✕ Quirky cuisine
- ⛺ Rooms with a skew
- ✳ Attractions
- ! Just plain weird
- ☆ Locations with more than one of the above

N

Bradt

0 _____ 100km
0 _____ 100 miles

CALIFORNIA: REGIONS

The Eccentric Year

JANUARY

Historic Longboard Revival Series Ski Races, Blairsden
www.easternplumaschamber.com (page 73)
Huntington Beach Pier Polar Plunge, Huntingdon Beach (Jan 1)
www.hbvisit.com/events/index.html (page 113)

FEBRUARY

Banana Slug Derby, Crescent City www.northerncalifornia.net (page 51)
Chinese New Year's Treasure Hunt, San Francisco (Jan/Feb)
www.sftreasurehunts.com (page 12)
Crab Races, Crescent City www.northerncalifornia.net (page 51)
Hysterical Walks, Sacramento www.hystericalwalks.com (page 77)
National Date Festival and The Blessing of the Dates, Riverside www.datefest.org (page 145)
SPAM Festival, Isleton www.isletoncoc.org (page 74)
Valentine's Day Sex Tour, San Francisco www.sf200.org (page 28)

MARCH

Bark & Whine Ball, San Francisco www.sfspca.org/barkandwhine (page 16)
Nuts for Mutts Dog Show, Woodland Hills www.nutsformutts.com (page 132)
Pi Day, San Francisco (Mar 14) www.exploratorium.edu/ (page 7)
Swallows Week, San Juan Capistrano www.missionsjc.com (page 108)
Urban Iditarod, San Francisco www.urbaniditarod.com (page 17)

APRIL

Pacific Coast Dream Machines, Half Moon Bay
www.miramarevents.com/dreammachines (page 86)
Pegleg Smith Liars' Contest, Borrego Springs (page 143)
San Francisco Earthquake Commemoration Ceremony (Apr 18) (page 15)
St Stupid's Day Parade, San Francisco (Apr 1)
www.saintstupid.com/parade.htm (page 17)
Teddy Bear Convention, Nevada City (Apr 1–3) www.teddybearcastle.com (page 71)

Memorial Day Weekend

Horned Toad Derby, Coalinga www.coalingachamber.com (page 86)

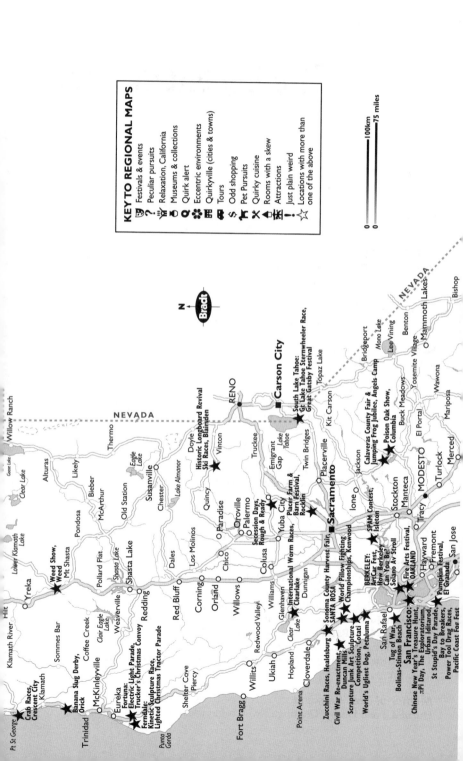

KEY TO REGIONAL MAPS

- 🎪 Festivals & events
- ❓ Peculiar pursuits
- ☝ Relaxation, California
- 🏛 Museums & collections
- ❓ Quirk alert
- ✿ Eccentric environments
- ⊞ Quirkyville (cities & towns)
- ⛪ Tours
- $ Odd shopping
- 🐾 Pet Pursuits
- ✕ Quirky cuisine
- 🛏! Rooms with a skew
- ! Just plain weird
- ☆ Locations with more than one of the above

0 ————— 100km
0 ————— 75 miles

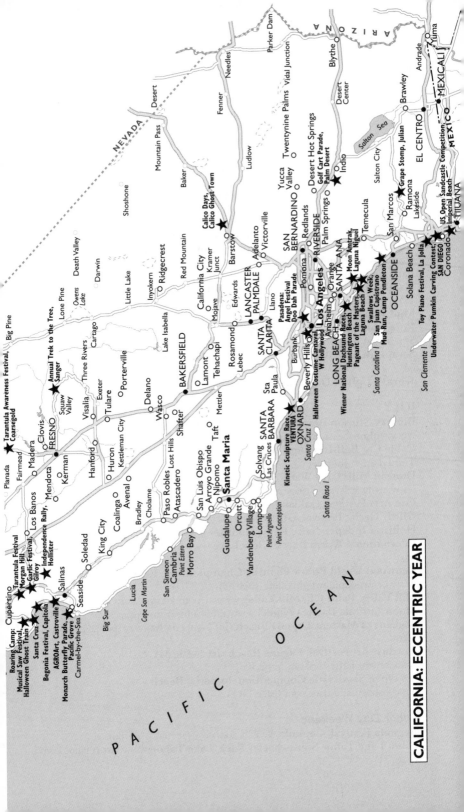

CALIFORNIA: ECCENTRIC YEAR

MAY

AGROArt, Castroville www.artichoke-festival.org (page 74)
Bay to Breakers, San Francisco www.baytobreakers.com (page 11)
Calaveras County Fair and Jumping Frog Jubilee, Calaveras County www.frogtown.org. Third weekend in May (page 161)
Carnaval, San Francisco www.carnavalsf.com (page 14)
Coyote Howl, Coulterville Third weekend in May (page 163)
How Weird Street Faire, San Francisco www.howweird.org (page 12)
Kinetic Sculpture Race, Ferndale www.kineticsculpturerace.org (page 49)
Power Tool Drag Races, San Francisco www.qbox.org (page 15)

JUNE

Absolut Chalk, Pasadena www.absolutchalk.com (page 112)
Big Dog Parade and Canine Festival, Santa Barbara www.bigdogs.com/bigdogclub/bdfoundation.asp (page 89)
Faux Queen pageant, San Francisco www.klubstitute.com (page 14)
Haight-Ashbury Street Fair, San Francisco www.haightstreetfair.org (page 17)
Mud Run, Camp Pendleton www.camppendletonraces.com (page 143)
Rough and Ready Secession Days www.roughandreadychamber.com. Last Sun in Jun (page 73)
Scrapture Junk Art Sculpture Competition, Cotati www.garbage.org (page 53)
World's Ugliest Dog, Sonoma www.sonoma-marinfair.org (page 54)

JULY

Bolinas–Stinson Beach Tug of War, Bolinas & Stinson Beach (Jul 4) www.stinson-beach.org (page 52)
Cable Car Bell-Ringing Contest, San Francisco www.cablecarmuseum.org. Third Thu in Jul (page 7)
Duncan Mills Civil War Re-enactment, Duncan Mills www.civilwardays.net (page 53)
Fire Arts Festival, Oakland www.thecrucible.org (page 53)
Gilroy Garlic Festival, Gilroy www.gilroygarlicfestival.com (page 86)
Hollister Independence Rally, Hollister www.hollisterrally.com (page 87)
International Worm Races, Clear Lake www.clearlakechamber.com (page 53)
Kenwood World Pillow Fighting Championship, Kenwood (Jul 4). www.kenwoodpillowfights.com (page 58)
Mill Valley Paint Off, Mill Valley www.depotbookstore.com (page 52)
Moon Amtrak, Laguna Niguel www.moonamtrak.org (page 104)
pageant of Masters, Laguna Beach (Jul 1–Aug 31) www.foapom.com (page 105)
Sawdust Art Festival, Laguna Beach (Jul 1–Aug 31) www.sawdustartfestival.org (page 108)
US Open Sandcastle Competition, Imperial Beach www.usopensandcastle.com (page 146)

Labor Day Weekend

Begonia Festival, Capitola www.begoniafestival.com (page 88)
Great Lake Tahoe Sternwheeler Race, Lake Tahoe www.virtualtahoe.com (page 71)

AUGUST

Banana Slug Derby, Orrick www.parks.ca.gov/?page_id=415. Third Sat in Aug (page 71)
Great Gatsby Festival, Tea, and Fashion Show, South Lake Tahoe (Aug 14–15) www.tahoeheritage.org (page 71)
Home Movie Day, San Francisco www.sfm.org (page 10)
Musical Saw Festival, Roaring Camp www.sawplayers.org (page 85)
pageant of Masters, Laguna Beach (Jul 1–Aug 31) www.foapom.com (page 105)
Sawdust Art Festival, Laguna Beach (Jul 1–Aug 31) www.sawdustartfestival.org (page 108)
Toy Piano Festival, La Jolla. www.orpheus.ucsd.edu/music/ (page 145)
Zucchini Races, Healdsburg (page 59)

SEPTEMBER

Art Car Fest, Berkeley www.artcarfest.com (page 40)
Folsom Street Fair, San Francisco www.folsomstreetfair.com (page 14)
Ghirardelli Square Chocolate Festival, San Francisco www.ghirardellisq.com (page 7)
Gold Rush Days, Sacramento www.oldsacramento.com (page 74)
Grape Stomp, Sonoma www.sonomavinfest.org (page 54)
Gravity Festival, San Francisco www.cora.org/sfgf.html (page 10)
How Berkeley Can You Be? Parade and Festival, Berkeley www.howberkeleycanyoube.com (page 40)
Julian Grape Stomp, Julian www.julianca.com (page 145)
Kinetic Sculpture Race at Ventura www.kineticrace.com (page 111)
Lobster Festival, Redondo Beach www.lobsterfestival.com (page 111)
Pacific Coast Fog Fest, Pacifica www.pacificcoastfogfest.com (page 87)
Poison Oak Show, Columbia www.columbiagazette.com/poison.html (page 164)
Port of Los Angeles Lobster Festival, San Pedro www.lobsterfest.com (page 110)
Solano Avenue Stroll, Berkeley www.solanoavenueassn.org (page 41)
Sonoma County Harvest Fair, Sonoma www.harvestfair.org (page 55)

Columbus Day Weekend
Calico Days, Calico www.calicotown.com (page 161)

OCTOBER

Angel Festival, Sierra Madre www.theangelfestival.com (page 112)
Burning Man Decompression, San Francisco www.burningman.com/blackrockcity_yearround/special_events/decompression/index.html (page 10)
Calaveras Grape Stomp, Murphys www.calaveraswines.org (page 163)
Exotic Erotic Halloween Ball, San Francisco www.exoticeroticball.com (page 16)
Floating Homes Tour, Sausalito www.floatinghomes.org (page 52)
Half Moon Bay Pumpkin Festival, Half Moon Bay www.miramarevents.com/pumpkinfest (page 86)
Halloween Costume Carnaval, West Hollywood www.visitwesthollywood.com (page 104)
Halloween in San Francisco (page 14)

Love Parade, San Francisco www.loveparadesf.org (page 16)
Monarch Butterfly Parade, Pacific Grove www.pacificgrove.org (page 87)
Placer Farm & Barn Festival, Rocklin www.placerfarmandbarnfestival.com
(page 74)
Roaring Camp Railroad Halloween Ghost Train, Roaring Camp (Oct 31)
www.roaringcamp.com (page 85)
Tarantula Awareness Festival, Coarsegold www.coarsegoldchamber.com
(page 164)
Tarantula Festival, Morgan Hill www.coepark.org (page 88)
Underwater Pumpkin Carving Contest, San Diego
www.oceanenterprises.com. End of Oct (page 147)
Wiener National Dachshund Races, Huntingdon Beach
www.oldworldvillage.net (page 112)

NOVEMBER

Doo Dah Parade, Pasadena www.pasadenadoodahparade.com (page 108)
Palm Desert Golf Cart Parade, Palm Desert www.golfcartparade.com (page
145)
Trannyshack, San Francisco www.heklina.com (page 14)
Weed Show, 29 Palms www.msnusers.com/29palmshistoricalsociety (page 147)

DECEMBER

Ferndale Lighted Christmas Tractor Parade, Ferndale (Dec 14)
www.victorianferndale.org/chamber/ (page 59)
Fortuna Electric Light Parade, Fortuna (Dec 12)
www.chamber.sunnyfortuna.com (page 58)
Santa Paws, San Francisco www.sfspca.org (page 11)
Trek to the Tree, Sanger www.sanger.org. Second Sun in Dec (page 163)
Trucker's Christmas Convoy, Eureka (Dec 13) www.eurekachamber.com
(page 59)

AND KEEP IN MIND . . .

Urban Golf Association's Bi-Annual Emperor Norton North Beach
Open, San Francisco www.urban-golf.org. Various times throughout the year
(page 18)

San Francisco Bay Area

SAN FRANCISCO
Festivals and events

Not surprisingly, Ghirardelli Square, formerly home to the famous chocolate factory, is home of the **Ghirardelli Square Chocolate Festival**. The highlight of the affair is the 'hands-free' Earthquake Sundae-Eating Contest in which contestants plough face first into giant sundaes made with eight scoops of various ice-creams smothered with eight different toppings. The winner takes home his or her weight in Ghirardelli chocolate. Kids have their own version of the contest, with the winner getting an entire basket of chocolate.

> **Ghirardelli Square Chocolate Festival** takes place at Ghirardelli Square in September. Ghirardelli Sq, 900 North Point St, San Francisco, CA 94109; ✆ 415 775 5500; www.ghirardellisq.com. Free. Directions: Ghirardelli Sq is on North Point St between Beach and Larkin.

Part of the charm of San Francisco's cable cars is the sound of their clanging bells, rung manually by the cable car conductor as they make their way up and down the city's steep hills. Each conductor develops their own style when it comes to ringing, and the **Cable Car Bell-Ringing Contest** has been a showcase for their talents for decades. Now a San Francisco tradition, the contest began in 1955 as a way to promote the cable cars as a tourist attraction after the newly elected mayor saved the system from extinction. Today entrants include cable car crew members, retired bell-ringing champions, celebrities, and non-profit organizations. Some champions, who admit to practicing on cable car bells at home, have won the title multiple times. There's a free cable car museum at the cable car barn at Washington and Mason Streets.

> **Cable Car Bell-Ringing Contest** takes place on the 3rd Thursday in July in Union Square. Contact the Cable Car Museum, 1201 Mason St, San Francisco, CA 94108; ✆ 415 474 1887; www.cablecarmuseum.org.

Even if you aren't big on math, you've *gotta* love Pi. Pi is the number you get when you divide the circumference of a circle by its diameter: 3.1415926535 . . . ad infinitum. Pi has a cult following in the math world, and San Francisco's Exploratorium throws a party every March 14 to celebrate this mathematical marvel. Officially known as **Pi Day**, this celebration combines math with the more familiar comforts of freshly baked pie. Lots and lots of pie. The festivities commence, as they should, at exactly 1.59pm, ensuring that the event appropriately honors Pi by taking place on the third month, the fourteenth day, at 1.59pm. In

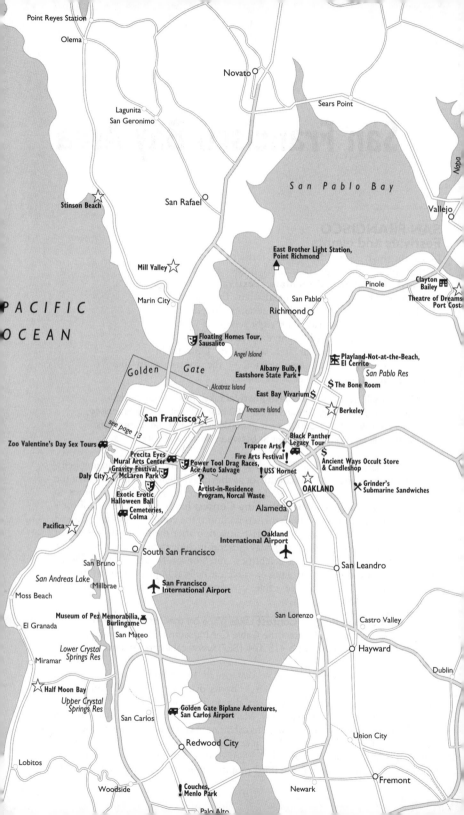

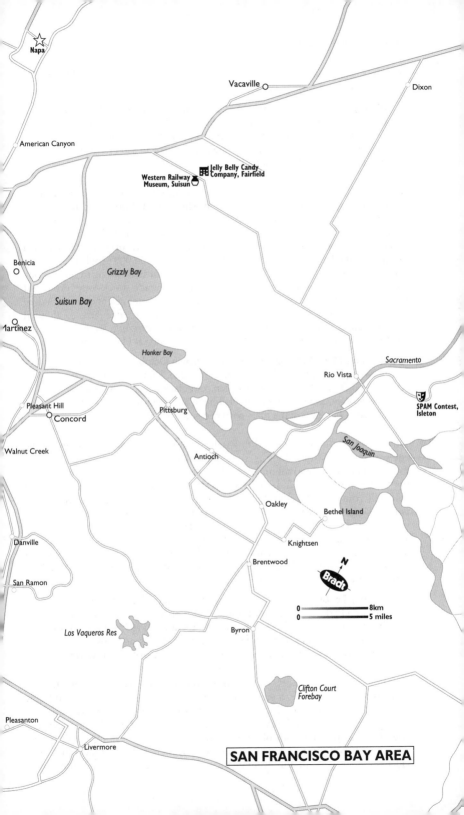

Napa

Vacaville

Dixon

American Canyon

Jelly Belly Candy Company, Fairfield

Western Railway Museum, Suisun

Benicia

Grizzly Bay

Suisun Bay

Martinez

Honker Bay

Sacramento

Rio Vista

SPAM Contest, Isleton

Pleasant Hill
Concord

Pittsburg

Walnut Creek

Antioch

San Joaquin

Oakley

Bethel Island

Danville

Knightsen

San Ramon

Brentwood

N

Bradt

0 ——————— 8km
0 ——————— 5 miles

Los Vaqueros Res

Byron

Clifton Court Forebay

Pleasanton

Livermore

SAN FRANCISCO BAY AREA

addition to eating pie, revellers can view the museum's 'Pi Shrine', add beads to a 'Pi string', listen to various Pi speakers, and maybe even catch a Pi-inspired film.

> **Pi Day** takes place on March 14 at the Exploratorium in San Francisco. Contact the Exploratorium, 3601 Lyon St, San Francisco, CA 94123; Ø 415 EXP LORE; www.exploratorium.edu. Directions: the Exploratorium is in the Palace of Fine Arts building in San Francisco's Marina district, just off Marina Blvd.

Some of what makes Burning Man so visually compelling can be seen at **Burning Man Decompression**, the annual **Heat the Street Faire** that follows the Nevada extravaganza by about a month. Famous for its large-scale art installations, theme camps, performance art, art cars and people dressed in the most peculiar of fashions, the mother party spawns this final chance to play 'playa style', so named for the vast and barren desert location that attracts up to 30,000 people every Labor Day. Spread over a four-block area, the faire attracts 'burners' trying to eek just one more day of eccentric camaraderie out of the year's week-long event. At Decompression you'll see bits and pieces of the flamboyant celebration, including some very provocative art, interactive performances, fire artists, themed environments, multi-media Burning Man images, amazing art cars, and the strangest assortment of costumes this side of the Castro at Halloween.

> **Burning Man Decompression** takes place in October on Indiana St, between Mariposa and 21st St in San Francisco. Contact Burning Man; ➤ 415 TO FLAME; www.burningman.com/blackrockcity_yearround/ special_events/decompression/. Half-price admission with a Burning Man costume. Directions: the main entrance is at 19th and Minnesota.

Why anyone would want to hurl themselves – at up to 60mph – down one of the city's steepest, twistiest hills is something that only competitors in the San Francisco **Gravity Festival** understand. Mounting their skateboards, street luges, buttboards, inline skates and gravity-speed bikes, they hurtle down a hay bale-lined half-mile course in McLaren Park to earn International Gravity Sports Association points. Launch rules vary and they're not known for their gracefulness. Street lugers begin by paddling crab-like 20ft before taking off; gravity bikes launch with a kick, bobbing and weaving until riders manage to get control. The stand-up downhill skateboarding is perhaps the most thrilling event, as well as the one most unforgiving of errors. All the events take nerves of steel, youthful bravado, and the ability to pretend that spills don't hurt.

> **Gravity Festival** takes place in September on John F Shelley Dr in McLaren Park. Contact the California Outdoor Rollerskating Association, Explorer Post #582, San Francisco, CA; ➤ 415 752 1967; www.cora.org/ sfgf.html. Directions: the entrance to McLaren Park is on Mansel St. From Hwy 101 in San Francisco, take the Paul Ave exit and head west.

San Francisco has its very own **Home Movie Day**, sponsored by the San Francisco Media Archive, a group that acquires, preserves and screens old home movies. Unlike commercial movies, home movies are an accurate record of our history, viewed through the eyes of the people who lived it. On home movie day you're invited to bring your old movies to the center for cleaning, repairing and screening. If you want to donate your movies to their archives, they'll make free videotapes for you. In the evening they showcase charming and entertaining examples of life as it was in the 30s through the 60s. Stephen Parr, director of **Media Archive**, also gives occasional weekend showings of some of the 50,000 offbeat films he's amassed over the last 20 years. Recent programs included Crash Cinema, an evening of police training and car crash clips, and Sex and Drug Cinema with historical/hysterical sex and drug scare films. Reservations recommended.

> **Home Movie Day** is usually held the second week in August. San Francisco Media Archive, 275 Capp St, San Francisco, CA 94110; ☎ 415 558 8117; www.sfm.org. Check the website for film screenings.

Santa Paws is a holiday tradition at the San Francisco SPCA. This too-cute-for-words event, during which pets can have their pictures taken with Santa, takes place in early November so their proud Mommies and Daddies will have plenty of time to mail out their holiday cards. There are a number of photo ops from which to choose, including two different backdrops, a choice of posing in costumes or going it *au naturel*, and posing pet-only or with their people. A Furry Merchants' Corner and a middle school band playing Christmas music keeps patrons entertained while waiting their turns. Proceeds go to the SPCA.

> **Santa Paws** happens at the San Francisco SPCA in December. Contact the SFSPCA, 2500 16th St, San Francisco, CA 94103; ☎ 415 554 3000; www.sfspca.org. Directions: the SFSPCA is on 16th St between Florida and Alabama St.

San Francisco hosts the wildest, largest, and one of the oldest (since 1912) foot races in the world. The **Bay to Breakers** draws 75,000 to 110,000 participants, ranging from elite runners down to casual joggers as well as costumed partygoers and centipedes (groups of 13 people tethered together). While the world-class runners compete for cash prizes, the world-class party joggers vie for costume recognition. One group, calling themselves the Spawning Salmon, runs upstream against the dense waves of rushing humanity. Racers may be dressed as anything from animals and plants to landmark buildings like Coit Tower and the Transamerica Pyramid. Live bands entertain the runners and fans along the 7.5-mile route, with the elite runners leading the pack followed by serious, then not-so-serious joggers. The 'Back of the Pack' is a special section for walkers and baby strollers.

You'll see a lot of political statements among the costumed runners along with a few expressing themselves by wearing nothing at all. Every year there are around 200 naked runners, some of whom compete bravely as members of the 'Bare to Breakers'. (Bare members get their own commemorative pins although wearing them during the race is problematic. According to official police policy, clothes must be donned at the finish line but this rule isn't always strictly obeyed.) After the race the party moves to the **Footstock Festival** at the Polo Field in Golden Gate Park. Prizes are awarded for the best costumes at the 4-mile mark of the 7.5-mile course. Don't even think about driving in the city on Bay to Breakers Sunday as the course cuts across the entire city, from the Bay to the ocean, and traffic is chaotic. Special public transportation is scheduled to handle the hordes.

> **San Francisco Bay to Breakers Race** is held annually in May in San Francisco, CA. Contact Bay to Breakers at ✆ 415 808 5000; www.baytobreakers.com. Registration required. Directions: the race starts at Embarcadero and Spear and finishes at the ocean side of Golden Gate Park. Footstock Festival immediately follows the race at the Polo Field in Golden Gate Park in San Francisco, CA.

The largest benefit treasure hunt in the country, the **Chinese New Year's Treasure Hunt** sends a sell-out crowd – 1,800 strong – through the streets of San Francisco, pursuing clues that take them right through the noisy tumult of the Chinese New Year parade. The two events, while not affiliated, take place at the same time, adding to the drama of this rigorous game of urban exploration. The hunt, encompassing North Beach, Union Square, Chinatown and the financial district, covers a one-square-mile area. Teams of four to eight players receive a packet containing elaborate clues, puzzles and riddles, all leading to mystery locations at which additional challenges need to be met. It takes about four hours to complete the adventure, with the first hour best spent in planning. Knowledge of San Francisco geography is useful but not required. Most of the clues relate to popular culture, current events, and the kind of general knowledge you haven't dredged up since college. You can register as a group or join one at hunt time.

It does help to come prepared with a flashlight, comfortable shoes, layered clothing, and perhaps a San Francisco guidebook. (The website offers suggestions as to what reference materials might come in handy as well as clues for pre-hunt research.) Some long-time players come armed with GPS systems and laptop computers. Most of the area is closed to traffic for the parade, and you'll be dashing about the districts, ducking and weaving around the parade festivities and making your way through throngs of spectators while seeking out obscure landmarks, secret views, and hidden treasures. The payoff is a memorable evening since the prize is just a bottle of champagne and bragging rights. Tickets usually sell out well in advance so it pays to pre-register.

> **Chinese New Year's Treasure Hunt** takes place late January/early February. Contact SF Treasure Hunts, PO Box 2229, Danville, CA 94526; ✆ 415 564 9400 or 925 866 9599; www.sftreasurehunts.com. Registration is required.

Howard Street becomes 'How Weird Street' during the **How Weird Street Faire**. This annual gathering of self-expressionists, a sort of springtime Halloween, turns the district into a carnival of quirkiness featuring performance art, music, dancing, shopping at the Bizarre Bazaar, and a peculiar assortment of costumes, some limited to just full body make-up. At this event the participants *become* the entertainment, performing all manner of unique self-expressions. Eccentricity is the norm, not just with the attendees but with the street vendors and artisans as well. You'll probably see stilt walkers, belly dancers, circus acts, and wandering musicians, as well as witness consciousness expanding before your very eyes.

> **How Weird Street Faire** is held in April or May from the intersection of Howard and 12th Streets through the SOMA (South of Market) district. Contact the World Peace Through Technology Organization, 150 Folsom St, San Francisco, CA 94105; ✆ 415 371 8706;

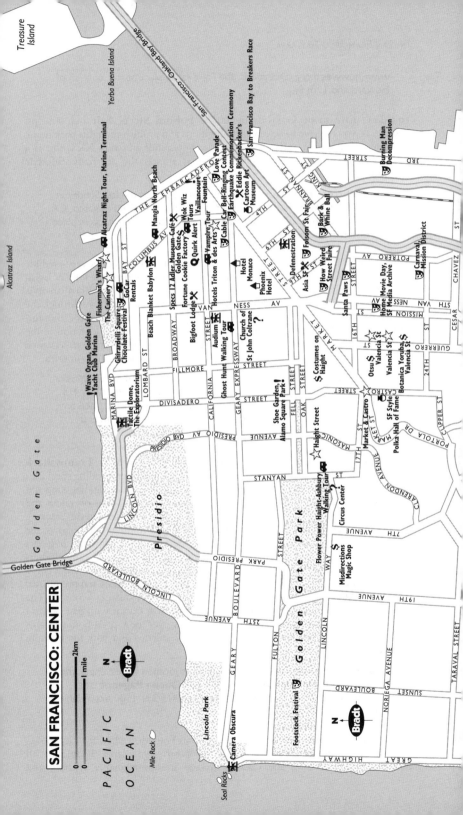

www.howweird.org. Directions: the Faire takes place at the junction of Howard and 12th St.

You don't have to be kinky to attend the **Folsom Street Fair** but it helps. Regardless, you do have to leave your inhibitions and prudish thoughts back home if you're to enjoy this outlandish spectacle. Very adult and very XXX, this is a world-class event for leather aficionados that attracts the alternative lifestyle community from all over the world.

> **Folsom Street Fair** takes place on Folsom Street on the last Sunday in September. Contact Folsom St Events, 584 Castro St, San Francisco, CA 94114; ✆ 415 861 3247; www.folsomstreetfair.com. The fair takes place on Folsom St between 7th and 12th St.

It may not be Rio, but San Francisco's Mission District puts on a very credible Brazilian-style **Carnaval** complete with a grand parade featuring the kind of lavish floats and wildly costumed dancers you'd expect to see in Rio. Brazilian-style samba contingents, some with hundreds of members, dance their way through the streets showing off production numbers they've been practicing for months. Considered the largest multi-ethnic, community-based artistic celebration in the state, Carnaval is an exuberant display of music and dance from regions as varied as the Caribbean, Mexico, Africa, Polynesia, Japan, China and South America.

> **Carnaval** takes place in the Mission District in May. Contact the Mission Neighborhood Centers, 362 Capp St, San Francisco, CA 94110; ✆ 415 920 0125; www.carnavalsf.com. Directions: the festival takes place on Harrison between 23rd and 16th St. The parade starts at 24th and Bryant, then runs along 24th St, Mission St, and 17th St.

It just wouldn't be San Francisco without events like the **Miss Trannyshack Pageant** and the **Faux Queen Pageant**. Both of these gender-bending spectacles spoof traditional beauty contests with bawdy good humor, judging drag king and queen contestants not just on style (they're loaded with it!), but on talent and personality as well. Trannyshack is a prestigious drag club considered the 'last stop of Bohemian San Francisco'. Famous for their Tuesday midnight drag shows, the club's pageant brings admirers from all over the state to see their favorite drag stars impersonate celebrities and show off their sequins and swimwear. Competition is fierce and the winners become legends. As for the faux queen event, here it gets a bit complicated as faux queens are actually women, drag queens trapped in real women's bodies who enjoy impersonating men impersonating women. The competition is open to any genetically challenged drag queen who just wants a chance to behave outrageously and dress way, way over the top. At both pageants you'll see helmet-hair wigs, feather boas, size 12 stilettos and faux fur in more combinations than you ever thought possible.

> **Trannyshack** takes place in November. The location varies; check the website for details: www.heklina.com. **Faux Queen Pageant** takes place in June at Slim's. Contact Klubstitute; ✆ 415 331 1500 ext 3438; www.klubstitute.com.

Halloween is an especially revered time in San Francisco when the city moves from weird, which is the norm, to the positively insane. People of all persuasions descend on the Castro, dressed in unimaginably creative and outlandish costumes. This is the place to see and be seen as an average of 250,000 people turn out for this major San Francisco holiday. Originally the predominantly gay Castro district was the hub of activities, but the celebration became too large to fit into the district. With the crowds now spread out between the Castro and the Mission district, it's easier to see and appreciate the artistry that's gone into the costumes. Some people spend months working on their Halloween finery and it's not uncommon to see costumes in the workplace during the days leading up to the holiday. From outrageous to flamboyant, from creative to costume-shop rentals, the scene is exuberant and, believe it or not, safe as no alcohol is allowed at the party and police are stationed at checkpoints to make sure everyone behaves.

Food booths line the streets alongside face-painting and henna-tattooing stations for those who show up sans costume. (Many feel that Halloween simply isn't a spectator sport in San Francisco.) The city has come a long way from the time in 1961 when a person could be arrested for impersonating the opposite sex. Halloween is October 31.

Halloween in San Francisco is centered around Market and Castro Streets, extending down Market towards downtown and into the Castro and Mission districts. No alcohol or weapons are allowed, so leave the devil's pitchfork at home.

The **Power Tool Drag Races** attract guys, geeks, engineers and artists in a strange event that's part science and part art. Sponsored by QBOX, an organization that encourages both established and emerging artists to create mechanical, kinetic and electronic art, the event showcases art that has absolutely no value other than its ability to entertain. You'll see all kinds of contraptions made from bits and pieces of machinery, household equipment, power tools and scrap, and the setting is most appropriate: the 75ft 'speedway' at San Francisco's Ace Junkyard. Prizes are given for the most impressive engineering, the most pathetic engineering, the most spectacular crash, the most dangerous machine and the machine most likely to get its creator laid.

Power Tool Drag Races takes place in May at the Ace Auto Salvage in the Bayside district of San Francisco. Contact QBOX; ☏ 415 307 3482; www.qbox.org. Directions: Ace Auto Salvage is at 2255 McKinnon, San Francisco (between Upton St and La Salle Ave).

The only event in San Francisco that beings at precisely 5.13am, the annual **Earthquake Commemoration Ceremony**, draws hundreds of celebrants willing to rise before dawn to remember that fateful April day in 1906 that so defined the city's history. With some dressing in period costume, they come to honor the dwindling number of survivors (just 7 in 2005) who gather at Lotta's Fountain at Market and Kearny Streets, a spot that served as a meeting place and communications center in the chaotic days following the earthquake. Another earthquake tradition is that of watching a coat of gold paint being applied to the fire hydrant at 20th and Church Streets. The pump is honored for miraculously managing to pump water after the quake, thus saving the Mission district from destruction.

Earthquake Commemoration Ceremony takes place on April 18 at 5.13am in several locations, including Lotta's Fountain at Geary, Kearny and Market Streets and 20th St & Church, the upper corner of Dolores Park.

The annual **Love Parade**, new as of 2004, is all about dancing in the streets. Originating in Berlin in 1989, this techno-music event is now hoping to make San Francisco its home. The idea is simple: DJ's, dance clubs, and bands from all over the country form a giant parade of sound system floats while attendees dance in the streets as the parade moves along its route. Disrupting traffic is nothing new to San Francisco so, if this parade finds its audience, it will be yet another reason to party and another reason not to drive in the city on weekends.

> **Love Parade** takes place in San Francisco in September/October. Contact Loveparade San Francisco, 1388 Haight St #149, San Francisco, CA 94117; ↘ 415 820 1449; www.loveparadesf.org. Directions: the parade begins at Mission St and Beale, then runs down the Embarcadero to Terry Francois Blvd.

It's *the* place to see and be seen if you're a dog in San Francisco. The SPCA's **Bark & Whine Ball** brings indulgent dog owners and SPCA patrons together for a Mardi Gras type fundraiser with everyone 'oohing' and 'ahhing' at the doggie costumes and watching carefully where they step. The dogs are all decked out in their party best (top hats, feather boas and sparkly accessories), as are their owners. A portrait photographer is on hand to capture the moment.

> **Bark & Whine Ball** takes place in March at the San Francisco Gift Center. Contact the SFSPCA, 2500 16th St, San Francisco, CA 94103; ↘ 415 522 3535; www.sfspca.org/barkandwhine. Directions: the San Francisco Gift Center is at 888 Brannan St.

Wild, infamous, and wicked, the **Exotic Erotic Halloween Ball** is one of two uninhibited celebrations of erotica in the state. Originally an underground, bizarre-erotica gathering, the ball has gone more mainstream, if you can call the world's largest and sexiest masquerade party mainstream. Fifteen thousand people attend and many spend all year planning their costumes – or lack of them, as the case may be, for this is one event at which what you don't wear is as important as what you do. The ball is ribald and carnal, a place for people of all sexes and persuasions to let it all hang out and in California that means pretty much everything. Celebrities like Nicolas Cage, Joe Montana, Madonna and Dennis Rodman lend their panache, although the event hardly needs celebrities to achieve notoriety. With $10,000 in prizes for the winners of the Mr and Miss Exotic Erotic and other costume contests, there's no shortage of shocking, electrifying creativity. Around a hundred vendors showcase the latest in erotic fashion and playthings at the accompanying Exotic Erotic Expo.

> **Exotic Erotic Halloween Ball** held annually in October at the Cow Palace in San Francisco. Contact the Exotic Erotic Ball; ↘ 888 EXOTIC6 or ↘ 415 THE BALL; www.exoticeroticball.com.

Quirk Alert

It's not illegal to perform naked yoga in San Francisco, not even at Fisherman's Wharf or at the cable car turnaround. This 2004 ruling came about as a result of charges against George Davis, the 'Naked Yoga Guy', who gives impromptu demonstrations to promote his book and nude lifestyle. 'Simply being naked on the street is not a crime in San Francisco,' said Debbie Mesloh, a spokeswoman for the district attorney's office. 'To bring a case, a person would have to exhibit lewd behavior, block traffic or impede pedestrians on a sidewalk, something along those lines.' The only charge left is that of being a public nuisance and San Franciscans consider him more like a street performer.

Around 100,000 people descend on the Haight during the annual **Haight-Ashbury Street Fair**. The fair aims to relive the district's famed 60s' heyday and Summer of Love with a laid-back, do-your-own-thing kind of feel. Reminiscently aromatic, the fair transforms the street from grungy to colorfully grungy with all manner of hippies, faux hippies and former real hippies relishing a day from the past. Music and entertainment anchor both ends of the street. For a tour of the Haight at other times, see the Flower Power tour listing.

> **Haight-Ashbury Street Fair** is held annually in June on Haight Street. Contact the Haight Ashbury Street Fair, 1621 Haight St, PMB #134, San Francisco, CA 94117; ✆ 415 863 3489; www.haightstreetfair.org. Directions: the fair takes place on Haight between Stanyan St and Masonic Ave.

Dress in costume and bring noise makers, confetti and socks to be part of the April Fool's Day **St Stupid's Day Parade** put on by the First Church of the Last Laugh. The parade, pure political satire that mocks the religion of business, has been marching through San Francisco's financial district since 1979, stopping to stage mini-events in front of public and corporate buildings. For example, the Pacific Stock Exchange is the setting for the sock exchange. Workers lean out their windows to watch as marchers pass by chanting, 'No more chanting!' and covering up the private parts of statues along the way. Past marchers include the Deep Fat Friars, a unicycle drill sergeant, and a group calling itself Save the Billionaires. The **First Church of the Last Laugh** has a website explaining its philosophy and practices. Among other things, you're encouraged to acknowledge the power of stupid in your life. Their secret handshake is a hi four: hand up, palm towards partner, fold thumb across palm, slap hi four, and then say, 'Ouch, we gotta change that!'

> **St Stupid's Day Parade** is always held at noon on April Fool's Day (April 1) in San Francisco, CA. Contact First Church of the Last Laugh; www.saintstupid.com/parade.htm.

What could be more delightfully absurd than San Francisco's **Urban Iditarod**, held the same date as the real thing up in Alaska? In the Alaskan version, dog-sled teams race across frozen tundra, risking life and limb for 1,150 miles in pursuit of fame and fortune. In this version three-dozen costumed, barking teams of humans,

many dressed like dogs, pull their shopping-cart sleds through the city's most touristy areas, making noisy and outlandish spectacles of themselves and taking mandatory 'rest' stops at local watering holes to water the dogs. The 3.5-mile course generally goes from the Market Street cable car turnaround through Union Square, up to Chinatown, through Washington Square, down to Fisherman's Wharf and along the water to Fort Mason. But then it could change given the nature of these mushers. The website posts a map of both the course and the rest stops. The event is free. If you want to participate, register through the website.

Urban Iditarod takes place in March in San Francisco. See the website for course details; www.urbaniditarod.com. Registration required to participate.

A golf club (any club will do) and a tennis ball are all you need to play in the **Urban Golf Association's Bi-Annual Emperor Norton North Beach Open**. Generally held each spring and fall, this wacky event is brought to you, not surprisingly, by the same folks who hold the Urban Iditarod. The 'course' is right in the middle of the city, nine holes and nine bars. Any place that serves liquor can be designated a hole and the course is built around getting there, hitting your tennis ball from street to street, from curb to pothole, and from tire to bus stop until you land in the hole. Wear your gaudiest golfing attire.

Urban Golf Association's Bi-Annual Emperor Norton North Beach Open is held on varying dates and locations in San Francisco. Check the website for dates and maps; www.urban-golf.org.

Peculiar pursuits

Believe it or not, the San Francisco dump has an artist in residence! One of only two such programs in the United States (the other is in New York), the residency provides workspace for up to eight artists each year at the San Francisco Solid Waste Transfer and Recycling Center, otherwise known as the town dump. While you might think this would be an easy gig to get, it's not. Dozens of artists apply each quarter for the opportunity to go to work – unpaid – in a completely empty warehouse-like space, furnishing it completely from what they can scavenge during several daily trips to the household-trash dumping site. Once they've found enough tables, chairs, shelves, and the like, they spend the next 12 weeks creating any kind of art they wish using exclusively found materials. The facility does provide certain supplies and equipment such as a kiln, welding tools, a sewing machine and a darkroom. At the end of their residency (they don't sleep at the dump, they just work there) they hold a reception at which time the public is invited to see and purchase their work.

The goal of the **Artist-in-Residence Program** is to use art to inspire people to recycle and conserve more. The artists are expected to talk to school and adult groups throughout their residency about the experience of turning trash into treasure and to make a few pieces for the company's permanent collection. Some contribute to the sculpture garden, a lush green oasis incongruously situated on the property amid the rumbling of passing dump trucks. Dump employees also have their own bizarre garden, of sorts, above the dumpsite, displaying their Tonka truck fleet, a giant tiger, a coffin, various mannequins, and anything else that they feel is deserving of display.

Most of the art ends up reflecting the political views of the artists, especially as it relates to environmental issues. Spending that much time seeing what society considers trash is bound to affect their perspective and much of the result is assemblage work, collage and mixed media. According to Sharon Siskin, in residence the summer of 2004, the most frequent categories of dumped items are photos, wallets, purses, handkerchiefs, old records, lace, cooking utensils, crutches, school texts, mirrors, and pictures of the *Last Supper*. She used these discards to make an exhibit that honored old memories while making a statement about environmental issues.

Artist-in-Residence Program Contact Norcal Waste, 1 60 Pacific Ave, Suite 200, San Francisco, CA 94111; ☎ 415 875 1205; www.norcalwaste. com/AIR/air_about_us.htm. Directions: shows of the art created by the Artists In Residence are held throughout the year. See the website for details.

Jazz lovers are familiar with the legendary John Coltrane, the jazz saxophonist who played with the Miles Davis quintet in the 50s and who later played with Thelonious Monk. But they might be surprised to learn that San Francisco claims a genuine church, the **Church of St John Coltrane**, dedicated to his memory and to his music. Holding services every Sunday morning surrounded by pictures of their saint, the congregation sways to the rhythm of the band and to the crooning of the Sisters of Compassion. The church was started by Franzo King, a former hairdresser and now Bishop King, who first heard Coltrane play in the mid 60s. So inspired was he by the experience that he converted a room in his apartment into a chapel and founded a temple dedicated to his inspiration. In 1982, after affiliating with a branch of the African Orthodox Church, he changed its name from the One Mind Temple Evolutionary Transitional Body of Christ to the Church of St John Coltrane. As for why Coltrane is deserving of sainthood, it seems he had a spiritual awakening in 1957, beating a heroin addiction, swearing off drugs and booze, and devoting the last decade of his life to composing pieces infused with religious passion. He was just 40 years old when he died. Services are open to anyone and are usually standing-room only with plenty of dancing in the aisles.

Church of St John Coltrane 930 Gough St at Turk, San Francisco, CA 94102; ☎ 415 673 3572; www.saintjohncoltrane.com. The church is sharing premises with another church: services are at 12 noon on Sundays.

If you have a large enough group (six or more), you can arrange for your own private circus class at the **Circus Center**. Available weekend afternoons, their sampler program introduces anyone over the age of five to a variety of circus skills, including low tight wire, trampoline, static trapeze and juggling. The flying trapeze, also available weekend afternoons, is a special class for those ten and up. You don't need any special ability other than a bit of nerve. They'll teach you basic skills first on the static trapeze and then let you climb up to the flying one to try your hand at making a 'catch'. And if you miss? You'll be wearing safety belts and there's a safety net underneath you as well.

Quirk Alert

If you come across something really weird going on that involves red noses and funny wigs, it's likely **Clownarchy** is at work, or, rather, at play. This group of non-violent, non-destructive activist clowns makes its political points by surprising people in the most outlandish of ways. Their gags are like theater, performance art designed to shock and amuse while making subtle and not-so-subtle social statements. For example, 20 of them rode BART trains en masse, explaining that the world had become a circus and telling perplexed observers that George W Bush was giving clowning a bad name. They organized a million-clown march on Washington, DC but that, sadly, never materialized. Their manifesto decrees that they shall honor the role of clowns despite the behavior of a few politicians who foolishly tarnish the image of all clowns.

Clownarchy Contact Clownarchy: www.clownarchy.org. Events take place at various locations through the year.

Circus Center 755 Frederick St, San Francisco, CA 94117; ➘ 415 759 8123; www.circuscenter.org. Directions: the center is on Frederick St south of the Kezar Stadium in Golden Gate Park, between Arguello and Willard St.

Dolphin Club members swim year around in the chilly to frigid Bay waters of **Aquatic Park** where temperatures range from 50 degrees Celsius in the winter to 61 degrees in the summer. You're welcome to join them, but keep in mind that real dolphins never wear wetsuits or fins. Just stay inside the line of buoys that runs parallel to the shore and marks the quarter-mile point. While most of the swimmers just get their kicks paddling around in cold water, some members aspire to swimming the Golden Gate or the English Channel or they may be training for the 'Escape from Alcatraz' triathlon. That event involves swimming 1.5 miles from Alcatraz to Aquatic Park, then bicycling 14 miles across the Golden Gate Bridge to Mill Valley, and then finally running 13 miles over Mount Tamalpais to Stinson Beach and back to Mill Valley. By the way, the Dolphin Club Polar Bear champion in 2004 was a 51-year-old man who logged 356 miles in a single winter swim season.

Dolphin Club of San Francisco 502 Jefferson St, Aquatic Park, San Francisco, CA 94109; ➘ 415 441 9329; www.dolphinclub.org. Events are held at various times and locations through the year: see the website for details.

Museums and collections

If you just can't bear to start the day without your comics, you'll love the **Cartoon Art Museum**. Created in 1987 with an endowment from Charles Schulz (of *Peanuts* fame), the museum explores how comics have influenced our politics and our pop culture. The only museum in the country dedicated to the preservation and exhibition of cartoon art in all forms, it houses 6,000 original favorites. Exhibits constantly rotate and cartoonists are always showing up for presentations and book signings. There's even an artist-in-residency program and Saturday morning cartooning classes. The first Tuesday of every calendar month is 'Pay What You Wish Day.'

Cartoon Art Museum 655 Mission St, San Francisco, CA 94103; ☎ 415 CARTOON; www.cartoonart.org. *Open Tue–Sun 11am–5pm.* The museum is on Mission St between New Montgomery and 3rd St.

Like all musical styles, polka is affected by the dialect in the region where it was created. If you're in Chicago you get Polish-style polka. If you're in Cleveland you get the more Slovenian variety. And much like the city itself, San Francisco-style polka is eclectic, combining elements of punk, jazz, rock, and even country-and-western music with a traditional polka beat. This combination has developed quite a cult following and, like all cult followings, it gets its own Hall of Fame, even if the 'Hall' itself is nothing more than the wall of a pizza parlor. The **San Francisco Style Polka Hall of Fame** was inaugurated in 2003 at Escape from New York Pizza in the Castro. The founding inductees were SF-polka-style pioneers Polkacide, Big Lou's Polka Casserole, and The Squeegees. The exhibition itself does justice to the accordion aristocracy of San Francisco with three separate boards of memorabilia encased in plastic and hung on the wall. You'll find feature album covers, a Zippy the Pinhead comic strip that mentions Polkacide, the flyer from that band's debut gig at the old Mabuhay Gardens (with the group's name misspelled), and other pieces of San Francisco-style polka's illustrious history.

San Francisco Style Polka Hall of Fame located at Escape from New York Pizza, 508 Castro St, San Francisco, CA 94114; ☎ 415 252 1515; www.accordionprincess.com/sfsphof/. Directions: the pizza parlor is on Castro between 18th and 19th St.

The **Wax Museum at Fisherman's Wharf** is a dynamic, state-of-the-art facility with 280 figures in settings so realistic you almost feel like you're intruding. Murals, music and sound effects add to the eerie reality, as does the drama of the settings themselves. Stars are well represented, including Robin Williams, Julia Roberts, and Jim Carrey. Hitler shares a war room with Mussolini and Tojo and Eisenhower and MacArthur stand among sand bags and a World War II jeep in front of an elaborate mural. Bill Gates looks suitably nerdy next to distinguished scientists Freud and Newton. The *Last Supper* scene is fully narrated, while a Van Gogh painting is rendered in a 3D wax display.

Wax Museum at Fisherman's Wharf 145 Jefferson St, San Francisco, CA 94133; ☎ 800 439 4305 or ☎ 415 202 0400; www.waxmuseum.com. *Open daily 10am–9pm.* Directions: the museum is on Jefferson St between Taylor and Mason St.

San Francisco's **Ripley's Believe It or Not Museum** features a toothpick sculpture of the Golden Gate Bridge made by artist Steve Blackman. Steve worked on the 13ft-long sculpture for two-and-a-half-years, using 30,000 toothpicks in the process. It's lit by more than 100 LEDs that are operated by a single nine-volt battery. You can also see a self portrait of Van Gogh made out of toast (yes, toast!) that uses 63 pieces of toasted white bread, as well as a matchstick cable car made from 270,836 matchsticks (can you imagine counting all those?), 21 pints of glue and 940 hours of labor.

Ripley's Believe It or Not Museum 175 Jefferson St, San Francisco,
CA 94133; ↘ 415 771 6188; www.ripleysf.com. Directions: the museum
is on Jefferson St between Taylor and Mason St. Steve Blackman has his
own website at www.toothpickart.com.

It's a small museum, but then you don't need a lot of space to display almost every
Pez candy dispenser ever made: 550 in all. The **Burlingame Museum of Pez
Memorabilia** represents more than a decade of collecting by Gary and Nancy
Doss who readily admit their strange fixation has taken over their lives. Pez, the
quirky plastic statues that spit candy from their necks, are beloved by young and
old alike. The museum, along with their website, draws collectors from all over the
world. A Make a Face model from the 1970s can fetch $4,500 if it's still in the box;
a 1960 model with a working slide rule can run to $800. An interactive display tells
you everything you'd ever want to know about Pez. Gary only needs half a dozen
more containers to make his collection complete; unfortunately, those last six will
set him back around $18,000.

Burlingame Museum of Pez Memorabilia 214 California Dr,
Burlingame, CA 94010; ✆ 650 347 2301; www.spectrumnet.com/pez.
Open Tue–Sat 10am–6pm, Sat 10am–5pm, closed major holidays. Free.
Directions: the museum is on California Dr, between Burlingame Ave
and Howard Ave, 2 blocks from the Burlingame Caltrain station.

Tours

The corner of Castro and Market streets is known as the 'gayest four corners on
earth'. That's where you meet Trevor Hailey for her **Cruisin' the Castro Tour**,
a four-hour walking tour of the Castro from a highly entertaining and historical
point of view. Trevor radiates with personality as she puts the gay and lesbian
experience – and the city itself – in sociological and psychological perspective. By
the time your tour – more like a field trip, really – is over, you'll have a much better
understanding of the chain of events that allowed California, San Francisco and the
Castro district to become such meccas of tolerance. You'll learn how the district's
sociological roots go all the way back to the Gold Rush days and then progress to
the drag queens of the 20s, the gay bars of the 40s, the impact of World War II, the
Summer of Love in the Haight, on up to the influx of so many gays into the Castro
beginning in the 70s.

The tour includes a lovely, leisurely lunch so you have plenty of time to ask
questions and discuss current issues. Trevor is uncommonly charismatic and
knowledgeable; her tour is really something special.

Cruisin' the Castro Tour leaves from Harvey Milk Plaza, Castro &
Market Streets; ↘ 415 550 8110; www.webcastro.com/castrotour. Cost
$45 (including lunch). Tours available Tue–Sat, May through November.

Colma's claim to fame is its population: 1.5 million, but only 1,100 of them are
breathing. That's because the town, named the City of the Dead, is designated as
the official burial ground for San Francisco, a city without enough land to devote
to cemeteries. Anybody who was anybody in the Bay Area now rests in Colma,
including Wyatt Earp, Levi Strauss, William Randolph Hearst, 'Emperor' Norton,
and baseball legend Joe DiMaggio. Tina Turner's dog is buried in the Pet
Cemetery in his owner's mink coat and Harry 'the Horse' Flamburis, past and
passed president of the Hell's Angels motorcycle club, is buried there on his
Harley. The Historical Association sells a book with a map of each cemetery and a

EMPEROR OF SAN FRANCISCO

San Francisco is a fertile breeding ground for eccentrics. One of its most famous was **Emperor Norton**, a flamboyant businessman who proclaimed himself Emperor of the United States in 1859 after he suffered the trauma of losing all his money. Immensely popular, people greeted him with a bow or a curtsy and saw to it that the penniless eccentric had a decent place to live and that he never went hungry. He ate free of charge wherever he pleased and the city made him a new uniform when his became too tattered. Three seats were reserved for him at public performances: one for the emperor and two for his well-behaved canine companions. Dressed in naval regalia he attended every public function and made daily rounds of his domain, making sure that order and harmony were maintained. He would anoint do-gooders with titles like 'Queen for a day', resulting in people following him around and hoping for a chance to help an old lady across the street while in his presence. Norton even printed his own currency which was accepted everywhere in the city without question. If he needed money he'd levy a 'tax' for a dollar or two. When he died in 1880 tens of thousands attended his funeral. He's buried at Woodlawn Cemetery in Colma, San Francisco's adjacent cemetery town.

In late 2004 the San Francisco Supervisors voted a resolution to re-name the newly refurbished San Francisco–Oakland Bay Bridge after Emperor Norton because he was famous for issuing proclamations – one of which, in 1872, decreed that a bridge be built joining San Francisco and the East Bay. A flurry of public comment, most of it sarcastic, ensued. Oakland, especially, took a dim view of the suggestion, either claiming complete ignorance of the man's existence or charging that the Emperor was strictly a San Francisco weirdo who had no business reflecting poorly upon their city. Other comments included snide remarks about the appropriateness of San Francisco honoring a lunatic with delusions of grandeur and one about how this would 'solidify red state opinions about San Francisco'.

guide to all the famous people buried there. They also offer tours by prior arrangement.

Colma Cemeteries Colma Historical Association, 1500 Hillside Blvd, Colma, CA 94014; ☎ 650 757 1676; email: colmahist@sbcglobal.net. *Open Tue–Sun 10am–3pm.* Directions: there are 17 separate cemeteries located on Hillside Blvd and El Camino Real. Take the Mission St (CA-82) exit of Hwy 280 and head south, turning left onto Hillside Blvd.

Meet the ghosts who call San Francisco home with Jim Fassbinder, a genuine member of the International Ghost Hunter's Society and the Institute for Paranormal Research. Jim, who has been seeing ghosts since he was a small boy, leads quite a convincing tour around elegant Pacific Heights on his **San Francisco Ghost Hunt Walking Tour**. Dressed in a black cape and top hat, his passion for his subject is obvious. 'The spirits tell us if they're willing to have visitors today,' he says. He does his part by building a profile of each ghost and by setting the mood, telling their stories based on documented research. You do yours by getting

Quirk Alert

Keep an eye out for two identical, impeccably dressed, sweet little old ladies when you're in the Union Square area. Known as the San Francisco Twins, Vivian and Marian Brown, who were once chosen 'most identical' at a twin convention, have been making their rounds for decades in their carefully matched outfits. They're happy to pose for pictures if you ask nicely. You may be able to see them at the Nob Hill Café at 1152 Taylor Street (between Sacramento and Clay). They usually eat dinner there at their regular window table on Tuesdays and Fridays.

into the spirit of the hunt. By the time you've heard the stories, and seen the haunts of half a dozen ghosts, you may become a believer yourself, especially when you see the spot where a key jumps mysteriously in the palm of your hand. Jim has been seen on the Travel Channel's *Haunted Hotels* program.

San Francisco Ghost Hunt Walking Tour departs every Mon, Wed, Fri, Sat and Sun at 7pm, year around, rain or starshine from Queen Anne Hotel, 1590 Sutter, San Francisco, CA; ☎ 415 922 5590; www.sfghosthunt.com. The Queen Anne hotel is at the corner of Sutter and Octavia St.

For a unique perspective on the Bay, climb into Loree and Harry Hirshman's shiny red open-cockpit biplane, pull on goggles and a cloth helmet, and take off like Snoopy going after the Red Baron. The plane, a modern 1994 Waco YMF-5C, is a replica of those flown during the golden age of aviation when pilots wore racy white scarves and leather flight helmets and entertained those on the ground with breathtaking loops and rolls. The Hirshmans, however, stick to strictly level flights at **Golden Gate Biplane Adventures**, putting their combined 18 years of Navy piloting skills to good use. Their plane holds two passengers sitting snugly side by side in the front compartment or you can go solo, getting a chance to control the stick yourself for a moment or two.

Golden Gate Biplane Adventures San Carlos Airport, Airport Dr, San Carlos, CA 94070; ☎ 650 325 3253; www.flysf.com. Directions: the flights depart from San Carlos Airport. On Hwy 101, take the Holly St exit towards Redwood Shores Parkway (east, towards the Bay). Airport Dr is the first traffic light: turn right. Skyway Blvd is the first street; the office is located at the corner of Airport and Skyway.

It's one thing to see **Alcatraz**, the infamous island prison in the Bay by day, and quite another to see it at night. But, unlike the crowded day tours, the **night tour** of 'The Rock' is a more comprehensive and a substantially freakier experience. For starters, the narrated ferry takes you all the way around the island, docking just before sunset so you get an idea of the tantalizing views the prisoners endured during their dismal incarcerations. Then you're met by an interpreter who escorts you up to the cell house and sets the stage for the audio tour. As night falls and eerie shadows envelop the cellblock, you wander the cellblocks, even sitting in a cell or two. After the audio tour you get to experience several special programs that aren't covered on the day tour, things like tours of the hospital (very creepy) or of the gun towers. Every year there's an annual Alcatraz Reunion, open to the public, where guards, their families, and former prisoners gather for a very strange 'living history' day right there on the grounds.

Alcatraz Night Tour Pier 41 Marine Terminal, San Francisco, CA 94133; ✆ 415 705 5555; www.blueandgoldfleet.com. Reservations are strongly recommended. The tour departs from Pier 41 next to Fisherman's Wharf.

For more than two decades the **Basic Brown Bear Factory** has been making teddy bears and now they offer the opportunity to make your own bear following a tour of the factory. The bear gets its start in life with a designer sketching a pattern, cutting the soft plush fabric into pieces, attaching eyes and then sewing it together. Next – this is where you come in – you get to use a stuffing machine to plump it full of just the right amount of polyester and air, and then fluff it up with a pressurized air machine before giving it a name and a hug. Owner Merrilee Woods made the very first basic brown bear back in 1976 for her son Sam who was three at the time; that bear now sports a mustache, eye patch and Hawaiian shirt and lives in the tour room. The factory makes an average of 600 bears a day.

Basic Brown Bear Factory 2801 Leavenworth St, Cannery, 2nd Level, San Francisco, CA 94133; ✆ 866-5BB-BEAR; www.basicbrownbear.com. Directions: the store is located in the Cannery, on Leavenworth St between Jefferson and Beach St.

City Guides Neighborhood Walks offers dozens of *free* walking tours given by individuals with a specific expertise and a passion to share it with visitors. Cityscapes and Public Places is a good one if you want to understand the city's infamous insistence on political correctness. Other offerings include Bawdy & Naughty, a two-block exploration of the professional women of the Gold Rush era and the contribution they made to the city's growth; the Coit Tower Murals, created during the Depression; a tour of the newly renovated Ferry Building; and the Landmark Victorians of Alamo Square, also known as 'postcard row'. In May and October, their busiest months, they add additional tours such as the City Hall Ghost Walk, a fascinating tour involving disinterred remains, assassinations and the cemetery that once covered Civic Center; an Earthquake and Fire Walk; Scalawag and Sin Sites, where early 'pros' and 'cons' plied their trades; and Sacred Places, a tour of the city's diversity as reflected in its places of worship. All told, City Guides offers at least three-dozen tours year around with another two-dozen added in May and October.

City Guides Neighborhood Walks depart daily from various locations around San Francisco. Contact City Guides, c/o San Francisco Public Library, Main Library, 100 Larkin St, San Francisco, CA 94102; ✆ 415 557 4266; www.sfcityguides.org.

The Mission is a neighborhood where life takes place on the streets and where Latino culture is vibrantly displayed on building façades and on alley fences. Almost everywhere you turn in the Mission you'll come upon murals depicting everything from political and social themes to community and cultural ones. You'll find them on the walls of businesses, schools, garages and churches, as well as fences. Balmy Alley is one of the most famous, with 70 brightly colored murals decorating the rear fences of the homes lining the alley. Some of the murals cover

SHOWING OFF THE CITY

The ideal companion guide to *Eccentric California* is **San Francisco As You Like It**, with touring suggestions arranged by theme depending on your interests – or those of your guests. There are 23 tour itineraries in all, tailor-made for intentional or accidental tourists like cynical natives, green fiends, artsy aunties, shopaholics, fitness freaks, the romantically inclined, gender blenders, and the politically correct. Arranged with morning, noon and night suggestions, specific destinations and logical itineraries, this guide is both funny and incredibly useful. Author Bonnie Wach understands that who you are determines how you want to see this most alluring and quirky of American cities.

entire buildings. Walking tours of the district are offered every weekend by **Precita Eyes Mural Arts Center**, an association of muralists involved with the creation and preservation of more than 800 murals in the neighborhood. The Sunday tour goes into more depth than does the Saturday one and includes a slide show on the history and process of mural art. You can also pick up a map of the murals at the arts center if you want to explore them on your own.

> **Precita Eyes Mural Arts Center** 348 Precita Ave, San Francisco, CA 94110; ☏ 415 285 7311; www.precitaeyes.org. The tours depart on Sat and Sun at 1.30pm.

If you'd rather get your history sitting in comfort in a luxury limo, try **Russell's SF Crime Tour**, a two-and-a-half-hour trip through the city's notorious past and present. Russell, descendant of an Alaskan gold miner, takes his heritage seriously, presenting the history of the city's seamier side with knowledge and enthusiasm. You'll hear stories of outlaws like Al Capone and Black Bart, the world's most poetic stage-coach robber; of the 'hanging' vigilante committees of the early Gold Rush days; of the Fatty Arbuckle murder trial in 1921; and of various dastardly deeds like the kidnapping of Patty Hearst, the murders of city supervisor Dan White and Mayor George Moscone, and the unsolved serial murders by the Zodiac Killer.

> **Russell's SF Crime Tour** 388 Second Ave, San Francisco, CA 94118; ☏ 415 387 1549; www.sfcrime.com.

Explore the Gothic side of Nob Hill with Mina Harker, a vampire-ette reputedly created by Count Dracula in London in 1897 and later banished by him to the USA. Lucky for us she's now giving tours of her above-ground haunts and you're invited to come in costume if the spirit moves you. Taking her all-in-fun history with a twist **Vampire Tour of San Francisco**, you'll visit eight famous Nob Hill locations, learning not just their history, but the role that vampires played in San Francisco's past. (Well, if drinking the water didn't cause the city's weirdness, maybe the vampires did.)

> **Vampire Tour of San Francisco** ☏ 650 279 1840; www.sfvampiretour.com. Tours start at 8pm at the corner of California and Taylor Streets.

Most visitors to San Francisco marvel at the variety and quality of the food, but if you're unsure of where to begin your culinary pursuits, consider a food/history tour. **Wok Wiz** offers a daily walking tour of Chinatown that explores the history, folklore, culture and cuisine of the largest Chinatown in America. Besides a tea-tasting ceremony and a visit to a herb shop, you'll enjoy a dim sum lunch at a Chinatown restaurant. They also offer a food-lovers 'I Can't Believe I Ate My Way Through Chinatown' tour and an evening tour that includes a Chinese banquet and an explanation of feng shui, the Chinese art of placement.

Wok Wiz Tours 654 Commercial St, San Francisco, CA 94111; ↘ 650 355 9657; www.wokwiz.com. Reservations required. Tours depart from the Wok Wiz cooking center at 654 Commercial St, between Kearny and Montgomery.

If Italian is more your style, GraceAnn Walden, a food writer for the *San Francisco Chronicle*, offers **Mangia North Beach**, a four-hour extravaganza that covers North Beach cuisine from appetizers to dessert. Everyone who takes this tour gives the same advice: be hungry when you arrive. You'll eat, drink, and learn some history while she threads your group through the streets to an authentic Italian bakery, a deli, and a truffle maker as well as to an Irish pub for a beer. Plus, you get lunch. This is a real behind-the-scenes kind of tour, a look into the way things used to be done in days past.

Mangia North Beach ↖ 415 397 8530; email: gaw@sbcglobal.net. Sat only, reservations required. Tours meet at the corner of Stockton and Columbus in front of the Bank of America at 10am.

Explore the tie-dyed cradle of hippie culture with a guide who was part of it all at the **Flower Power Haight-Ashbury Walking Tour**. The Haight was heart of the 60s counter-culture movement, the center of the Summer of Love and Be-Ins, and home to music greats like Jimi Hendrix, Janis Joplin and Jerry Garcia. (One resident, Manny the Hippie, used to appear regularly on David Letterman's late-night talk show, teaching America how to talk hippie.) You'll see the Grateful Dead house and the stairs where they posed for the famous poster, the house where kidnapped Patty Hearst was held hostage, and learn how a dense mass of confused humanity managed to get along sleeping in vans and sharing way too few bathrooms. The tour, about 60% hippie history and 40% neighborhood culture, takes you through restaurants, bars, and shops into which you might not otherwise venture.

Flower Power Haight-Ashbury Walking Tour PO Box 170106, San Francisco, CA 94177; ↖ 415 863 1621; www.hippygourmet.com. Tue and Sat. Reservations required, tours depart from the corner of Stanyan and Waller.

The Haight isn't just all about hippies. During the **Haunted Haight Walking Tour** you'll 'meet' spirits that lived in the Haight more than 100 years ago as well as visit haunted houses and explore the urban legends and macabre past of one of the city's most famous districts. You'll also learn what it was like when the Native Americans lived there from licensed tour guide Tommy Netzband who created the tour through endless hours of in-depth research. His resources include old newspaper articles, publications and personal accounts from local residents who have proclaimed their houses to be haunted. The tour starts in front of a real haunted store.

Haunted Haight Walking Tour ℃ 415 863 1416; www.hauntedhaight.com. Reservations required. Tours depart from Planetweavers, 1573 Haight St, between Ashbury and Clayton at 7pm daily.

It's a big, red, shiny Mack fire engine and you get to ride on it, bells clanging, from the waterfront across the Golden Gate Bridge to Sausalito and back again on a campy tour called **San Francisco Fire Engine Tours and Adventures**. Owners Robert and Marilyn Katzman dress you in fireman coats, pile on the blankets and charge off to dramatic vista points around the bridge as well as on it. The tour in their 1955 open-air truck is hardly low key as Marilyn quickly has you singing silly ditties while people on the streets gawk in amazement. As you pass under the south tower of the bridge Marilyn explains to you how she managed to tap dance on *top* of it. She regales you with stories, including little-known fire-fighting facts such as that in the old days, before city fire departments, volunteer brigades were paid by the fire and there was lots of competition among them to get to a fire first and claim the rewards. When more than one unit arrived at the scene, there was considerable fighting – not of the fire, but between units. The fire engine also tours North Beach, Chinatown and Pacific Heights. The Katzmans live in a real restored firehouse bought from the city when modern fire trucks became too large to fit through the doors. They even have a Dalmatian and a real pole to slide down from the upper floors.

San Francisco Fire Engine Tours and Adventures ℃ 415 333 7077; www.fireenginetours.com. Daily except Tue. Tours depart from The Cannery at Fisherman's Wharf.

It's all about romance and lust, animal style, at the **San Francisco Zoo Valentine's Day Sex Tours**. The tram tour, hosted by a zoo guide who explains novel ways to love your lover, takes you from the birds and the bees to animals that may – or may not – co-operate by demonstrating their amorous techniques. While the tour is intended to be entertaining, it's also educational, sharing information on the way animals choose their mates, raise their families, and defend their territories. For example, you'll learn that penguins are monogamous, that rhino foreplay lasts for a month, and that orang-utans can mate upside down. The tour ends with champagne, truffles, and a mashed-potato bar.

San Francisco Zoo Valentine's Day Sex Tours held annually in February. Contact San Francisco Zoo, 1 Zoo Rd, San Francisco, CA 94132; ℃ 415 753 7080; www.sfzoo.org. The Zoo is located on Sloat Blvd, just off Hwy 35 (Great Hwy) in San Francisco.

If you're looking to go clubbing, doing it with **Three Babes and A Bus** adds an edge to what already promises to be an energetic evening. Leaving every Saturday evening at 9pm, their 50-seat party bus visits four clubs, returning you safe, if not exactly sane, around 01.30. You never know who your companions might be, but there's a good chance that inflatable body parts will be involved since the bus is popular with bachelorette party groups. The tour guides are suitably sassy and you need to dress to impress.

Three Babes and A Bus ✆ 800 414 0158; www.threebabes.com. Sat only. Tours depart from Ruby Skye, 420 Mason St between Post and Geary.

'Where's the F'ing Beach in North Beach' is just one of ten comedy tours of San Francisco led by the accomplished comedians at **Foot! Tours**, working professionals who delight in making you laugh while you learn. One tour, 'Nude, Lewd, and Crude' covers the rise of strippers, comics, and beats in North Beach; another, 'Instant City – Just Add Gold' deals with the glitter, greed, and growth of San Francisco. 'Drugs, Thugs, Crimps & Pimps' covers the red-light district where you'll learn the story behind the city's opium dens, arson gangs, ruthless kidnappers, illegal gamblers and notorious prostitutes. 'Flashback' visits the Haight-Ashbury district while 'Hobnobbing with Gobs of Snobs' explores San Francisco's *nouveau riche*. Founder Robert Mac describes his company a combination 'comedian-guided game-show and historical walking tour'. You'll hear all kinds of offbeat tales while playing along in a walking game show that involves misfortune cookies and valuable imaginary prizes. It's a highly entertaining way to learn about this most eccentric of cities from some of its more eccentric inhabitants.

Foot! Tours ✆ 415 793 JEST; www.foottours.com. Reservations required.

Sister Carmen Barsody and Reverend Kay Jorgensen lead a 'tour' of a different kind, one where the itinerary and activities are left up to you. One to two times a month they arrange **Street Retreats**, orienting you to the Tenderloin neighborhood around their **Faithful Fools Ministry** that is largely populated by the poor and homeless, and then sending you out for a day of wandering in an environment you would normally avoid. The challenge in taking a street retreat is in facing your fears about mingling with those living in poverty and deprivation and in experiencing viscerally the hardships that come with simply existing moment to moment when you're living on the streets. One of the hardest parts of the retreat is just wandering without a plan, with nowhere to sit and with nothing to do, just like the homeless do all day, every day. But that's part of the enlightenment that comes with the experience. This isn't for everyone, but people from all walks of life who are looking for such a spiritual experience are welcome.

Street Retreats ✆ 415 474 0508; www.faithfulfools.org. Reservations required; retreats happen several times a year.

For a quirky way to experience San Francisco's waterfront area, consider taking the **San Francisco Electric Tour**, a scenic three-hour trip piloting your very own Segway®. Segway Human Transporters are personal, self-balancing scooter-like things guided forward and backward by your body's movements. They can maneuver most walkable areas, including paved surfaces, dirt roads, grass, and inclines, traveling at an average 5mph. While anyone 12 and up (and under 250lb) can participate, you do have to wear a helmet and take a training class before starting the tour. You'll even become a tourist attraction yourself! Guided tours depart several times daily, stopping for periodic refreshments and photo ops.

San Francisco Electric Tour 165 Jefferson St, Suite 2F, San Francisco, CA 94133. ✆ 877 474 3130 or ✆ 415 474 3130; www.sfelectrictour.com. Reservations are a must; tours limited to ten riders per tour. Tours depart from 165 Jefferson St, at the corner of Jefferson and Taylor.

Another novel way to see the sights is in a **GoCar**, a strange little three-wheeled putt-putt of a car that talks to you. This bright yellow, open-air car is a fun way to explore the city as the built-in 'tour guide' in the dash uses a global positioning system to trigger recorded information as you drive past a tourist attraction. Accurate to within 17ft, the car can even give suggestions on where to turn to see more of the sights. You control the car with motorcycle-style handles, throttles and handbrakes while wearing a safety helmet. The computer is programmed to direct you on a two-hour loop covering the Marina, Fisherman's Wharf, Golden Gate Park, the Presidio, and Haight-Ashbury.

> **GoCar rentals** 2715 Hyde St, San Francisco, CA 94109; ☎ 800 91
> GoCAR; www.gocarsf.com. Reservations recommended. Priced per
> hour. The rental location is at 2715 Hyde St, between Beach and North
> Point.

Odd shopping

With three stores in the Bay Area, **Good Vibrations** is a friendly, well-lit, well-stocked place for 'personal' toys, the kind of place you could send your mother were she so inclined. Started in the mid 70s by Joanie Blank, the store was the first of its kind where Mr & Mrs America could feel comfortable browsing 'adult' merchandise, the kind normally associated with men in stained raincoats. A democratically run and worker-owned co-operative, the staff of approximately 100 people are all impressively well educated about their product lines. One corner of the Valencia Street store is dedicated to the **Antique Vibrator Museum**, a display of electric vibrators once prescribed by doctors in the late 1800s and early 1900s to help treat 'female disorders'. Also called 'hysteria', it was the most common health complaint among women of the day. Most of them look like power tools or gadgets in need of explanation on a television shopping channel. Joni's collection dates from the late 1800s up to the 1970s. (Believe it or not, the first vibrator was a steam-powered massager.) Women had to use the vibrators in their doctor's offices to induce 'hysterical paroxysm', standard treatment for what was then considered a disease. The vibrator was later marketed as a home aid for health, vigor and beauty. One manufacturer claimed their product 'makes you fairly tingle with the joy of living'. The Polk Street and Berkeley stores have smaller antique vibrator collections.

> **Good Vibrations** 603 Valencia St, San Francisco, CA 94110; ☎ 415 522
> 5460; 1620 Polk St, San Francisco, CA 94109; ☎ 415 345 0400; 2504 San
> Pablo Ave, Berkeley, CA 94702; ☎ 510 841 8987; www.goodvibes.com.
> The Valencia St store is at the corner of Valencia and 17th St. The
> Berkeley store is on San Pablo Ave between Dwight and Parker.

The Mission District is also home to several other exquisitely eccentric stores. **826 Valencia** is a combination pirate-supply/writer center, the brainchild of author Dave Eggers who wrote *A Heartbreaking Work of Staggering Genius*. The front of the store sells such quirky merchandise as eye patches and peg legs while the rear is a dedicated reading and writing lab for underprivileged kids. There's a large bin of lard (pirates past used lard for cooking) that serves today as a tactile curiosity. A sign outlines the 'Goals for the Voyage': Plunder, Meet New People, Learn Valuable New Skills. You shouldn't miss this place; it's wonderfully weird. Another is **Paxton Gate**, a store carrying oddities such as framed and mounted insects, taxidermy, fossils, carnivorous plants and scientific supplies. Its insect collection is wide-ranging, with the critters being collected in their native habitats and then received at the store in dried and packaged form. The beetles are then soaked in hot water, and the butterflies are kept in a humid container, until they've softened and their legs and wings can be pinned in the desired positions. Look for the costumed, stuffed mice made by an artist/taxidermist. Paxton Gate has been described as a '*Smith and Hawken* (a gardening catalogue) on LSD'. Where else can you find glass eyes for your bobcat? **X21** is a store of 'stuff you never see', crammed to the gills with vintage merchandise that ranges from the hi-brow to the low, from quality modern to downright funky. It's impossible to browse here without laughing or squealing, 'Oh, I remember that!' The stores are located on Valencia between 19th and 20th St.

826 Valencia 826 Valencia St, San Francisco, CA 94110; ✆ 415 642 5905; www.826valencia.org. *Open daily 12 noon–6pm.*

X21 890 Valencia St, San Francisco, CA 94110; ✆ 415 647 4211; www.x21modern.com. *Open Mon–Thu 12 noon–6pm, Fri and Sun 12 noon–7pm, Sat 12 noon–8pm.*

Paxton Gate 824 Valencia St, San Francisco, CA 94110; ✆ 415 824 1872; www.826valenica.org. *Open Sun–Thu 12 noon–8pm, Fri and Sat 12 noon–9pm.*

The Haight district was the hub of the 'tune in, turn on, drop out' hippie movement of the 60s. Today the district still attracts teenage weekend pretenders who descend from the suburbs to shop and 'do the Haight', trying on personas like they try on shoes. The shops are as individualistic as their owners; Ben and Jerry's ice-cream and a Gap store are about the only 'corporate' presence. The movie theater, the Red Vic, is worker owned and operated. When Safeway Foods tried to move in, protesters filled up carts with food and then left the store. Within three months Safeway was gone. At the Haight Goodwill young hipsters shop right alongside the homeless. The district is filled with health food stores, retro, vintage, costume and head shops, cafés, and body shops. You won't find hair salons like Sassoon's or shoes like Nordstrom's on Haight, but you will find some very odd gifts for very odd people.

Far Out Fabrics, located in the rear of Mendel's Art Supplies, is the source for wild psychedelic furs, lycra spandex, oil cloth, and animal prints. **Costumes on Haight** has an outfit for every occasion, from politician masks to super-hero characters, from drag wear to straight wear. **Piedmont Boutique** is world famous, with locations in The Village in Manhattan as well as in San Francisco. A shop for cross-dressers and drag queens, they carry the most outrageously fun, originally designed clothing, lingerie and gowns fit for a king-sized queen. They produce their own peacock feathers, furry angel wings, glitzy cowboy hats, feather boas, tights with feathered cuffs, jewelry, thongs, pasties, fingerless gloves, and fake fur G-strings. The wig selection is huge, ranging from stunning to funky, and you'll see enough rhinestones to bring Liberace back from the other side. Look for their 'sign', the legs protruding from the second-floor window.

Far Out Fabrics/Mendel's 1556 Haight St, San Francisco, CA 94117; ✆ 415 621 1287; www.mendels.com. *Open Mon–Sat 10am–5.30pm, Sun 11am–4pm.*

Costumes on Haight 735 Haight St, San Francisco, CA 94117; ✆ 415 621 1356; www.costumesonhaight.com. *Open Mon–Sat 11am–7pm, Sun 12 noon–6pm.*

Piedmont Boutique 1452 Haight St, San Francisco, CA 94117; ✆ 415 864 8075; www.piedmontsf.com. *Open daily 11am–7pm.*

You don't have to eat in a Chinese restaurant to get your fortune cookie. You can buy them at **Golden Gate Fortune Cookie Factory**, located on a narrow street in Chinatown. Since 1962 they've been producing 200,000 cookies annually, some of them with custom fortunes tucked inside. You'll probably smell this tiny place before you see it.

Golden Gate Fortune Cookie Factory 56 Ross Alley, San Francisco, CA 94108; ☎ 415 781 3956. *Open 9am–midnight*. Directions: Ross Ave is off Jackson, between Grant and Stockton St.

Otsu is a Japanese word meaning both strange and stylish, a word that aptly describes one of the country's only vegan boutiques. Carrying quality 'fairly made' shoes, belts, wallets, bags, paper products, and shirts free of all animal products, the store caters to those practicing a strict vegan lifestyle. Vegans shun meat, poultry, seafood, dairy, eggs, wool, silk, leather, goose down, glue, and even honey, so shopping is quite a challenge for them. The *Vice Cream Cookbook* is especially popular since ice-cream is also taboo.

Otsu 3253 16th St, San Francisco, CA 94114; ☎ 415 255 7900 or ☎ 866 HEY OTSU; www.veganmart.com. *Open Tue–Sun 11am–7pm*. Directions: between Guerrero and Dolores.

With a reputation as one of the country's premier magic shops, and with an obsessive fan base that fills the store each day with budding magicians, **Misdirections Magic Shop** supplies everything that the professional or novice needs, including lectures by the country's best and brightest on how to use the merchandise. Demonstrating each and every effect, and teaching you how to do it yourself, is their hallmark, and the store exudes a genuinely friendly aura that can't be conjured up using one of their products. Owner and mentor Joe Pon likens the shop to a neighborhood bar where everyone knows your name and everyone cares about your progress. He also runs a magic club, brings in visiting pros for lectures, and hosts two annual competitions.

Misdirections Magic Shop 1236 9th Ave, San Francisco, CA 94122; ☎ 415 566 2180; www.misdirections.com. *Open Mon–Sat 11am–6pm, Sun 11am–5pm*. Directions: the store is on 9th Ave between Lincoln Way and Irving St.

Botanica Yoruba is a fascinating place to browse for spiritual products used to summon saints, banish sinners, and appease the gods of many religions, including Voodoo, Santeria, Catholicism and various other faiths practiced in Africa, Cuba, Mexico and the Caribbean. Most of the candles, statues, potions, herbs, incense, powders and washes are meant to be used in rituals and ceremonies designed to influence your luck, balance harmony, or get the attention of gods and goddesses in a position to improve or change a situation. For example, 'Boss Fix' oil, when added to your bath water and combined with prayer, should improve things at work. A Miracle Healing Candle is said to help cure what ails you while other concoctions are helpful for casting love spells or attracting financial success. The owner and staff are known as spiritual consultants.

Botanica Yoruba 998 Valencia St, San Francisco, CA 94110; ☎ 415 826 4967; www.geocities.com/botanicayoruba/. Directions: the store is on Valencia St, between Liberty and 21st St.

Quirky cuisine

This isn't a biker bar, but you'll still find plenty of bikes here, about $700,000 worth, suspended from the ceiling at **Eddie Rickenbacker's Restaurant**. Hanging above you as you dine are several dozen classic, early 20th-century motorbikes. It's perfectly OK to just peek in and gawk if you wish. You may even see the 1930 Lionel train that runs on elevated tracks around the dining room.

> **Eddie Rickenbacker's** 133 2nd St, San Francisco, CA 94105; ☏ 415 543 3498. *Closed Mon.* Directions: the restaurant is on 2nd street between Minna and Natoma St.

Bigfoot in the city? Yep, at the **Bigfoot Lodge**, a frontier-in-the-city bar and music club, you come face to face (well, not quite, unless you're very tall) with a life-sized Sasquatch created by famous tiki artist Crazy Al. He also made the faux fur bear heads that are mounted at either end of the bark-lined bar which itself features a miniature forest fire blazing away. Not even the fireplace fire is for real, but the atmosphere amid the faux log-cabin walls is both campy and realistic. Expect kitsch everywhere from the paintings and posters to stuff like taxidermy squirrels and the hatchet stuck in the front door.

> **Bigfoot Lodge** 1750 Polk St, San Francisco, CA 94109; ☏ 415 440 2355; www.bigfootlodge.com. Directions: the lodge is located on Polk between Washington and Clay St.

They call themselves 'gender illusionists' and they'll likely be the most memorable servers you'll ever encounter. They work – or more accurately, perform – at **Asia SF**, providing additional entertainment (besides being superb in drag) between courses on a red runway in the center of the dining area. The décor, as dramatic as the wait staff, is exotically Asia Modern with atmospheric lighting – like a color-changing wall – to enhance the decidedly surreal experience. After dinner you can follow the fiber-optic lighting downstairs into the Dragon's Belly for a pulsating dance floor and mysterious lighting effects. Reservations are a must for the three nightly seatings.

> **Asia SF** 201 9th St, San Francisco, CA 94103; ☏ 415 255 2742; www.asiasf.com. Directions: the restaurant is on 9th St between Howard and Folsom St.

Exuding gritty charm, **Specs 12 Adler Museum Café** has been home to the city's bohemian types since 1968. Founded by Specs Simmons, resident sage and storyteller nicknamed for his signature eyeglasses, the cluttered North Beach bar is a legendary haven for beats, poets, and eccentrics wanting to commiserate with their own kind. (Seeing as the bar is located directly across the street from City Lights Bookstore, this pretty much explains its clientele.) The walls are covered with faded signs and mementos from Specs's travels – a shark's jaw, a walrus's penis bone, and stuffed critters like armadillos, cobras, and mongoose – and the atmosphere is the antithesis of trendy. If you wish to drink undisturbed, there are cards for your use with sayings like 'Sir, the lady does not wish your attention' and 'Madam, the gentleman prefers to sulk in silence.'

Although he's nearing 80, the irascible Specs is fond of saying, 'If I'm not in bed by midnight, I go home.'

> **Specs 12 Adler Museum Café** 12 Adler Pl, San Francisco, CA 94134; ☏ 415 421 4112. Directions: Adler Pl is off Columbus, between Broadway and Pacific.

While the Haight was famous for its residents smoking illegal substances from pipes, the **Kan Zaman Café** is famous today for a different kind of pipe-smoking experience. Diners at this Middle Eastern restaurant can smoke the hookah after their meal, a water pipe filled with various flavors of tobacco such as apple, honey, or apricot. The experience is best had at night when the décor benefits from low lighting and red lamps. You sit on the floor at knee-high tables amid fake palm trees, eating hummus and baba ghanoush while watching belly dancers perform.

Kan Zaman Café 1793 Haight St, San Francisco, CA 94117; ☎ 415 751 9656. *Closed Mon.* Directions: the Café is on Haight St between Schrader and Cole.

Rooms with a skew

As the staff at the **Hotel Triton** is fond of pointing out, you don't come to San Francisco for the predictable, so why should your hotel be so? Hardly ordinary, the Triton, with its cutting-edge jewel-tone décor, is known for its wacky-but-cool publicity stunts such as putting stunt men on the roof and drag queens and go-go dancers in the lobby. Fire-eaters and a full-scale fashion show draw throngs of gawkers, too. On their politically correct eco floor the air is purified, the water free of chemical conspiracies, and the bed linens made from naturally grown cotton. The entire hotel is cleaned with 'green' and pets are welcome except on the eco floors. Nine local artists contributed to the décor with whimsical, creative, upscale furnishings that are both inspiring and comfortable. Zen Dens are smaller rooms for one with incense and a *Book of Buddha*. Celebrities like Woody Harrelson and Anthony Kiedis of the Red Hot Chilli Peppers decorated their own theme suites, with the hotel donating 10% of Woody's room fees to an ecological preserve. A variety of packages entice, such as the 'So Hip It Hurts' that includes a tattoo or piercing at a Haight Street body shop.

Hotel Triton 342 Grant Ave, San Francisco, CA 94108; ☎ 800 800 1299; www.hotel-tritonsf.com. Directions: the hotel is on Grant Ave between Bush and Sutter.

PECULIAR PERFORMANCES

You'll see street performers all over the city, particularly at Pier 39, Union Square, and at Fisherman's Wharf. Especially keep an eye out for the opera singer at the foot of Maiden Lane just off Union Square, the tap dancer at the Powell Street cable car turnaround, and the white guy in the trashcan at the wharf. Beware, however, the infamous **Bushman of Fisherman's Wharf**.

With the Bushman, aka David Johnson, anyone can become part of the performance. He spends his days on the wharf lurking behind a bunch of eucalyptus branches waiting for unsuspecting passers by. Crouched behind his foliage, he watches the crowds, carefully waiting until his target has almost passed. Then he leaps up, waving the branches frantically and crying, 'ugga-bugga!' His goal is not only to frighten his target, but to amuse those watching this peculiar performance in the hopes they'll give him some cash. The Bushman has been alternately amusing and horrifying onlookers for over 25 years, and his back-to-basics scare tactics make him one of the most well-known street performers in San Francisco.

An upscale boutique hotel, the **Hotel Monaco** takes pets very seriously with their Bone-A-Petit package. Realizing that your dog is probably accustomed to a relatively high level of indulgence, the package includes bottled water, a dog bowl, Good Dog towels, premium chew toys, gourmet doggie cookies, the hotel's temporary dog tags and, of course, clean-up baggies. They even offer *Lassie*, *Babe*, and *Dr Doolittle* videos in case Fido or Fifi need a bedtime story. If you can't bring your pet with you, they'll supply a substitute with a program called Guppy Love. Just ask and they'll loan you a relaxed, quiet goldfish to keep you company during your stay. You don't even need to feed it; housekeeping takes care of that.

Hotel Monaco 501 Geary St, San Francisco, CA 94102; ✆ 415 292 0100; www.monaco-sf.com. Directions: the hotel is on Geary St, between Jones and Taylor.

'Peace Through Tourism' is the motto at the **Red Vic Bed and Breakfast and Art** where you can live like the hippies lived in the 60s. Originally a 'country resort', San Francisco's Red Vic is the embodiment of the Haight, located right in the heart of the famous hippie capital. This hotel has seen it all, from the peace movement to the ecology movement to the movement for social justice. True to its heritage, it has a meditation room, motivational videos, meditative art and visual poetry. Its funky theme rooms have names like Flower Child and Summer of Love, decorated with Grateful Dead posters, tie-dyed bed covers and lava lamps. One of the shared hall bathrooms has an aquarium where fish swim in the pull-chain toilet's tank. The mirror in the Sunshine Room is meant to reflect the viewer back to themselves as the world sees him or her, not the mirror image you're accustomed to seeing. Owner Sami Sunchild likes to think of the place an alternative to corporate tourism (which it certainly is), stressing the conversations around the breakfast table and international friendships in the making. She's founder of the Peaceful World Traveler's Network, a group that strives to make the world a better place by assuring travelers that their travel dollars will be invested back in local environmental or social causes.

Red Vic Bed and Breakfast 1665 Haight St, San Francisco, CA 94117; ✆ 415 864 1978; www.redvic.com. Directions: the hotel is on Haight, between Cole and Belvdere.

While the exterior is Victorian, there's nothing old fashioned about **Hotel des Arts**. From the lobby to the guest rooms the entire interior is an artistic experience. Using local, sometimes underground artists to transform a tired tourist hotel into a bold environmental gallery, art collector Hero Nakatani's vision was for the art itself to be the focal point and for the building to play second fiddle. Six of the rooms feature wall-to-wall, floor-to-ceiling murals, painted by emerging artists, that envelop you totally within the space. In others the colors are muted and the furnishings minimalist so the art, much of it edgy, can take center stage. Some of the walls are even done by actual graffiti artists. Most of the art is for sale and the pieces change every few months. Some of the rooms in this dynamic, spotless hotel have shared bathrooms.

Hotel des Arts 447 Bush St, San Francisco, CA; ℓ 866 285 4104; www.sanfrancisco.com/hoteldesarts. Directions: the hotel is on Bush St, between Grant Ae and Kearny St.

If the idea of a hotel that offers free tattoos upon check in appeals to you, then the **Phoenix Hotel** is right up your tenderloin district alley. Not in the city's best neighborhood, the hotel nevertheless oozes style with each 50s-style bungalow room sprouting bamboo furnishings, tropical plants and colorful fabrics and art. But go for more than the rooms, as this place rocks in the kind of way that families and couples looking for a quiet getaway probably wouldn't appreciate. The hotel is known as a fun and funky one with a lounge that draws a chic crowd and guides to the city written by the staff.

Phoenix Hotel 601 Eddy St, San Francisco, CA 94109; ℓ 415 776 1380; www.tablethotels.com. Directions: the hotel is on Eddy St, between Polk and Larkin.

Attractions

Your sense of touch becomes your best friend in the **Tactile Dome**, a fixture at the San Francisco Exploratorium since 1971. Created by Dr August Coppola (brother of filmmaker Francis and father of Nicolas Cage), the one-way maze is soundproof and pitch black; the only way you can get out is to feel your way through. Coppola built the attraction so that one climbs, crawls, and slides though the Dome to get to the end, encountering a variety of textures and objects along the way. Often voted one of the best places to bring visitors to San Francisco, the Tactile Dome is fun for older kids and adults alike. You can also rent the Dome for your own personal party if you have a minimum of 15 people, which makes for a great birthday party or other special event. Suffice to say, the Tactile Dome is not for the claustrophobic.

Tactile Dome The Exploratorium, 3601 Lyon St, San Francisco, CA 94123; ℓ 415 EXP LORE; www.exploratorium.edu. Directions: the Exploratorium is in the Palace of Fine Arts building in San Francisco's Marina district, just off Marina Blvd. *Admissions Tue–Sun at 10.15am, 12 noon, 1.45pm, 3.30pm, 5.00pm, and 6.45pm.* Additional charge on top of admission to the Exploratorium; reservations required. Not recommended for children under the age of seven.

Amusing America is a look back at the days when fun had nothing to do with joysticks or keyboards. You enter this world of mechanized, coin-operated machines through Laughing Sal, the giant sentry that once stood at Playland at the Beach, and find yourself not just amid the clatter and clang of these marvelous old machines from the now-defunct Musée Mecanique, but of exhibits chronicling the history of the city's playful past. Years of research went into the exhibition that tells the story of the city's most renowned amusement parks, World Fairs, arcades, dance pavilions and plunges. Many of these fortune-telling, love-telling, strength-testing and games-of-chance machines will still entertain you for a quarter.

Amusing America San Francisco Museum and Historical Society, Pier 45, San Francisco, CA 94142; ℓ 415 775 1111; www.sfhistory.org. Directions: the exhibition is located on Pier 45 (Fisherman's Wharf) at the foot of Taylor St.

The last remaining structure of San Francisco's famous Playland at the Beach, **Camera Obscura** is an entertaining relic, a camera-shaped building that offers a

360-degree image of the oceanfront projected onto a large viewing surface inside the structure. The oldest freestanding, original-location Camera Obscura in the country, it was threatened with destruction until dedicated preservationists managed to get it added to the National Register of Historic Places in 2001. The building itself is an example of architecture known as 'duck' or 'signature', a style of building that invites exploration due to its unique shape.

Camera Obscura Cliff House, San Francisco; ☎ 415 750 0415; www.giantcamera.com. Directions: the camera is located on the lower terrace behind the Cliff House at the foot of Geary Blvd.

Audium is an unusual San Francisco experience to say the least. The only sound-sculpture theater in the world, its 169 speakers produce sound that you not only hear, but feel as well as it moves over, under, and right through you. While you sit in the dark in the small, 49-seat theater, you're enveloped by compositions that are performed live at each program by a tape artist who directs the sounds through a custom-designed console to various combinations of speakers. The sounds thus become sculpted as their movement, direction, speed and intensity vary in the space around you. The performance space itself consists of concentric circles, sloping walls containing the speakers, a floating floor, and a suspended ceiling. 'Audiences should feel sound as it bumps up against them, caresses, travels through, covers and enfolds them,' says composer, creator, and musician Stan Shaff. 'It could be to sound what virtual reality is to sight.'

Audium 1616 Bush St, San Francisco, CA 94109; ☎ 415 771 1616; www.audium.com. Performances Fri and Sat at 8.30pm. Directions: Audium is on Bush St between Gough and Franklin St.

Just plain weird

You expect to find furniture *in* a building, not *on* it. But at an abandoned tenement at Sixth and Howard Streets, artist Brian Groggin launched a project he called **Defenestration**, defined as the 'act of throwing a person or thing out of a window.' Twenty-three pieces of seemingly animate furniture hang out the windows and run down the sides of the four-story building, looking, perhaps, to escape the bleakness of the abandoned building. Tables, chairs, lamps, grandfather clocks, a refrigerator and couches hug the walls, the fire escapes and the roof, their legs seeming to grasp the surface like insects. The furniture, like the neighborhood, is cast off, and Brian rescued the pieces, 're-animating' them for their new role. For the installation itself, Brian held an Urban Circus with artists, performers and musicians, many dressed as clowns, putting on freak shows and vaudeville-style acts. Participants included members of the Church of the Subgenius, the Cacophony Society, Circus Redickuless, First Church of the Last Laugh and the Sisters of Perpetual Indulgence, all outrageous San Francisco institutions accustomed to misbehaving. The property was donated by the owners who have the building up for sale – with or without the furniture.

Defenestration 214 Sixth St at Howard, San Francisco, CA; www.defenestration.org and www.metaphorm.org. Directions: the building is at the corner of Sixth and Howard Streets south of Market St.

If you're going to see just one show while in San Francisco, make sure it's **Beach Blanket Babylon**. This fast-paced, satirical musical review, famous for its ludicrous headdresses and zany characters, has been playing to sell-out crowds

Quirk Alert

Only in San Francisco can a strange guy who feeds birds end up writing a local bestseller about his experiences. **The Wild Parrots of Telegraph Hill** was written by the once-homeless Mark Bittner, aka The Birdman, who now teaches experts about the behavior of wild parrots based on the decade he spent observing the now-famed flock of wild parrots that make the hill their home. Bittner began befriending the flock, originally numbering around two-dozen, while living in a cottage as a rent-free caretaker. At the time, having no idea that wild parrots were notoriously difficult to study, he became intimate with the flock, naming its members and caring for them when they became sick or injured. The flock today has grown to about 130 and you're likely to see them as you wander about Telegraph Hill.

since 1974. It's the quintessential San Francisco experience: irreverent, topical, and joyously funny. The premise is built around Snow White who is fed up with waiting for her Prince Charming. So she hits the road in search of him, traveling the world in her quest for true love. Along the way she meets pop-culture and not-so-pop-culture icons from history and from current events; characters that cavort in the most riotous of ways. Nothing is sacred – religion, sex and politics are all targets for ludicrous, sarcastic songs. Inanimate objects come to life too, singing and dancing along with the people they're spoofing. The costumes are as over the top as their subjects, with extremely large hats that upstage the actors. The signature San Francisco skyline hat is 8ft wide, 12ft high and weighs 200lb. You'll ache from laughing and you'll come away with a better understanding of the California point of view. The staff meets every day to tweak the show's content so the skits are always current.

Beach Blanket Babylon Club Fugazi, 678 Beach Babylon Blvd, aka Green St, San Francisco, CA; ☎ 415 421 4222; www.beachblanketbabylon.com. Performances at 5pm and 8pm.

Long the subject of controversy, the **Vaillancourt Fountain** is once again flowing. Depending on your point of view, this is either a blessing or a curse, but, in typical San Francisco style, the controversy over whether this enormous, concrete, Lego-like structure should be demolished is likely to rage for another 25 years, just as it has done since the work of public art was installed in 1971. The sculpture makes more sense when it's a working fountain but, from 2000–04, the city couldn't afford to pay for the electricity and water to run it so the bone-dry eccentrocity became home to the homeless and various other undesirables. It also made more sense when there was a concrete freeway overhead, a structure that had to be torn down after the 1989 earthquake.

Vaillancourt Fountain is on the Embarcadero, between the Embarcadero Shopping Center and the Ferry Building.

There's a garden with a twist tucked away in a corner of Alamo Square Park, home to the picture-perfect postcard view of the row of Victorian houses known as the painted ladies. Look for a shed in the garden at the top of the park and you'll see the **Shoe Garden** with its various styles of shoes serving as planters. Gardener David Clifton started the garden using shoes left behind in the park. Now it's not uncommon for folks to drop by to contribute a pair specifically to see them planted. There are quite a variety of shoes all reflecting the variety of people in the neighborhood: cowboy boots, red patent leather heels, sneakers and roller skates.

Shoe Garden is located at the top of Alamo Square Park at the junction of Steiner and Hayes.

The Bay itself is the composer of the 'music' you hear at the **Wave Organ**, a wave-activated acoustic sculpture tucked away on a tiny peninsula behind the Golden Gate Yacht Club. Created by Peter Richards in 1986 while he was an artist-in-residence at the Exploratorium Science Museum, the organ is an inviting experience, not just for the subtle sounds it produces, but for the stunning views and quiet solitude of its plaza as well. Richards was inspired to construct the organ by a recording of sounds he heard that were made by water flowing in and out of a concrete dock in Australia. The structure itself is a jumble of carved granite and marble slabs, material salvaged from a demolished cemetery, that forms the platforms and walkways. Protruding from the slabs are listening tubes where you sit, lean or crouch to hear. The 'organ pipes' themselves are made of PVC and concrete and are scattered about the installation at various elevations to take advantage of the rise and fall of the tides. The sounds you hear, like drums, cymbals, and thunder, are caused by the impact of the waves against the pipe ends and the flow of water in and out of the pipes. The best time to visit is at high tide but it's a soothing experience at any time.

The Wave Organ is located at the end of Yacht Rd. Directions: the Organ is at the end of the jetty that forms the north side of the Golden Gate Yacht Club Marina. Walk past the yacht club to the end of the jetty.

EAST BAY
Festivals and events

When it comes to sizzle, it doesn't get much hotter than the **Fire Arts Festival** sponsored annually by the Crucible, an arts educational center that teaches, among other things, fire dancing, fire eating and fire blowing. This one-of-a-kind event is a chance for fire and light artists from all over the world to show off their flaming talents in a comfortable, indoor setting. Held in the Crucible's huge industrial arts building, the festival features such performances as fire cascading through water, dancers spinning in fiery vortexes, and musicians creating rhythm by rapidly lighting and stopping gas jets. Other artists create with a more stable source of brightness – light – making illuminated and special-effects sculptures from a variety of light sources. Burning Man is a participant in this event so you get a chance to see some of the art destined for, or hauled back from, the desert as well as attendees dressed in their playa best.

Quirk Alert

The Cacophony Society is a loose network of free spirits responsible for two spectacles you may witness if you're around when these pranks are perpetrated. The first is **The Brides of March**, always held on the Ides of March, where gangs of 'brides', all genders, roam the downtown area, shopping at fancy stores for things like rings and lingerie and buying pregnancy test kits at Walgreens. The second is **SantaCon** when hundreds of Santas swarm the tourist areas, singing raucous carols and handing out inappropriate gifts to startled passers-by. Intended as an anti-consumerism holiday message, the SantaCons are viewed by some as invasions or rampages rather than as harmless pranks.

Brides of March takes place in March in various locations in downtown San Francisco. SantaCon takes place in December. Contact the San Francisco Cacophony Society; www. sf.cacophony.org.

Fire Arts Festival takes place over five nights in July at the Crucible, 1260 7th St, Oakland, CA 94607; ✆ 510 444 0919; www.thecrucible.org. Directions: the Crucible is on 7th St in Oakland between Mandela Parkway and Union St.

Berkeley, sometimes referred to as Berserkly, holds its own spoof version of the already irreverent Pasadena Doo Dah Parade during the city's **How Berkeley Can You Be? Parade and Festival**. The vibrant diversity of cultural, political, and ethnic groups that make up the town, home to the University of California, is a perfect breeding ground for this most eccentric of events and Berkeley residents look forward all year to this opportunity to dress up and act extra silly. Ninety organizations, about a thousand marchers in all, show up to make fun of themselves or others. Past entrants included Billionaires for Bush carrying signs with slogans like 'Thanks for Paying Our Share'; giant pink bunny slippers and electric muffin 'cars'; a café that catapulted giant meatballs onto a huge plate of spaghetti; pregnant mothers from Birthaways marching with synchronized contractions; the Explicit Players naked marchers, and around 80 of the country's most delightfully daft art cars.

> **How Berkeley Can You Be? Parade and Festival** is held annually in September in Berkeley, CA. Contact Epic Arts at ✆ 510 849 4688; www.howberkeleycanyoube.com.

Art cars are vehicles that have been transformed into mobile, public folk art, their owners merging their adoration for the cars with their need to express themselves in a very public, extroverted way. The West Coast's largest gathering of art cars, **Art Car Fest** brings around one hundred of these highly individualistic car owners together for a four-day festival, caravan and fashion show during which they show off their cars and bond with fellow creatives who understand the strange passions that drive them to drive such things. These gentle extroverts converge first on Berkeley, then caravan to various Bay Area cities during the weekend, sometimes stopping to visit schools and hospitals and usually spending a day parked at a museum or plaza where you're welcome to gawk at will. Day four is always spent riding in the How Berkeley Can You Be? parade. The fashion show displays some pretty weird, over-the-top wearable art, some of which co-ordinates with the cars. The schedule changes every year so check the website for the current year's listings of places and events. These folks don't punch a clock, though, so their arrivals don't always match their expectations.

Art Car Fest is held annually in Berkeley in September. Contact Art Car Fest, 322 Cortland Ave, PMB #23, San Francisco, CA 94110; ✆ 800 391 9673; www.artcarfest.com. Events happen at various locations: see website for details.

The **Solano Avenue Stroll**, also called the 'Mardi Gras of the West' is a giant day-long festival that attracts 150,000 people to a mile-long stretch of boulevard stretching from Berkeley to Albany. The parade that launches the stroll is a good place to view the region's multitude of art cars, decorated vehicles that reflect their eccentric owners' quirky personalities and their views of the world. More than 100 entertainers take part in the parade, including 50 different bands. Gasoline engine floats are banned (except for art cars and city vehicles). If it can be pushed, pulled, ridden or rolled, it can be entered so you may see all kind of weird modes of transport including wheelchairs, beds, rickshaws and strollers.

The festival that follows features dozens of ethnic dance groups, face painters, magicians, stilt walkers and puppeteers. The street is closed for the day so the crowd can enjoy the several hundred game, craft, restaurant and food booths. Since this is Berkeley, you can expect food that is organic, pesticide free and/or produced by sustainable agriculture with utensils made from recycled materials.

Solano Avenue Stroll happens annually in September in Berkeley. Contact the Solano Avenue Association, 1563 Solano Ave, PMB #101, Berkeley, CA 94707; ✆ 510 527 5358; www.solanoavenueassn.org. The stroll happens on Solano Ave between The Alameda and San Pablo Ave.

The historical re-creationists who belong to **PEERS**, Period Events & Entertainments Re-Creation Society, take their history quite seriously. Almost every month they attend full-dress theme balls and events, with many of those attending both dressing and behaving as if they're really living during whatever bygone era is being represented that evening. The society stresses audience participation and interaction at their events and strives for historical accuracy by offering classes in living history, historic dance, and costuming. Etiquette plays a key role for many as it isn't considered proper to disturb the period impression that people are trying to create by acting out of character. The events, many of which are full-dress balls, cover a wide range of historical periods with names like a *Canterbury Tales* Feast & Ball; an 18th-century Scarlet Pimpernel Ball; a Jane Austen Tea, Fete and Assembly; a 1941 Evening in Casablanca; an Opera Masquerade Ball, and their famous annual Le Bal des Vampires, a recreation of a 19th-century French costume ball. Within each event there may be a concert, play, or musicale. Attracting fans from all over the Bay Area, most events are held in San Mateo at the Masonic Temple except for the annual Le Bal des Vampires which is held in Pleasanton. It's OK to attend out of costume and just observe, perhaps taking in one of the dance lessons offered before each event. The website has all the details.

Quirk Alert

There's a good reason that the **Benicia Camel Races** are occasionally held in this small East Bay town. Camels are part of the town's history, having been headquarters for the US Army's Camel Corps for two short months in 1864. The beasts were originally shipped in from Turkey with the thought that they'd be ideal for transporting ammunition through the arid desert regions of southern California. But the plan was abandoned when soldiers pushed the animals beyond their limits, killing many of them. So 35 of the remaining beasts were shipped up to Benicia where they lived around the armory for two months until sold to miners. Today the town repeats history every few years by holding the camel races. There's a museum in the Camel Barn.

Benicia Camel Races Benicia Historical Museum, 2060 Camel Rd, Benicia, CA 94590; ✆ 707 745 5435; www.beniciahistoricalmuseum.org.

PEERS 2144-B Buena Vista Ave, Alameda, CA 94501; ✆ 510 522 1731; www.peers.org. Events take place first Saturday every month (except December and June) in various locations.

Peculiar pursuits

With locations in both Oakland and Lake Tahoe, you have two opportunities to fly through the air, if not with the greatest of ease, at least with a modicum of style. The set up at **Trapeze Arts** is just like you see in the circus, only with plenty of nets and safety harnesses. People of all ages and abilities usually manage to overcome their fears after practicing pulling themselves up and hanging by their knees on a stationary bar. Then it's up the ladder and into the air. The experience is awesome whether you participate or just watch. Part sport and part art, the secret is in technique and form, not in brute strength. Regulars do it for fun, for physical fitness or because it's cheaper than a therapist. Trapeze Arts also teaches trampolines, aerial arts and wire walking. With just a single class you might progress from 'no way am I doing that' to launching yourself from the platform, swinging by your knees and catching the arms of an instructor in mid air. Call first: you need to reserve a spot in class.

Trapeze Arts 1822 9th St, Oakland, CA 94607; ✆ 510 419 0700 and 235 Squaw Valley Rd, Olympic Valley, CA 96146, ✆ 866 435 9386; www.trapezearts.com. Directions: the Oakland location is at the corner of 9th St and Pine. The Tahoe location is open seasonally late June through late August.

As battlegrounds go, the **Albany Bulb** is a pretty picturesque one with its prime wetlands, wildlife and sections of the Bay Trail spread along the shore of Richmond's inner harbor. But this idyllic piece of parkland has a sorry history, starting life as a pile of rubble from construction projects, part of Albany's former city dump. In 1985 the city abandoned the dump, allowing nature to reclaim what it could of the landfill. While Mother Nature was busy improvising, the homeless moved in, setting up an encampment village that was eventually destroyed by authorities in 1999. Artists drawn to junk sculpture found the area attractive as well and their public art pieces have been decorating the landfill ever since the dump was abandoned. For now the place is pretty wild, open to artists at will and to dog walkers appreciative of the freedom to let their pets run off leash. In typical California style, however, the Bulb is the center of controversy. The state has plans to construct an organized park complete with design review for artists and leash laws for dogs. Opponents of the plan want to preserve the wildness that nature started and to protect the right of 'outsider' artists to create their work from the abundance of flotsam and jetsam still washing up on the shore.

> **Albany Bulb** is part of the planned Eastshore State Park. Contact the East Bay Regional Parks District, 950 Peralta Oaks Court, Oakland, CA 94605; ℃ 510 562 PARK; www.ebparks.org/parks/eastshpk.htm or www.albanyletitbe.com. Directions: On I-80 near the Golden Gate Fields racetrack in Albany, take the Albany exit and head towards the Bay on Buchanan St. Parking is alongside the racetrack fence. As the park is still in the planning stage, access may be limited at times.

Quirkyville

There are several reasons to visit tiny Port Costa. The first is to visit **Clayton Bailey** on the way into town. You'll know you've reached this sculptor and robot maker's compound when you see the 27 gargoyles atop his redwood fence. Clayton's yard and workshop represents 40 years of passionate sculpting and tinkering, producing weird 'scientific' ceramic oddities, a mad doctor's laboratory of quack medical devices, and a robot gallery of shiny tin men made from galvanized parts from paint sprayers, vacuum cleaners and the like. (He happily hands you a popgun so you can shoot corks at his menagerie.) His pottery morphs into all kinds of strange shapes because he's always trying to break the laws of physics, displaying his melts, bloats, and breaks in a pottery chamber of horrors. Clayton, with his long Fu Manchu mustache, admits to being influenced by *MAD Magazine* as a child. He is open, by prior appointment only, every Sunday at 2pm.

In Port Costa proper, a ramshackle one-horse, one-block town, there are two worthwhile stops. Most of Port Costa's 250 residents are either artists or performers and that explains the enchanting **Theatre of Dreams**, a store and shadow-puppet performance space carrying 'practical and fantastical, usable and inexcusable' merchandise. Owner Wendy Addison's store is always a 'work in progress' as she uses vintage materials and techniques to make such eclectic merchandise as glass glitter stars, sheet-music cones, masks, top hats, tags, spangled fantasies and message boxes. In Wendy's words, her creations are 'objects for an imaginary life'. Every year she has a special Christmas showing of collectible ornaments. She's open only the first Saturday of every month plus her special performance and holiday shows.

Finally, visit the **Warehouse Café**, basically the only gathering place in town, where everyone drinks their pints from Mason jars. Known for their selection of more than 400 beers from around the world, the Warehouse is a cavernous building filled with stuff, stuff, and more stuff – as in an enormous polar bear standing in a glass case, an elevator pit, a train station waiting room, a birthday booth, light fixtures sprouting plastic grapes, and a meandering Marilyn Monroe theme.

Clayton Bailey 69 Carquinez Scenic Dr, Port Costa, CA 94569; ☎ 510 787 1168; www.claytonbailey.com. Tours are by appointment only at 2pm on Sundays. Directions: on I-80 south of the Carquinez Bridge, take the Crockett/Port Costa exit and turn east onto Pomona St. Pomona turns into Carquinez Scenic Dr, then look out for the gargoyles on the fence and the rocket ship in the front yard.

Theatre of Dreams 11 Canyon Lake Dr, Port Costa, CA 94569; ☎ 510 787 2164. Open first Saturday of the month, and for special performances only.

Warehouse Café 5 Canyon Lake Drive, Port Costa, CA 94569; ☎ 510 787 1827. Dinner served on Fri and Sat only. Directions: on I-80 south of the Carquinez Bridge, take the Crockett/Port Costa exit and turn east onto Pomona St. Pomona turns into Carquinez Scenic Dr, then turn left onto Canyon Lake Dr.

Tours

If you're interested in the civil rights movement in the West, Black Panther Tours provides a **Black Panther Legacy Tour** by bus that takes you to sites meaningful to the party and to the movement. The tour covers sites of many of the party's community service programs as well as the shootout site where Huey Newton was arrested and later convicted of voluntary manslaughter of a police officer.

Black Panther Legacy Tour ☎ 510 986 0660; www.blackpanthertours. com. Tours depart from the West Oakland Public Library at 18th Ave and Adeline.

Odd shopping

Bones and bugs clutter **The Bone Room**, an eccentric natural history shop that draws skeleton lovers from all over the west to shop amid this huge collection of human and animal skulls, embalmed insects, fossils, animal remnants and insect jewelry. Mainly of interest to scientists, museums, artists, designers, doctors and photographers, the just plain curious are also welcome, often purchasing earrings made from mink penis bones or lucite bracelets and rings with beetles, spiders or scorpions inside. There's an entire drawer of freeze-dried moles plus displays of hominid fossil casts, real fossil dinosaur and shark teeth, shark-tooth necklaces, and all the insect-collecting equipment you'll ever need. The skeletons may include those of a camel's skull, a full-size wallaby, or a walrus skull complete with tusks the size of a man's arms. This is one of only three stores in the country that deals in human bones, selling them mainly to medical schools and teachers. Rick Cauble, owner of the Bone Room and a former rocket scientist, is an amateur archaeologist, a passion that led to his opening the Bone Room.

The Bone Room 1569 Solano, Berkeley, CA 94707; ☎ 510 526 5252;
www.boneroom.com. *Open Tue–Sat 11am–6pm.* Directions: the store is
on Solano, between Peralta and Tacoma Ave.

Some boys just never get over their fascination with creepy crawly critters and the
East Bay Vivarium serves their needs nicely. Carrying one of the largest
selections of reptiles and herpetological supplies in the country, the Vivarium also
has a fine selection of live insects, insects that give new meaning to the word
creepy. Here you'll find tarantulas, scorpions, Madagascar hissing cockroaches and
spiders as big as post-it notes. Their selection of reptiles – snakes, lizards, turtles
and frogs – is so diverse that they attract buyers from all over the world and they
breed the food that keeps them fat and happy in the back of the store. (Think trays
of live rodents.) Spot, a cuddly 6ft water monitor lizard, is the store pet. They have
a traveling reptile program for schools, parties, and social events that features,
among several dozen other things, a bug that smells like Ceasar salad and a frog
that can kill a horse.

East Bay Vivarium 1827-C 5th St, Berkeley, CA 94710; ☎ 510 841
1400; www.eastbayvivarium.com. *Open Mon–Fri 11am–7pm, Sat and Sun
11am–6pm.* Directions: the store is on 5th St between Delaware St and
Hearst Ave.

Ancient Ways Occult Store and Candleshop specializes in merchandise
designed to influence your life in positive ways. Among their huge selections are
stones containing spiritual and healing properties that you choose based on your
intuition. Then you cleanse the stone in a ritual involving time, herbs, and a burial
in the earth for a bit. The herb inventory is extensive, used for medicinal and tea
purposes as well as for money, love, and protection spells. Baths, soaps, and
powders have names like Fast Luck, Come to Me, and Jinx Removing. Candles in
glass jars, called Seven-Day Candles, rely on faith and prayer for their effectiveness
and are 'dressed' with various oils such as those that attract money or love. Even
the color of the candle has meaning, with blue signifying health and peace; green,
money and abundance; orange, safety from enemies; red, love and sex; purple,
overcoming problems; white, truth and purity; and black, thought to remove bad
vibrations and extract retribution. They also carry several dozen kinds of sacred
incense, hold classes and special events, and hold the largest annual pagan
convention in the western US.

Ancient Ways Occult Store and Candleshop 4075 Telegraph Ave,
Oakland, CA 94609; ☎ 510 653 3244; www.ancientways.com. *Open daily
11am–7pm.* Directions: the store is on Telegraph Ave between 40th and
41st St.

A quasi-retirement home for mannequins past their prime, **Mannequin Madness**
provides a new lease on life for outdated models no longer deemed fashionable
enough for shop displays. Judi Henderson, owner of the company that sells and
rents the dummies and their body parts, has been passionate about collecting them
since 2000 when she stumbled across a man with 50 of them to sell. Since then she's
become an avid collector and spokesperson, giving them names and imagining
personalities for them much like girls do with their Barbie dolls. The basement and
garage of her home is littered with bodies, thousands of them, some without heads
and, for some, heads without bodies. Tall ones, skinny ones, fat ones, thin ones.
Bendable or rigid, gender specific or gender neutral, and of all ethnicities, they share

space just waiting to be adopted or rented out. At the holidays well-turned legs are in demand as people try to find parts to make a lamp like the one they saw in the movie *A Christmas Story*. Judi's business also prides itself on recycling body parts, preventing them from being dumped in the landfill. CSI, anyone?

Mannequin Madness 564 Kenmore Ave, Oakland, CA 94610; ☎ 510 593 0623; www.mannequinmadness.com. Visits by appointment only; please call Sylviette Gamble for an appointment.

Contrary to popular belief, fortune cookies as we know them didn't originate in China at all. They're as American as apple pie, invented, depending on which legend you want to believe, either by the Chinese 49ers as a substitute for lotus-nut moon cakes or by a Japanese American who invented them in 1914 as thank-you notes for his Japanese Tea Garden restaurant. Made from midwest wheat, the recipe is almost identical to that of crêpes but with all the air bubbles forced out. You can learn all this, as well as see how these popular desserts-with-a-message are made, at a visit to the **Fortune Cookie Factory** where 50,000 cookies are shipped worldwide each day. They'll make custom cookies to order with your own personal message (100 cookie minimum) and you can buy bags of Misfortunes, broken bits that are otherwise not saleable.

Fortune Cookie Factory 261 12th St, Oakland, CA 94607; ☎ 510 832 5552. Directions: the factory is on 12th St between Harrison and Alice St.

Quirky cuisine

In a case of life imitating art, the scene at **Grinder's Sub Shop** is straight out of a *Seinfeld* episode. With an atmosphere much like that of the Soup Nazi's, patrons waiting in the rarely ending lines to order from hundreds of options had better know precisely what they want by the time they reach the register—with cash only, and no bills larger than a $20 – or else they'll be banished until they do. Owner Peter York doesn't mind being called the Sandwich Nazi although he's quick to point out that he was the first such, having opened in 1991. Newbies usually leave in a daze.

Grinders Submarine Sandwiches 2069 Antioch Ct, Oakland, CA 94611; ☎ 510 339 3721. Directions: the store is on the corner of Antioch and Mountain Blvd.

Rooms with a skew

For really getting away from it all, consider **East Brother Light Station**, a restored Victorian B & B operated by a non-profit organization formed in the 70s to save the structure from demolition when the Coast Guard automated the lighthouse itself. Perched atop an island in the straits that separate San Francisco and San Pablo Bays, you arrive by boat (ten minutes from the mainland) to find peace and quiet along with a gourmet dinner and breakfast. The library has a collection of stories about former keepers and shipwrecks.

East Brother Light Station 117 Park Pl, Point Richmond, CA 94801; ☎ 510 233 2385; www.ebls.org. Directions: on I-80, take San Rafael exit to I-580 west toward Richmond–San Rafael Bridge. Just before toll plaza, take Point Molate exit. Follow signs to Point San Pablo Yacht Harbor. The staff picks up visitors in front of the Galley Café.

Attractions

Richard Tuck is so enamored of arcade games that he acquired many of those that used to be at San Francisco's Playland at the Beach in order to open **Playland-Not-at-the-Beach**, his free interactive museum of artifacts from the famous amusement park that closed in 1972. Hundreds of volunteers, including artists, muralists, carpenters, electricians, architects, and members of the community have helped him create an amazing fantasy inside the nondescript building that houses his Playland, a world of carnivals, circuses, and county fairs of days gone by. An avid collector of amusement-park memorabilia, he's built an interactive world around such exhibits as a miniature Santa's Village, a 300,000-piece miniature circus from 1930, midway and sideshow dioramas, county fair 'skill' games, a penny arcade, and Haunted Manor, a spooky adventure séance. Not only that, you can play the 50 pinball games for *free*. Richard, who is positively besotted with toys, also owns a real traveling circus plus an extensive collection of toys and dioramas in his home. Playland-Not-at-the-Beach is Richard's own mini-Playland, always evolving and always welcoming you to join him at play. The exterior of the building will not in any way give away what's inside. That's part of the surprise. Once you walk through the door though, there's no doubt you're in Playland.

> **Playland-Not-at-the-Beach** PO Box 894, El Cerrito, CA 94530; ✆ 800 548 5318 ext 25; www.playland-not-at-the-beach.com. Please call to arrange a visit. Located on San Pablo Ave at Jefferson. Free.

Just plain weird

Two hundred ghost sightings are said to have taken place in recent years on the USS *Hornet*, reputedly the country's most haunted ship. The former aircraft carrier was commissioned during World War II, becoming one of the most decorated ships in the Navy by destroying 1,400 Japanese aircraft, sinking enemy submarines and battleships, supporting amphibious landings, and destroying or damaging more than a million tons of enemy shipping. With a combat record like that, it's not surprising that some suddenly departed souls, many killed by tragic shipboard accidents or by suicide, would hang around looking for closure. Time after time, crews and visitors alike report strange goings-on, like slamming doors, vanishing tools, objects moving by themselves, toilets flushing of their own accord, ghostly images passing by and, finally, to feelings of being grabbed or shoved. The ship, docked in the Bay off the island of Alameda, is open daily.

Quirk Alert

An underground diner? Rumor has it that there's an Italian diner/speakeasy housed inside an old 1947 bus hidden away somewhere in the East Bay. According to an article – with pictures – in the *San Francisco Chronicle*, the diner has been operating since 2003, serving traditional Italian food under cover of darkness to patrons lucky enough to have a friend who knows the secret location and who will vouch for you. 'Open' just one night a week, the 'bustaurant' can't go legal since it's against the law to, among a host of other things, cook in an antique bus. Getting a seat on the bus isn't easy. You need a contact, a golden key and a secret number to eat at one of the five tables. Oh, and you have to know how to keep a secret.

Quirk Alert

It was supposed to be the start of something big, housing developments modeled after the too-sweet-for-words paintings of Thomas Kincaid. Also known as the 'painter of light', Kincaid paintings portray an idealistic view of an ideal world with flower-filled landscapes and fairytale-like houses filled, presumably, with perfect families enjoying heart-warming moments. The first 'Kincaid Community', a project within a cluster of others in a gated development, was a colossal failure and the builders quickly abandoned any marketing connections when it became obvious that no-one was going to spend half a million dollars based on an artist's unrealistic vision of the world.

USS *Hornet* Pier 3, Alameda Point, Alameda, CA 94501; ☎ 510 521 8448; www.uss-hornet.org. *Open Wed–Mon 10am–5pm, Tue 10am–3pm;* admission $14. Directions: on I-880 in Oakland, take the Broadway/Alameda exit and turn south on 5th St. Follow the signs to Alameda via the Webster St Tube (tunnel). Upon exiting the tube, follow Webster St to Atlantic Ave and turn right. Follow Atlantic Ave through the gate into Alameda Point (formerly Naval Air Station Alameda). Turn left on Ferry Point and proceed along the water towards the ships. NOTE: As of press time the *Hornet* was being threatened with closure so call first if you're hoping to visit.

Previous page AGROart™ Festival, Placer County (KS)

Above Sleep in a Cadillac in the '50s drive-in room at the Union Hotel & Victorian Mansion in Los Alamos (GC)

Below Salvation Mountain, a tribute to God made entirely of adobe and paint in southern California (LH)

North Bay/North Coast

FESTIVALS AND EVENTS

A kinetic sculpture is an artistic contraption built to travel on land, through mud, and over deep-harbor waters. These ludicrous machines can be simple crafts piloted by a single person or they can be quite complex, well-engineered vehicles powered by a team of pilots. Used bicycles, gears and machine scraps usually play a big role in their construction, as do a lunatic sense of humor and a wildly inventive brain. The **World Championship Kinetic Sculpture Race** covers a hopping 38-mile course that stretches from Ferndale to Arcata, drawing its participants from various other kinetic sculpture races held around the country. Over the course of the three-day event the craft have to cross sand dunes, plunge into open water, descend a steep, slimy mud slope, and make their way through the streets of three towns. It takes physical fitness and endurance to race in this event considered the triathlon of the art world.

Whatever the theme of the craft, the owner is usually dressed to match and equipped with theme-co-ordinated 'bribes' to sway the judges to overlook infractions of the quirky race rules, one of which stipulates that no pushing or pulling is allowed. The personal security rule requires that each sculpture carry a comforting item of psychological luxury, namely a homemade sock creature made from a not-too-recently washed sock. The honk and pass politeness rule requires yielding the right of way to another sculpture that wants to pass. (A one-finger salute is encouraged.) Time penalties are incurred for rule infractions, while time bonuses are given for carrying a passenger, called a barnacle, along the entire course. Past entries have included a six-man dinosaur, an eight-man iguana, a family of ducks, and a flying saucer. The Mediocre Award is given for finishing exactly in the middle. The Next to Last Award is highly coveted, making the end of the race particularly exciting. Awards are also given for best costume, the most memorable breakdown and the most spectacular water entry, or sinking, as the case may be.

The race, first held in 1969, was founded by sculptor Hobart Brown who was suggested for a Nobel Peace Prize in 1998 for 'recognizing unsung genius, promoting non-polluting transport and lifting the spirit' of the communities that hold the race. It all started when he welded extra wheels, seats and handlebars to his son's tricycle, creating a 6ft-tall vehicle he called a 'pentacycle'. His neighbor, a rival sculptor, made his own version and challenged Hobart to a race down Ferndale's Main Street. On race day, to their amazement, five other wacky contraptions showed up to compete and a legend was born. Hobart himself can be usually be found in his gallery dressed in his signature hi collar, cufflinks, overalls and stovepipe hat.

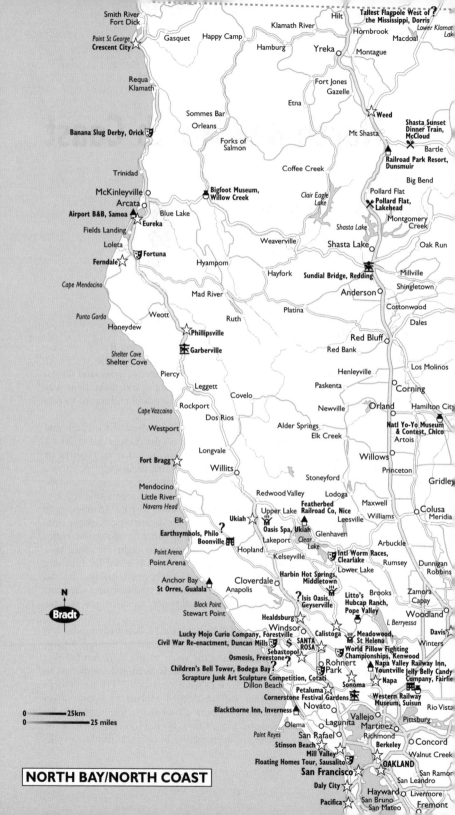

Smith River
Fort Dick

Klamath River

Hilt

Tallest Flagpole West of
the Mississippi, Dorris

Lower Klamat
Lak

Gasquet

Happy Camp

Hamburg

Hornbrook

Macdoal

Point St George
Crescent City

Yreka

Montague

Requa
Klamath

Fort Jones
Gazelle

Sommes Bar

Etna

Weed

Orleans

Banana Slug Derby, Orick

Mt Shasta

Shasta Sunset
Dinner Train,
McCloud

Forks of
Salmon

Coffee Creek

Bartle

Railroad Park Resort,
Dunsmuir

Trinidad

Clair Eagle
Lake

Big Bend

McKinleyville
Arcata

**Bigfoot Museum,
Willow Creek**

Pollard Flat

Airport B&B, Samoa
Eureka

Blue Lake

**Pollard Flat,
Lakehead**

Fields Landing

Montgomery
Creek

Loleta

Weaverville

Shasta Lake

Oak Run

Ferndale
Fortuna

Hyampom

Sundial Bridge, Redding

Millville

Cape Mendocino

Hayfork

Anderson

Shingletown

Mad River

Cottonwood

Punta Gorda

Weott

Ruth

Platina

Dales

Honeydew

Red Bluff

Shelter Cove
Shelter Cove

Phillipsville

Red Bank

Piercy

Garberville

Henleyville

Los Molinos

Leggett

Paskenta

Corning

Cape Vazcaino

Rockport

Covelo

Newville

Orland

Hamilton City

Westport

Dos Rios

Elk Creek

Alder Springs

Artois

**Natl Yo-Yo Museum
& Contest, Chico**

Longvale

Willows

Princeton

Gridley

Fort Bragg

Willits

Stoneyford

Mendocino
Little River

Redwood Valley

Lodoga

Maxwell

Navarro Head

Upper Lake

**Featherbed
Railroad Co, Nice**

Leesville

Williams

Colusa
Meridia

Elk

Ukiah

Oasis Spa, Ukiah

Clear
Lake

Glenhaven

Arbuckle

Earthsymbols, Philo
Boonville

Lakeport

Hopland

Kelseyville

**Intl Worm Races,
Clearlake**

Rumsey

Dunnigan
Robbins

Point Arena
Point Arena

Lower Lake

Zamora
Capay

Anchor Bay
St Orres, Gualala

**Harbin Hot Springs,
Middletown**

Brooks

Woodland

Cloverdale
Anapolis

**Litto's
Hubcap Ranch,
Pope Valley**

L Berryessa

Black Point
Stewart Point

Healdsburg

**Isis Oasis,
Geyserville**

Davis

Lucky Mojo Curio Company, Forestville

Windsor

Calistoga

**Meadowood,
St Helena**

Winters

Civil War Re-enactment, Duncan Mills

**SANTA
ROSA**

**World Pillow Fighting
Championships, Kenwood**

Sebastopol

Osmosis, Freestone

Rohnert
Park

**Napa Valley Railway Inn,
Yountville Jelly Belly Candy
Company, Fairfie**

Children's Bell Tower, Bodega Bay

Scrapture Junk Art Sculpture Competition, Cotati

Dillon Beach

Sonoma

Napa

Petaluma

**Western Railway
Museum, Suisun**

Cornerstone Festival Gardens

Novato

Rio Vista

Blackthorne Inn, Inverness

Olema

Lagunita

Vallejo

Martinez

Pittsburg

Point Reyes

San Rafael

Richmond

Concord

Stinson Beach

Berkeley

Walnut Creek

Mill Valley

Floating Homes Tour, Sausalito

OAKLAND

San Ramon

San Francisco

San Leandro

Daly City

Hayward

Livermore

Pacifica

San Bruno
San Mateo

Fremont

N

Bradt

0 — 25km
0 — 25 miles

NORTH BAY/NORTH COAST

Quirk Alert

While you're in Arcata, try to pick up a copy of the **Arcata Eye** (www.arcataeye.com), an obscure weekly newspaper famous for its **Police Log** feature. Ostensibly a column about the week's criminal activities in the region, it's a combination of humorous reporting, biting social commentary, and tell-it-like-it-is editorializing as well as the occasional poem or two. Author Kevin L Hoover is famous for such entries as:

The delicate fluorescent ambiance of a 24-hour doughnut shop was either shattered or enhanced, depending on your perspective, by a public he–she frisson. The feuding fuss-budgets took their leave.

A drummer's frenetic flamboyance
Resulted in noise deemed non-joyous
To one so appalled
The cops were soon called
To temper the sonic annoyance.

We now know that if you leave a drum in a tent in your front yard in the 700 block of J Street, it might disappear.

Some guy's writhing face-hole erupted with halitosis-borne verbiage that made up in volume for what it lacked in decency at Ninth and H Streets. A brush with adult beverages preceded the event.

Kinetic Sculpture Race is held annually in May, usually Memorial Day weekend. Contact the Ferndale Arts and Cultural Center that also serves as the **Ferndale Kinetic Sculpture Museum** 580 Main St, Ferndale, CA 95536; ☎ 707 845 1717 or ☎ 707 834 0529; www.kineticsculpturerace.org. Directions: the race starts at 9th and G Streets in downtown Arcata, just off Hwy 101. **Hobart Galleries** 393 Main St, Ferndale, CA 95536; ☎ 707 786 9259.

The Dungeness crab caught for the **Crab Races** in Crescent City is lucky indeed because those that race get to avoid the crab pot. The event, which has been going on for decades, involves a racetrack with chutes to keep the crabs from doing what comes naturally – going sideways. On race day you can catch your own racing crab or rent one, competing in either the kid or adult divisions. Business groups also race against one another, displaying unusual fervor. The lucky chosen crabs are released back into the ocean where they presumably pass on their winning survival strategies to the next generation. Crescent City is also home to the annual **Banana Slug Derby**.

Crab Races are held annually in February at the Del Norte County Fairgrounds in Crescent City. **Banana Slug Derby** is held annually in August at the Prairie Creek Redwoods State Park. Contact the Crescent City & Del Norte County Chamber Of Commerce, 1001 Front St, Crescent City, CA 95531; ✆ 800 343 8300; www.northerncalifornia.net. Directions: the Del Norte County Fairgrounds are just off Hwy 101 at the Crescent City exit. The Prairie Creek Redwoods State Park is 25 miles south of Crescent City on Newton B Drury Scenic Parkway off Hwy 101.

The floating home community that resides in the coastal town of Sausalito is an eclectic bunch, as are the homes they live in. Drawn to the unconventional lifestyle that's a defining feature of the Sausalito waterfront, these dockside inhabitants live colorful lives in 440 colorful homes that vary from converted tugboats to multi-million dollar, multi-level marine mansions. Every year the Floating Homes Association offers a **Floating Homes Tour,** a chance to visit the eccentric, quirky structures that house about a thousand people in a tight-knit community of free-spirited artists, writers, entrepreneurs and just plain folk drawn to live at the water's edge. Today all houseboats (those with a source of propulsion) and floating homes (those without any source of propulsion) must meet the same building and safety codes as do houses on land and prices for these homes are on par with others in this pricey area. During the tour you might see a home that incorporated an entire railroad car and another with three levels, a circular kitchen and an atrium.

Floating Homes Tour is held annually in October in Sausalito. Contact the Floating Homes Association, PO Box 3054, Sausalito, CA 94966; ✆ 415 332 1916; www.floatinghomes.org. Directions: tour leaves from the Kappas Marina in Sausalito, with parking at the Gateway Shopping Center. Exit Hwy 101 at Sausalito/Marin City. At the light at the end of the off ramp turn right. At the next light, turn right into the Gateway Shopping Center where you will be directed to a parking space.

The decades-long rivalry between the costal towns of Stinson Beach and Bolinas (see *Quirkyvilles*) is played out each July 4 at the **Bolinas–Stinson Beach Tug of War**. Men's and women's teams gather on both sides of the Bolinas Lagoon shoreline, fiercely clutching the huge rope stretched across the spit separating their towns and determined not to be dragged into the water by their opponents. The rules are simple: no digging in of feet and no sitting down.

Bolinas–Stinson Beach Tug of War is held annually on July 4. Contact the Stinson Beach Chamber of Commerce, PO Box 404, Stinson Beach, CA 94970; ✆ 415 868 1034. Directions: the Stinson Beach end of the rope is at the end of Seadrift Rd, off Hwy 1.

It's strange to think of artists competing against one another but that's just what they do at the **Mill Valley Paint Off**, a friendly competition sponsored by the local arts commission. Three-dozen artists set up easels at 10am in the town plaza and paint any scene visible to them, using the medium of their choice, until 3.30pm. Then the artists themselves vote for first, second, and third places. There's also a people's choice award and an award for the most creative and original work. Some of the artists dress quite artfully for this event.

Mill Valley Paint Off is held annually in July outside the Depot Bookstore and Café in Mill Valley. Contact the Depot Bookstore, 87 Throckmorton Ave, Mill Valley, CA 94941; ✆ 415 383 2665; www.depotbookstore.com. The painting starts at 10am, the judging happens at 3.30pm. Directions: take the Mill Valley exit from Hwy 101, follow E Blithedale Ave all the way into Mill Valley, then left onto Throckmorton Ave. Continue 1 block to Lytton Square Plaza.

Garbage Reincarnation Inc is the spark behind Cotati's annual **Scrapture Junk Art Sculpture Competition**. The event draws participants dressed in colorful recycled costumes who compete in four categories: professional, amateur, families, and children. Awards are given for best costumes and sculptures, and everyone sings dumpster diving songs and eats junk food.

Scrapture Junk Art Sculpture Competition is held annually in June in the La Plaza Park in Cotati. Contact Garbage Reincarnation Inc; ✆ 707 795 3934; www.garbage.org. Directions: take the W Sierra Ave exit from Hwy 101 towards Cotati. La Plaza Park is half a mile along on the right.

The Casini Ranch Family Campground and the California Artillery Historical Association are sponsors of the **Duncan Mills Civil War Re-enactment**, the largest such war re-enactment on the West Coast. Around 6,000 spectators show up to watch 1,000 dedicated re-enactors stage battles using horses, muskets, bayonets, full-size cannons, and Civil War-era fighting techniques. Between battles you can wander the Union and Confederate camps, taking in demonstrations of life in the mid 1800s and wondering what motivates the 100,000 or so avid Civil War re-enactors nationwide to spend their free time wearing scratchy, ill-fitting uniforms and dying over and over again for a cause long since fought. (Note: It's less expensive to fight for the Union as the gear is more plentiful. Most rebel uniforms were little more than rags by the war's end.)

Duncan Mills Civil War Re-enactment Casini Ranch Family Campground, Duncan Mills, CA (Russian River area). Event held every July. ✆ 831 751 6978; www.civilwardays.net. FROM THE EAST BAY/SACRAMENTO/CENTRAL VALLEY: take either the San Rafael Bridge (East Bay) or Hwy 37 (Sacramento/Central Valley) to Hwy 101 and head north to Santa Rosa. North of downtown Santa Rosa take the River Rd exit west, continuing a total of 25 miles to Duncan Mills, passing through the town of Guerneville along the way. At Duncan Mills turn left onto Moscow Rd, cross the bridge and make a hard right onto Freezeout Rd. Follow the signs. FROM THE SOUTH BAY: take either Hwy 101 or I-280 north to the Golden Gate Bridge, proceeding north on Hwy 101. Follow the directions from the East Bay above. FROM THE COAST: take Hwy 1 to Hwy 116 (River Rd) and go east until you reach Duncan Mills, approx 4 miles. Turn right onto Moscow Rd, cross the bridge and make a hard right onto Freezeout Rd. Parking at the second gated entrance off Freezeout Rd (called Mendocino Redwood Co Rd).

The worms may not be clear on either the concept or the rules, but their handlers get a kick out of the **International Worm Races**. During this event worms are dropped onto a bull's-eye and the first one to make it past the outer circle wins. You can bring your own worm or rent a fully trained Clear Lake variety. A tradition for more than three decades, the races originated to compete with the Calaveras County Frog Jumping Jubilee.

> **International Worm Races** are held annually in July in Redbud Park, Clear Lake. Contact the Clear Lake Chamber of Commerce, 4700 Golf Ave, Clearlake, CA 95422; **℄** 707 994 3600; www.clearlakechamber.com. Directions: take the 40th Ave exit from CA-53, turn left onto Lakeshore Dr. Redbud Park is on the right.

With faces and rumps only a mother could love, several dozen of California's most aesthetically challenged dogs vie for the title of the **World's Ugliest Dog** at the annual Sonoma-Marin Fair. Hairless, wrinkled, perhaps dentally deprived, several dozen beloved – if not lovely – pets compete in two classes, pure bred and mutt, with the winners of these two events facing each other in a mug-off for the current year's title. But it doesn't end there. A final round pits the newly crowned pooch against all former Ugliest Dog winners that have returned to defend or regain their titles, parading before a standing-room-only crowd on the Kiwanis Stage near the main concourse. Dogs also keep the judges busy during the **Crazy Dog Tricks** event, doing back flips, balancing balls, yowling tunes or playing a variety of instruments. Seeing the dog's owners cajoling their pets into performing is just as entertaining as the trick itself.

The fair also features a **Decorated Shoe Contest** during which sculptors, seamstresses and shoe fanatics submit shoes made from, or embellished with, paint, fiber, paper, or other sculptural media. The shoes are on display throughout the fair's five-day run.

> **World's Ugliest Dog** is held annually in June at the Sonoma-Marin Fair in Petaluma. Contact the Sonoma-Marin Fair, 75 Fairgrounds Dr, Petaluma, CA 94952; **℄** 707 283 3247; www.sonoma-marinfair.org. Directions: from Hwy 101, take the Washington St exit and go west. The Fairgrounds will be on the left between the second and third stop lights.

California is ground zero for the **Rock Paper Scissors** movement, a sport (of sorts) based on the schoolyard hand game often used to resolve disputes. The unlikely headquarters for the game is **Roshambo Winery** named after the slang verb that describes the challenge. Each year they hold a Rock Paper Scissors Pro-Am Invitational competition, the winner going on to the international finals in Toronto, headquarters of the World RPS society. The game goes back centuries to England where it is called Paper Scissors Stone. In 1842 a law was passed declaring 'any decision reached by the use of the process known as Paper Scissors Stone between two gentlemen acting in good faith shall constitute a binding contract.' For those of you who don't remember the rules, here they are: Rock beats scissors, which beats paper, which wins over rock (it wraps it).

> **Rock Paper Scissors Pro-Am Tournament** takes place in June at the Roshambo Winery, 300 Westside Rd, Healdsburg, CA 95448; **℄** 707 431 2051; www.roshabowinery.com. Directions: from Hwy 101, take the Central Healdsburg exit and head west on Westside Rd. The winery is about 3 miles down this road.

When wine was made by hand, the crushing was done with the feet, a skill you'll find not all that easy to replicate during **Grape Stomp** at the Valley of the Moon Vintage Festival. Contestants not only have to jump in a wine barrel filled with

Quirk Alert

The Bohemian Grove is the infamous summer gathering place of the most powerful and influential politicians and business leaders in the country. It is strictly members only at this Republican enclave deep in the heart of the redwoods, a faux summer camp of 2,700 acres where the chosen few, all of them men, spend two weeks each July bonding, peeing in the woods, and making deals out of the public eye. Well hidden from media scrutiny, future politicians are anointed while a are 'pass-the secret' network dispenses the kind of vital information – off the record – that can have worldwide implications. Secrecy is sacrosanct among the members and security is so tight that sentries hang from trees with binoculars.

If all this sounds just too weird, consider this: the opening ceremony involves red pointy hats, torches, and a 40ft owl altar. Every year an original play is written and presented, the women's parts played by men. There are 100 different campsites set up to handle the 2,000 campers, campsites with names like Sons of Toil and The Hillbillies, George H W Bush's camp. The club has a waiting list of about 3,000 hopeful powerbrokers and the average number of years spent on the waiting list is 15 to 20. Every Republican president since Coolidge has been a member. Nixon was quoted in 1971 as saying, 'the Bohemian Grove – which I attend, from time to time – is the most faggy goddamned thing you could ever imagine, with that San Francisco crowd. I can't shake hands with anybody from San Francisco.'

grapes, they have to try to stomp more juice out of the grapes than any other team. The festival also has a BUWB Contest, Best Use Of A Wine Barrel For Anything But Wine, and a Fireman's Water Fight during which opposing teams use fully charged hoses in a battle to control a wine barrel suspended across Spain Street. Past winners of the BUWB wine barrel contest include an airplane, a piggy bank and a cage for ring-necked doves.

> **Grape Stomp** is held annually in October at the Valley of the Moon Vintage Festival in Sonoma. Contact the Valley of the Moon Vintage Festival, PO Box 652, Sonoma, CA 95476; ☎ 707 996 2109; www.sonomavinfest.org. Directions: see the website for directions and recommended parking locations.

The **Sonoma County Harvest Fair** is a riot of funny competitions. While the focus of the fair is to celebrate the bountiful agriculture of the region, it's the events that bring in the crowds. You can't be a farmer to milk a cow at the Cow Milking Contest, a task that's harder than you'd imagine since the cows aren't used to amateur milkers and aren't all that co-operative. (Farmers and dairy workers are ineligible to compete.) The Just Call Me Martha event involves making a craft that would make her proud out of a pile of miscellaneous craft supplies. This is an individual rather than a team event and you get four hours to complete your creation before judging. The Lego contest is also an individual effort; the fair supplies the Lego and you have four hours to make a masterpiece. There's a Great

RELAXATION, CALIFORNIA STYLE

Northern California is filled with spas enticing you with mineral baths, hot springs, massage and relaxation experiences, some of them more than a bit out of the ordinary. The town of Calistoga, for example, is famous for its **mud baths**, with **Dr Wilkinson's Hot Springs and Resort** being one of the more famous of the several spas offering the unconventional treatment. The good doctor, a chiropractor, came to the area in the 40s, fascinated with the restorative possibilities of mineral hot water mixed with volcanic ash and peat. Originally used to treat arthritis, today the treatment is widely promoted for overall detoxifying and relaxation. The mud bath itself involves immersion in the heated muck followed by a mineral bath, a blanket wrap, and an optional massage. Accommodations are also available. Half a dozen other spas offer mud baths too, including **Indian Springs Resort & Spa**, **Mount View Hotel and Spa**, **Golden Haven Hot Springs**, **Oasis Spa**, and **Calistoga Oasis Spa**.

Dr Wilkinson's Hot Springs and Resort 1507 Lincoln Ave, Calistoga, CA 94515; ✆ 707 942 4102; www.drwilkinson.com

Indian Springs Resort & Spa 1712 Lincoln Ave, Calistoga, CA 94515; ✆ 707 942 4913; www.indianspringscalistoga.com

Mount View Hotel and Spa 1457 Lincoln Ave, Calistoga, CA 94515; ✆ 707 942 6877; www.mountviewhotel.com

Golden Haven Hot Springs 1713 Lake St, Calistoga, CA 94515; ✆ 707 942 6793; www.goldenhaven.com

Calistoga Oasis Spa 1300 Washington St, Calistoga, CA 94515; ✆ 800 404 4772; www.oasisspa.com. Directions: Calistoga is about 25 miles north of Napa on Hwy 29.

Oasis Spa 2605 Vichy Springs Rd, Ukiah, CA 95482; ✆ 707 462 9515; www.vichysprings.com.

Elsewhere, **Osmosis** is the only day spa in the whole country offering a cedar enzyme bath during which you're immersed in a mixture of finely chipped evergreen wood (basically sawdust) and rice bran mixed with heat-generating enzymes, sort of like being breaded before being fried. Afterward you can contemplate the utterly relaxing experience in their zen garden.

Osmosis 209 Bohemian Hwy, Freestone, CA 95472; ✆ 707 823 8231; www.osmosis.com.

Part treatment, part performance, the 'cascading stone massage' at **Meadowood** involves volcanic heated stones placed along your spine, between your toes and under your palms. Then two masseuses drench you in hot oils and rub you in a synchronized pattern from head to toe, adding chilled marble stones to the experience. The hot and cold rush is both invigorating and relaxing.

American Pumpkin Toss where distance, rather than the condition of the pumpkin upon landing (splat!) is what counts, and the Grape Spit, another distance event where the object is to spit a grape the farthest in a more-or-less straight line.

Kids especially love the Scarecrow Building Contest as well as the Mummy Wrap where group participants decide who gets to be wrapped up in a roll of toilet

Meadowood 900 Meadowood Lane, St Helena, CA 94574; ☎ 800 458 8080; www.meadowood.com.

The Tibetan sound massage combines a full body massage with vibrating sound waves from sacred Tibetan bowls at the **Claremont Resort & Spa**. Based on the ancient practice of using sound vibrations for healing and meditation, a 'singing bowl' is placed on your body after that part has been massaged. Each bowl is believed to produce vibrations that restore balance and alignment to your body's energy centers and encourage calm and spiritual development.

Claremont Resort & Spa 41 Tunnel Rd, Berkeley, CA 94705; ☎ 800 551 7266; www.claremontresort.com.

At **Orr Hot Springs** clothing is optional, the kitchen is communal, and the accommodations rustic (campsites, dormitories and a few duplex cabins). This place, formerly a 70s' commune, is a genuine throwback to the hippie era when the absence of creature comforts went largely unnoticed. Flowered skirts and love beads can be expected around the campfire. Day-use passes are available.

Orr Hot Springs 13201 Orr Springs Rd, Ukiah, CA 95482; ☎ 707 462 6277.

Nearby **Vichy Hot Springs** is no less historic but offers a different perspective. The waters here are naturally carbonated and have the same composition as do those at the famous springs in Vichy, France. The grotto looks exactly as it did when Mark Twain visited and he was expected to wear clothes just like everyone else. This is a far more upscale retreat, one with renovated rooms and lodging awards.

Vichy Hot Springs 2605 Vichy Hot Springs Rd, Ukiah, CA 95482; ☎ 707 462 9515; www.vichysprings.com.

Harbin Hot Springs is a California gem, a combination spa, retreat center and spiritual commune that leaves it up to you as to how you want to participate. You can simply enjoy the facilities – natural spring pools, conventional massages, WATSU water massage and spa treatments – or join in a variety of free events like yoga, 'unconditional' dance, and spiritual gatherings. Beyond that you can sign up for extended study workshops with names like Enlightened Warrior Training or Hot Wave Free Flow as well as Waterdance and Love, or Intimacy and Sexuality, one of their most popular retreats. Around 150 residents live at the center, maintaining and operating its facilities and extensive programs. Accommodations vary from camping to dormitories, from private rooms to cottages and there are cafés and a restaurant on the property. Clothing is optional; an open mind is not.

Harbin Hot Springs 18424 Harbin Springs Rd, Middletown, CA 95461; ☎ 707 987 2477; www.harbin.org.

paper. A Scarecrow UN-Building Contest follows. Pumpkin Carving By Committee involves groups of three or more and no-one can be voted off the island. Finally, there's the Team Scream with groups of five or more cheering on the Grape Stompers competing in the World Championship Grape Stomp. Teams of two, a stomper and a swabby, compete to see who can most successfully stomp

60lb of grapes into juice in five minutes. The stomper does most of the work; the swabby collects the results.

> **Sonoma County Harvest Fair** is held annually in late September/early October at the Sonoma County Fairgrounds. Contact the Harvest Fair office, PO Box 1536, 1350 Bennett Valley Rd, Santa Rosa, CA 95402; ✆ 707 545 4203; www.harvestfair.org. Directions: take Hwy 101 to Santa Rosa and exit onto Hwy 12, eastbound, towards Sonoma. Exit Hwy 12 at the Downtown exit. Upon reaching the surface street, Bennett Valley Rd, you will come to a stop light, and just in front of you on your right will be the Sonoma County Fairgrounds.

Remember those pillow fights you had as a kid? And how much fun it was to play in the mud? Well, you can do both at the same time at the annual **World Pillow Fighting Championships**. Anyone over the age of 14 can enter as long as they leave their maturity outside the arena. This absurd contest has been taking place each July 4 holiday for more than 40 years and begins after fire-fighters flood part of the main square to create an enormous mud pit. Competition begins by straddling a slippery wet pole suspended on the banks of the pit. Contestants select a pillow, dip it in the muck, and then slither as best they can along the pole to the starting position, an achievement in itself. Then

they go at it, pounding one another with the mud soaked pillows (average weight is 14lb) until one of them falls into the pit.

During combat their hands can't touch the pole and they can't use their feet to unseat their opponent. Their only weapon is the pillow that can be swung using one or both hands. They have to swing at least every 30 seconds. If a minute passes without anyone falling, the bout continues with one hand behind their backs. After yet another minute without a fall, fighting continues holding the pillow with both hands. The first contestant to topple his opponent into the mud wins the fall; two out of three falls wins the bout. Anyone prepared to fall down, get muddy and be laughed at is qualified to enter. Some contestants have been fighting for 30 years or more. Expect displays of American flags, beefcake, tattoos, and wet T-shirts. Sign in to play no later than 9am.

> **Kenwood World Pillow Fighting Championship** is held annually on July 4 in Kenwood, Sonoma County. Contact Kenwood Pillow Fights; ✆ 707 833 2440; www.kenwoodpillowfights.com. Directions: take Hwy 101 to Santa Rosa then Hwy 12 east to Sonoma. Hwy 12 goes through Kenwood. The fair is in Plaza Park on Warm Springs Rd, 2 blocks from the highway.

The tri-cities of Ferndale, Eureka and Fortuna put lights on just about anything that moves during their annual lighted parade weekend. Beginning on Friday night with the **Fortuna Electric Light Parade**, it continues Saturday with the

Trucker's Christmas Convoy and ends Sunday with the **Ferndale Lighted Christmas Tractor Parade**. These much-anticipated events involve pretty much everyone in town and pretty much everything (except plain old cars) that moves. Held rain or shine, the town folk line the streets to watch the decorated trucks, big rigs, farm tractors and wagons parade their holiday finery, decked out with thousands and thousands of lights. Many are decorated with elaborate themes such as the apple picker that was transformed into a fishing elf towing a rainbow trout. Flatbed trucks do their part by carrying music bands or partiers, and there's plenty of wassailing to keep you warm.

Fortuna Electric Light Parade is held annually in December in Fortuna. Contact the Fortuna Chamber of Commerce; 735 14th St, Fortuna, CA 95540; ☎ 707 725 3959; www.sunnyfortuna.com.

Trucker's Christmas Convoy is held annually in December in Eureka. Contact the Eureka Chamber of Commerce, 2112 Broadway, Eureka, CA 95501; ☎ 707.442.3738; www.eurekachamber.com.

Ferndale Lighted Christmas Tractor Parade is held annually in December in Ferndale. Contact the Ferndale Chamber of Commerce; ☎ 707 786 4477; www.victorianferndale.org/chamber. Directions: from Hwy 101, take the Ferndale exit.

It's mostly kids, 40–60 of them, who get involved in racing zucchinis at the **Zucchini Races** held each August at the Healdsburg Farmers Market. The vegetables race down a custom-made 20ft ramp, their wheels and decorations made of vegetables or toy parts. The best artistic design award once went to a gondola zucchini complete with gondolier holding a long pole. At Halloween they also race pumpkins.

Zucchini Races Healdsburg Farmers Market, North & Vine Streets, Healdsburg, CA; ☎ 707 431 1956. Dates vary in August.

PECULIAR PURSUITS

It's well known that the Egyptians were fond of cats. So is Loren Vigne, founder and chief priestess of **Isis Oasis**, a temple and retreat center honoring not only the Goddess Isis, but 20 cats of the ocelot, bobcat and jungle kind. Loren raised the wild cats in her backyard in San Francisco until the city outlawed the keeping of wild animals. Undeterred, she moved them to rural Geyserville, establishing a sanctuary both for her cats and for believers in the ancient queens and goddesses of Egypt. She also keeps llamas, goats, peacocks, pheasants, parrots, swans, and a living unicorn. The property, open most Sundays for tours, also houses an ornate Temple of Isis, a retreat house, a theater, and a lodge with bedrooms decorated in Egyptian décor honoring various goddesses. During the open houses you're welcome to participate in their temple ceremonies.

Isis Oasis 20889 Geyserville Ave, Geyserville, CA 95441; ☎ 800 679 PETS or ☎ 707 857 ISIS; www.isisoasis.org. Geyserville is 75 miles north of San Francisco on Hwy 101. Open houses most Sundays from 2pm to 4pm.

That strange three-tiered structure you see by the highway, the one with all the bells tinkling in the wind, is actually a powerful monument to the tragic 1994 shooting in Italy of a seven-year-old Bodega Bay boy, Nicholas Breen. Named the **Children's Bell Tower**, it commemorates the decision by Nicholas's parents to donate the boy's organs to seven Italians following his murder. One hundred and thirty bells adorn the monument, donated from churches, families, and schools all over Italy – school bells, cowbells, ships' bells, and mining bells. The centerpiece is a bell, made by the foundry that has been making papal bells for a thousand years. It was blessed by Pope John Paul II and contains the names of Nicholas and the seven sick people who received his donated organs.

Children's Bell Tower just off Hwy 1, Bodega Bay; ☎ 818 952 2095; www.nicholasgreen.org. Directions: the memorial is on the west side of Route 1, 1.5 miles north of Bodega Bay.

Patrick Amiot managed to get his neighbors to join him in his peculiar pursuit of displaying zany junk sculptures on front lawns. Known as the **Art Street in Sebastopol**, Florence Avenue is testimonial to the unifying power of art, a tribute to a community willing to let an eccentric into their midst. When Patrick and his wife Brigitte, both former ceramic artists, first moved to the small town of Sebastopol (pop 7,800), they confined their proclivity for weird art to inside their home, furnishing it with stuff from the flea market and city dump, including a carousel horse they hung from the dining-room ceiling and a chair they made from an old metal shopping cart.

Eventually, the clutter spilled outside, filling their yard, front porch and driveway and causing the neighbors concern. Then one day Patrick erected a giant 15ft-tall junk sculpture of a fisherman and his catch in his front yard and he was transformed from a weirdo to an artist in the eyes of the neighborhood. Even more amazing, some of them asked if he could build a sculpture for *their* front yards and pretty soon houses on both sides of the street, for several blocks in both directions, boasted one of his whimsical sculptures: a postal worker being chased by a dog, a fireman, Batman, a giant duck made from a motor home, and a surfer among them. Patrick's own yard now has a giant jukebox and the visitors' bureau proudly sends folks to wander the art street. You're welcome to visit his shop – you can't miss it. Fondness for his sculptures has spread to other parts of town as well.

Art Street in Sebastopol Florence Ave, Sebastopol; ☎ 707 824 9388; www.patrickamiot-brigittelaurent.com. Directions: take Hwy 101 to Hwy 116 west. At downtown Sebastopol turn left on Bodega Ave, then go 4 blocks and turn right on Florence.

A former scientist and biochemist, **Earthsymbols** creator Alex Champion now builds labyrinths and mazes, using sacred geometry and dowsing in his work. His designs are massive and complex, including a four-leaf-clover maze, the 3,000-year-old Cretan Labyrinth design, and a Viking-age horse trappings maze. Dozens of his earthworks are scattered around the state and you're welcome to visit five of those he's built on his property in Mendocino County. Just call first for permission to visit most days from 12 noon–5pm. The best time to see the Earthsymbols is in the spring when the grasses are short and green.

Earthsymbols 19020 Gschwend R, Philo, CA 95466; ✆ 707 895 3375; www.earthsymbols.com. Directions: follow Hwy 128 6 miles north from Philo. Turn left on Clark Rd, then left on Gschwend Rd. *Open by appointment only from 12 noon–5pm.*

MUSEUMS AND COLLECTIONS

A red car dangles from a tree; a cluster of arms reaches up from the grass; and a stack of file cabinets 60ft high pierces the meadow. These are all part of an non-intimidating-by-design art experience, the **di Rosa Preserve**, a 250-acre complex of almost 2,000 modern art pieces displayed in both indoor and outdoor settings. The collection is the passion of one man, Rene di Rosa, now in his eighties, who has been collecting emerging California artists for 40 years. Almost 750 artists are represented, their work chosen for no other reason than because di Rosa fell in love with it. Expressing an intense dislike for stuffy, pretentious art galleries, the work is displayed in a manner simply meant to be experienced and without explanatory signs of any kind. The preserve is di Rosa's legacy, a gift of art you needn't understand, just enjoy.

di Rosa Preserve 5200 Carneros Hwy, Napa, CA 94559; ✆ 707 226 5991; www.dirosapreserve.org. Viewing is through guided tours, reservations are required. *Tours are at various times, closed Sun and Mon.* Directions: from CA-29 North of Vallejo, turn left onto CA-12 West. The preserve is 2.5 miles along this road.

One of Fort Bragg's most famous residents is Madame Chinchilla, a renowned tattoo artist and owner of **Triangle Tattoo & Museum**. Both a museum and a working tattoo parlor, the place is a fascinating glimpse into a culture that most of us are curious about. Dispelling the notion that tattoos are only for angry young men, the displays explore the history, lore and culture of this misunderstood art. You'll see the historical designs of other cultures, those of the Japanese masters, military designs from World War II to the present and a collection of artifacts of the last living circus sideshow sword swallower. Eleven segments of a Discovery Channel documentary called *Tattoo! Beauty, Art and Pain* was filmed here. The Madame herself refers to her creations as 'art with a pulse'.

Triangle Tattoo & Museum 56 B North Main St, Fort Bragg, CA 95437; ✆ 707 964 8814; www.triangletattoo.com. *Open daily 12 noon–6pm.* Directions: the museum is on North Main St (Hwy 1) in Fort Bragg between E Oak St and E Alder St.

For such a quiet, unassuming man, *Peanuts* creator Charles M Schulz sure had an active imagination, entertaining the world with the escapades of his eccentric band of little characters. For Charlie Brown, Lucy, Snoopy and the rest of their cartoon world, there were no adults and no buildings, just universal truths expressed with humor and tenderness. The **Charles M Schulz Museum** honors the creator and his pals in a simple building housing 80% of the cartoonist's output along with a research center and promotional materials from *Peanuts*'s licensees. On the second Saturday of every month visitors have the chance to meet a professional cartoonist and to learn in mini-workshops. The Snoopy labyrinth contains paths totaling one-sixth of a mile with resting points in Snoopy's nose, eye, and ear.

Charles M Schulz Museum 2301 Hardies Lane, Santa Rosa, CA 95403; ✆ 707 579 4452; www.schulzmuseum.org. *Open Mon–Fri 12 noon–5pm;*

closed Tue, Sat and Sun 10am–5pm. Directions: north of Santa Rosa on Hwy 101, take the Guerneville Rd/Steele Lane exit. Turn left onto Steele Lane and bear right onto West Steele Lane. The Museum is on the corner of West Steele Lane & Hardies Lane, just past the Ice Arena.

Litto, the Pope Valley Hubcap King, collected more than 2,000 hubcaps over a 30-year period. He arranged them, decorated with bottles and pull tops, into various constructions that can be seen at **Litto's Hubcap Ranch** in Pope Valley.

Litto's Hubcap Ranch 6654 Pope Valley Rd, 2.1 miles northwest of Pope Valley, CA; www.janesaddictions.com/damonte01.htm. Directions: on CA-29 north of Yountville, turn right onto CA-128. Bear Left on Chilies Pope Valley Rd, then turn right on Pope Valley Rd.

It's hard not to become a believer, at least for a little while, after you've read the handwritten accounts of Bigfoot encounters at the **Bigfoot Museum** in the backwoods town of Willow Creek. This little museum tries mightily to make a compelling case for the existence of the big ape, aka Sasquatch, with plaster casts of big footprints, a map of northern California sightings, a diorama of Bigfoot on a bluff, and a video of the famous Patterson film that purportedly shows something apelike lumbering through grainy footage. Perhaps the most interesting evidence, though, is in the Bigfoot Memories Journal where folks have recorded their scary experiences in the woods, mentioning most often how foul smelling the creature is. The place is run entirely by dedicated volunteers.

Bigfoot Museum is located in the Willow Creek–China Flat Museum, PO Box 102, Willow Creek, CA 95573; ✆ 530 629 2653. Directions: Willow Creek is at the intersection of Hwy 96 and Hwy 299. *Open Wed–Sun 10am–4pm Apr–Oct. Open by appointment only at other times.*

The **Hand Fan Museum** is the only museum in the country dedicated just to hand fans, the kind you wave in your face on a hot day. The little museum presents the cultural and artistic history of the hand fan and, according to passionate collector and museum curator Pamela Sher, they tell the history of the cultures and people who used them. Fans have been used in fashion, in religion, in battle, and in ceremonies and can be made of anything from palm fronds to jewel-encrusted ivory.

Hand Fan Museum 327A Healdsburg Ave (on the grounds of the Healdsburg Hotel), Healdsburg, CA 95448; ✆ 707 431 2500; www.handfanmuseum.com. *Hours: varies, but typically Thu–Sun 11am–3pm. Closed for rainy days and holidays.* Directions: on Hwy 101 in Healdsburg, take the central Healdsburg exit. Follow Healdsburg Ave to the town plaza, where the hotel is on the right.

Displaying a number of wacky race vehicles from past kinetic sculpture races, along with videos, posters and photos from three decades of race history, the **Ferndale Kinetic Sculpture Museum** honors the brave and the foolish who make this event so memorable. The race rules posted on the wall are a hoot. It all started over a bet to see who could build the weirdest and best human-powered sculpture. (For more details see the *Kinetic Sculpture* entry under *Festivals and Events.*)

Ferndale Kinetic Sculpture Museum 580 Main St, Ferndale, CA 95536; ✆ 707 845 1717 or 707 834 0529 www.kineticsculpturerace.org. *Hours: vary; call before visiting.*

QUIRKYVILLES

The verbal equivalent of a secret handshake, Boontling is the language once spoken exclusively in **Boonville**, a tiny, isolated, gritty little town with a population of around 1,200. The 1,300-word language was widely spoken from the mid 1800s to the mid 1900s, but has slowly died out along with the 'codgy kimmies' (old men) who kept it alive. Boontling is considered one of the most extraordinary examples of homemade languages ever devised. For example, 'Burlappin'' is a verb refering to the time a shop clerk was caught in *flagrante delicto* atop a few burlap sacks; a 'bucky walter' is a pay phone, named after a buckey (a nickel) and the first person in the valley to have a telephone. You can read about this strange language when you stop for 'bahl gorms' (good food) or 'zeese' (coffee) in town but you better look quick when you're on the road. The town is only four blocks long. If you want to hang out in Boonville, check out the one-of-a-kind Boonville Hotel.

> **Boonville** Contact the Anderson Valley Chamber of Commerce, PO Box 275, Boonville, CA 95415; ☎ 707 895 2379; www.andersonvalleychamber.com. Learn more about harpin' boontling, the local lingo of the Anderson Valley, at www.avbc.com/visit/boontling.html. Directions: Boonville is on Hwy 128, between Philo and Yorkville. The Boonville Hotel Hwy 128 at Lambert Lane; ☎ 707 895 2210. Reservations by phone only.

Bolinas is hard to find. Feisty and independent, its residents opted decades ago to protect themselves from tourism and encroaching suburbanism by tearing down all the road signs directing you to their town. Populated then, as now, by 'free-spirits', the hamlet is a living, breathing microcosm of California stereotypes. From the café (Think Globally, Eat Locally) to the saloon to the community bulletin board, Bolinas exemplifies all that California was – and still is – known for: mystics, hippies, alternative therapies, green cuisine, feminism, and rampant social consciousness. Bolinas is a small place, shabby but not chic, and prefers to remain so.

This ultra-quirky place is famous for a wacky ballot measure that defines the town as a

> Socially acknowledged nature-loving town because to like to drink the water out of the lakes to like to eat the blueberries to like the bears is not hatred to hotels and motor boats. Dakar. Temporary and way to save life, skunks and foxes (airplanes to go over the ocean) and to make it beautiful.

The woman who initiated this extremely weird, grammatically incorrect, stream-of-conscious initiative exemplifies the eccentric nature of the town, wearing burlap and painting her face with chocolate. Rather than being shunned, she's been adopted by the townsfolk as a loveable loner.

> Directions: don't bother looking for road signs directing you to Bolinas: the 'Bolinas Border Patrol' tears them down as soon as they go up. To find Bolinas, take Hwy 1 north of Stinson Beach to C122. Look for the intersection sign and turn left about 2 miles past the Audobon Ranch. Two more lefts bring you into town. Wharf Rd dead ends at a lovely beach with no parking.

TOURS

Sex and politics are part of the commentary when you take a walk in Marin County's famous Muir Woods with **Tom's Scenic Walking Tours**. Tom Martell, an eco-guide with a comedic bent, has a decidedly California (read politically correct) perspective on the birds, the bees and hugging trees. You'll learn how redwood trees and spotted owls reproduce and, if you're lucky, you'll see thousands of ladybugs having a not very ladylike orgy. Be sure Tom tells you all about California's 'green' movement. Tours go through Muir Woods to Point Reyes or along the ocean bluffs. Besides spectacular scenery and the serenity that comes with being one with nature, you'll be entertained by Tom's knowledgeable and humorous commentary.

Tom's Scenic Walking Tours ☏ 415 381 5106; www.muirwalker.com

A tour through **Mrs Grossman's Sticker Factory** is pure delight for the kids as they see the source of America's largest art sticker factory. From teddy bears to dinosaurs to scrapbooking slogans and page borders, the factory prints 800,000 stickers an hour, 15,000 miles of them a year. Little is off limits to visitors as you tour the facility since Mrs Grossman loves having company and just wants people to be happy. The tour starts with an introductory film narrated by her dog so it's not surprising that her employees can bring their dogs to work as long as they're well behaved. Fido can stay at their owner's workstation all day or join a playgroup in the on-site kennel.

Mrs Grossman's Sticker Factory 3810 Cypress Dr, Petaluma, CA 94954; ☏ 800 429 4549; www.mrsgrossmans.com/tours. Tours are at 9.30am, 11am, 1pm, and 2.30pm, Mon–Fri. Reservations are required.

ODD SHOPPING

Catherine Yronwode's business card describes her **Lucky Mojo Curio Company** as a manufacturer and distributor of 'Paraphernalia of Conjure', meaning that she's one of the country's premier spiritual merchants, expert in the kind of products needed for hoodoo, voodoo and other religious rituals, including Catholic, Jewish and Buddhist. They make 2,000 different products designed to influence or change your luck, including anointing oils, crystals for baths and floor washes, zoological curios, folkloric amulets, and talismans. They carry body-part ritual candles, penis-bone charms (mostly made from raccoons), and things like 108 Buddha heads carved on a walnut. You can learn how to make your very own money altar using a money lamp and a variety of money-drawing oils, or a love altar with a keep-it-burning love light and oils like 'return to me' and 'peaceful home'. A seemingly endless supply of herbs, minerals and roots are available for casting spells to influence others to do your bidding. The company's incredibly well-organized retail store is located at the rear of their manufacturing facility, nestled under a redwood tree. As odd a shop as you'll ever find, this is a fascinating place to see tools for magical spell-craft as well as meet Dusty, a life-size wizard sculpture and Lefty, an 1880s' human skeleton that watches over the store from his redwood coffin.

Lucky Mojo Curio Company 6632 Covey Rd, Forestville, CA 95436; ☏ 707 887 1521; www.luckymojo.com. Directions: take the Covey Rd turning off Hwy 116 at Carr's drive-in in Forestville and go a block and a half north. Look for a post with the number 6632 on it and turn left into that driveway.

You might think they take their fashion way too seriously in **Mill Valley** when you see the **Fashion Police** handing out tickets at parades and civic events for infractions such as 'failure to yield to good taste'. Patrolling on roller blades in chic bike shorts, the 'clothes cops' are actually employees of a local clothing store. The bright yellow citations include fashion faux pas like 'did not listen to significant other', 'inappropriate dress for body type', and 'bad banana khaki karma'. If you've been cited you can bring in your ticket for a discount. Most men consider it an honor to attract their attention, dressing even more appallingly than normal.

Fashion Police of Mill Valley Contact Famous for Our Look, 96 Throckmorton St, Mill Valley, CA 94941; ✆ 415 388 2550.

Wendy Gold deals in toilet seats, expensive ones designed to make you laugh. While you might think the toilet a strange place for art, Wendy's **Arte de Toilette** decoupage creations grace well-heeled thrones and celebrity derrieres throughout the country. Making use of surf-board and auto-body repair technology so the products will stand up to the rigors of bathroom conditions, all her seats are one-of-a-kind, made to order in whatever theme strikes your fancy. For example, an embittered divorcee embedded pictures of her ex-husband and another decorated hers with her pre-nuptial agreement. But most of her seats are playful, like the one Sean Penn ordered as a gift for Jack Nicholson in which she made a collage of pin-up girls and snapshots of Jack. Others involve body parts, cityscapes, florals and sports themes. She also has a line of scales like 'Moment of Truth' featuring a devil beckoning with a cookie opposite an angel proffering a grapefruit half.

Arte de Toilette ✆ 415 990 5343; www.artdetoilette.com.

A combination store and museum, **Golden Gait Mercantile** is a delightful mixture of nostalgic merchandise and displays of the way folks looked as they shopped in the late 1800s. Proprietors Marlen and Sandra Messman live on the third floor of their 4,000 square foot establishment, stocking it with merchandise that Sandra remembers from her childhood in old Vermont. You can wander among the vignettes of life in Victorian times on the second floor and browse old display cases of things like Dutch Cleanser, Burma Shave and Fells-Neptha soap on the main floor.

Golden Gait Mercantile 421 Main St, Ferndale, CA 95536; ✆ 707 786 4891. Directions: Golden Gait Mercantile is on CA-1 in Ferndale, between Brown St and Washington St.

Sebastopol has its very own Little Shop of Horrors with the world's largest collection of carnivorous plants. No matter which way you turn at **California Carnivores** you're probably witnessing some mayhem. It may be showy, as when the infamous Venus flytrap ostentatiously snaps up a fly, or more likely subtle, as when the devious sundew plant traps its prey using a glue-like secretion. In all the store sells 120 varieties of plants that do lunch, eating everything from bugs to fish hatchings to rodents.

California Carnivores 2833 Old Gravenstein Hwy South, Sebastopol, CA 95472; ✆ 707 824 0433; www.californiacarnivores.com. *Open Thu–Mon 10am–4pm; closed Tue and Wed.* Directions: on Hwy 101 at Cotati, take the Cotati/Hwy 116 West exit. Head west on 116 towards Sebastopol. Go 6 miles, then turn right on Old Gravenstein Hwy at the Antique Society building. Drive 1.5 blocks.

QUIRKY CUISINE

Perhaps the strangest food combination you'll ever encounter can be found at **Tex Wasabi's**, a restaurant specializing in – believe-it-or-not – **Sushi-BBQ**. Mixing Texas-style barbeque with Japanese sushi, the place is bizarre-with-a-buzz, meaning that it's become a hot nightspot in downtown Santa Rosa. Fortunately you can order *either* sushi or barbeque or, if you're really adventurous, you can try combinations like the Kemosabe roll. The décor is a mix of Japanese and Texan, the big-screen TV plays Westerns and Japanese *Godzilla* movies and the logo is a cowboy digging his spurs into the sides of a koi carp.

> **Tex Wasabi's** 515 4th St, Santa Rosa, CA 95401; ☎ 707 544 8399; www.texwasabis.com. Directions: from Hwy 101, take the Downtown Santa Rosa exit, then turn right on 3rd St, then left on B St, then right on 4th St.

One of the most elegant meals you can eat in California is aboard the **Napa Valley Wine Train**, famous for its white-linen gourmet meals served aboard one of their luxuriously restored 1915–47 Pullman dining, lounge, parlor or Vista Dome rail cars. With brunch, lunch and dinner seating, the line also offers murder-mystery dinners and concert runs. Naturally, the meal is accompanied by Napa Valley boutique wines.

> **Napa Valley Wine Train** departs from Napa for brunch, lunch and dinner trips. Contact the Napa Valley Wine Train, 1275 McKinstry St, Napa, CA 94559; ☎ 800 427 4124; www.winetrain.com. Directions: on Hwy 29 in Napa, take the Lincoln Ave exit. Go east on Lincoln Ave. Turn right on Soscol Ave. Turn left at the lights onto First St then immediately turn left again onto McKinstry St.

A cross between a rustic saloon and a cozy English pub, the **Ace-In-The-Hole** is the country's first cider pub, serving a variety of ciders, some alcoholic, from the gleaming tanks behind the bar. Owner Jeffrey House spent two years perfecting his ciders that make use of the region's uniquely flavored apple juice.

> **Ace-In-The-Hole** 3100 Gravenstein Hwy North, Sebastopol, CA 95472; ☎ 707 829 1101; www.acecider.com/pub.html. Directions: on Hwy 116 at Graton Rd, 3 miles north of Sebastopol.

Copia is like a culinary theme park, a cultural museum and educational center that, in their own words, 'explores the interconnectedness of food, wine, and the arts.' Is that California enough for you? But the core exhibit at Copia, 'Forks in the Road: Food, Wine and the American Table', is a large and fascinating exhibition that explores the culture of Americans and their food. A series of interactive stations sprinkled throughout the exhibit invite you to do things like test your sense of smell, guess at the use of mystery kitchen gadgets, look at photos of unwrapped candy bars and try to identify them, and learn the language of short-order cooks. The whole experience is both educational and entertaining, ending with a funny film of movie scenes involving food. The rest of Copia involves eating at one of several restaurants, watching various cooking demonstrations, wine tastings, or signing up for various food and wine classes. All that plus gardens and the food-related art galleries. It's an odd blend of serious museum and tourist attraction.

> **Copia** 500 First St, Napa, CA 94559; ☎ 707 259 1600; www.copia.org. *Open daily 10am–5pm except Thu.* Directions: from Hwy 29 in Napa, take the Lake Berryessa/Downtown Napa exit and turn right (this becomes Soscol Ave). Turn right on First St and go 2 blocks. Copia is located on the left.

ROOMS WITH A SKEW

There's no shortage of quaint Victorian B & Bs in Eureka but if you want a touch of quirky with your quaint, try the **Elegant Victorian Mansion**. A stay here involves much more than just a bed and breakfast as innkeepers Lily and Doug Vieyra are infused with enthusiasm for the era. Everything in the house reflects the social and physical realities of the late 1800s, from reminders not to use matches to light the electrical lamps, to serving you lemonade and ice-cream sodas in the afternoon, to explaining the reasoning behind closed cupboards in kitchens. This is interactive living history at its best, where the guests are often referred to as students and playing house – Victorian style – becomes a memorable experience. Lily and Doug will even take you around town in a horseless carriage. Arthur Frommer called it 'the most authentic Victorian atmosphere we have ever encountered in the United States.'

> **Elegant Victorian Mansion** 1406 C St, Eureka, CA 95501; ✆ 707 444 3144. Directions: on C St, between 14th and 15th Ave.

Being able to park your airplane right outside your bedroom window at the **Samoa Airport Bed and Breakfast** is how men convince their wives to go flying with them. Built as a fly-in resort that couples could enjoy together, this restored 40s blimp base is located on the dunes just outside of Eureka. You don't have to be a pilot to stay there.

> **Samoa Airport B & B** Eureka Municipal Airport, 900 New Navy Base Rd, Samoa, CA 95564; ✆ 707 445 0765; www.northcoast.com/~airbb/. Directions: on Hwy 101 near Eureka, take the CA-255 exit and head west.

The last thing you'd expect to find among the ranches and vineyards of Sonoma County would be an authentic slice of Africa. Called **Safari West**, this 400-acre preserve is the passionate pursuit of Peter Lang and his wife Nancy, who have managed to create a safari experience closely resembling the real thing continents away. Opening their private facility to the public in 1992, the couple delight in sharing their home with human guests as well as 400 animals and birds representing 90 species. (About the only animals not represented here are lions, tigers, and elephants.) The variety of daily safari adventures include animal sightings of giraffe, cheetah, zebra, antelope (cheetah fast food!), Cape buffalo, white rhino, and warthogs, lovingly referred to as spare-parts animals. There's also a huge walk-in aviary. Throughout the year they hold special holiday events such as the one at Halloween where you come dressed as your favorite animal or the Valentine's Day Sex Tour that offers chocolate, champagne, and a mating rituals animal tour. Meals are available at the **Savannah Café**; non-safari guests are welcome to dine there with advance reservations. One of only six such ventures in the country to be admitted to the American Zoo and Aquarium Association, Safari West participates in the exchange and breeding of endangered species.

Safari West 3115 Porter Creek Rd, Santa Rosa, CA 95404; ☎ 800 616 2695; www.safariwest.com. Directions: on Hwy 101 north of Santa Rosa, take the River Rd exit and turn right onto Mark West Springs Rd. Remain on this road for 7 miles. At Franz Valley Rd, turn left directly into the entrance.

Clustered in an idyllic setting on the shores of Clear Lake, the **Featherbed Railroad Company** consists of restored train cabooses, each with all the comforts you'd expect in a more conventional bed and breakfast. The cabooses, all decorated differently, are painted in a variety of colors and surrounded by flowers, lawn, and trees. Breakfast is served in your private rail car or in the main station house.

Featherbed Railroad Company 2870 Lakeshore Blvd, Nice, CA 95464; ☎ 800 966 6322; www.featherbedrailroad.com. Directions: on Hwy 20 at Nice, make a right on Hammond Ave. At the end of Hammond, make a left and the Featherbed Railroad Company is on the left-hand side.

The **Napa Valley Railway Inn** is a cluster of antique rail cars – three cabooses and six refrigerator cars – converted into a bed and breakfast. Sitting on the now-defunct, original railroad tracks right in the heart of Yountville, the inn had a previous incarnation as rows of shops.

Napa Valley Railway Inn 6503 Washington St, Yountville, CA 94599; ☎ 707 944 2000. Directions: on Hwy 29, take the Yountville exit, turn right onto California St, and left onto Washington St.

A visit to the **Blackthorne Inn** is sort of like visiting eccentric relatives. After all, who else would build a Tudor-like treehouse with an octagonal bedroom perched on top? This whimsical inn comes with trap doors, narrow walkways, and spiral staircases among its five rooms, to say nothing of an outdoor tree-top potty reached by crossing a sky bridge. The Eagle's Nest on top is a glass-enclosed octagonal room with a 360-degree view of trees and sky. It was originally designed as a private residence.

Blackthorne Inn 266 Vallejo Ave, Inverness, CA 94937; ☎ 415 663 8621; www.blackthorneinn.com. Directions: about one hour's driving time north of the Golden Gate Bridge. Take Hwy 101 north, to the Sir Francis Drake Blvd/San Anselmo exit. Go west on Sir Francis Drake Blvd Olema. Turn right onto Route One/Shoreline Hwy and proceed north approximately 2 miles. Make a left turn just before the green bridge towards Inverness (this is Sir Francis Drake Blvd, but the road sign is often missing). Continue a little over 1 mile, and look for a green city sign saying 'Inverness Park'. Just around the next bend, you'll be taking a left onto Vallejo Ave.

You can't help but exclaim, 'What on earth is that?' when you drive along Hwy 1 past **St Orres**, a rough-hewn, heavy-timbered structure more reminiscent of Red Square than of the redwoods surrounding it. Built entirely of native timbers in a style best called 'Russian inspired', the inn and restaurant is the work of three partners who have been building on the site since 1977. With unique buildings that honor the Russian heritage of the area, the inn now encompasses the main hotel and restaurant with its eight handcrafted rooms reached by spiral staircase, eight creek-side cottages (one with an onion dome like the main house), and five meadow cottages. The restaurant is known for chef and partner Rosemary Campiformio's North Coast cuisine.

> **St Orres** 36601 Coast Hwy 1, Gualala, CA 95445; ☎ 707 884 3303; www.saintorres.com. Directions: located on Hwy 1, north of Gualala.

ATTRACTIONS

This is definitely not your Great Aunt's garden. With 300 pinwheel daisies, 120 nautical miles of monofilament, and a Monterey pine densely covered with sky-blue Christmas ornaments, **Cornerstone Festival of Gardens** is the first ongoing, gallery-type exhibit of landscape gardening in the United States. There are no rhododendrons and climbing roses here; instead, noted landscape architects and designers from around the world are invited to contribute gardens that are unconventional and thought provoking. Chris Hougie, inventor of those glow-in-the-dark stars seen nightly by millions of children on their bedroom ceilings, founded the gardens, inspired by a similar exhibit he saw in France. Captivated by its originality, he decided to bring something like it to the United States.

Designers are given approximately 1,800 square feet in which to express their creativity. For example, Break Out involves 32 screen doors, embedded within a massive maze of hay bales through which you can dart, sporadically opening and closing doors with a satisfying clang. A dying pine tree is saturated with 100,000 sky-blue Christmas balls so that it disappears against a blue sky while contrasting against a grey one. Some of the garden exhibits, like the ornament-festooned pine, are view-only while others, such as Earth Walk, a descending and ascending journey of smell, feel, touch and breath, are more interactive. The number of gardens on display varies from 15 to around 30, each remaining in place for one to two years.

> **Cornerstone Festival of Gardens** 23570 Arnold Dr, Sonoma, CA 95476; ☎ 707 933-3010; www.cornerstonegardens.com. Directions: Cornerstone Festival of Gardens is about 6 miles south of Sonoma on CA-121.

No trip to northwestern California would be complete without a drive along the **Avenue of the Giants**, a 31-mile portion of old Hwy 101 famous for its giant redwood trees. The route is also known for a number of gimmicky tourist attractions, among them drive-thru trees, chainsaw woodcarvings and Bigfoot memorabilia. You can also walk a cute, quirky Hobbitton redwood trail and see entire houses carved out of a single log. Eccentric entrepreneurs with a vision of the touristy possibilities that the future could bring created most of these attractions decades ago.

> **Avenue of the Giants** is off Hwy 101 between Phillipsville and Pepperwood; www.avenueofthegiants.net. Directions: the northern entrance to the avenue is at the Pepperwood exit of Hwy 101.
> **One Log House** 705 US Hwy 101, Garberville, CA 95542; ☎ 707 247 3717; www.oneloghouse.com. Directions: 8 miles south of Garberville.
> **The Chimney Tree & Hobbitton, USA** Avenue of the Giants, Phillipsville, CA 95559; ☎ 707 923 2265.
> **Chandelier Drive-Thru Tree** Legget, CA. Directions: follow the signs from Hwy 101 at Legget.
> **The Tree House** 26510 Avenue of the Giants, Redcrest, CA 95569; ☎ 707 722 4262. Directions: Redcrest is 4 miles south of the entrance to the Avenue of the Giants at Pepperwood.

ONLY IN CALIFORNIA

Only in California ... does feng shui, the ancient Chinese art of placing things so there is a positive flow of energy, become a voter issue. In the Marin County town of Sausalito plans for a new police and fire building were threatened because the location of the building would have 'cut off the mouth of Qi'. The issue became so divisive that it ended up on the ballot and opponents of the building were voted down. Now, peace and harmony flow once again in Sausalito despite the Qi-blocking building.

Only in California ... is one of the safest and most desirable places to live immediately outside a prison. The town of Point San Quentin Village offers prison housing on prison grounds and there's a waiting list to live there. Prison employees needed for emergencies get priority. The view includes San Francisco Bay, the big cell block, and the exercise yard.

Long a fixture of the northern California coast, the **Skunk Train** has been following its coastal 'Redwoods Route' since 1885. But today, instead of hauling logs, it carries passengers in vintage 20s' and 30s' rail-buses and open-air cars, the last remaining train of its kind in use. So named because the trains announced their arrival due to a mixture of pot-bellied stove smoke and gasoline fumes, the route runs from Fort Bragg 40 miles to Willits on Hwy 101. Besides sheer scenic-ness, the line also offers holiday and seasonal theme runs from Easter Egg Hunts and Halloween trains to a Father's Day ribs & beer run.

Skunk Train Fort Bragg Depot, foot of Laurel St, Fort Bragg, CA 95437. Willits Depot, 299 East Commercial St, Willits, CA 95490; ✆ 800 866 1690 www.skunktrain.com

FESTIVALS AND EVENTS

Dressing in vintage 1920s' clothes is half the fun when attending the **Great Gatsby Festival, Tea, and Fashion Show** on the shores of Lake Tahoe. The festival re-creates every aspect of life during the flapper era from cars to fashions and from games (like jacks, marbles and jump rope) to entertainment. Held at the Tallac Historic Site, the highlight of the two-day event is the fashion show of period costumes from the 1880s through the 1920s. Prizes are given for the best costume, the best hat created at the garden party, and the best antique tea-cup story, a story relating to an antique tea cup or other heirloom piece.

> **Great Gatsby Festival, Tea, and Fashion Show** takes place in August at the The Tallac Historic Site in South Lake Tahoe. Contact the Tahoe Heritage Foundation, PO Box 8586, South Lake Tahoe, CA 96158; ☎ 530 544 7383; www.tahoeheritage.org. Directions: the Tallac Historic Site is on CA 89 at Camp Richardson, a few miles west of South Lake Tahoe.

Nevada City becomes Teddy Town during the annual **Teddy Bear Convention**. Thousands of arctophiles (people who collect, or are fond of, teddy bears) gather for teddy bear games, teddy bear songs, teddy bear contests and a huge teddy bear collectors' trade show. The whole town gets involved and bears are displayed everywhere. The event is sponsored by the American Victorian Museum that displays several thousand teddy bears, miniature bear buildings and miniature teddies.

> **Teddy Bear Convention** takes place in April at the Miners Foundry, 325 Spring at Bridge St, Nevada City. Contact the Teddy Bear Castle, PO Box 328, Nevada City, CA 95959; ☎ 530 265 5804; www.teddybearcastle.com. Directions: the Miners Foundry is on Spring St between Bridge St and S Pine St, 2 blocks from Hwy 49.

You might want to bring along a book to the annual **Banana Slug Derby**, an afternoon of slug racing and slug tasting, the latter of the chocolate kind. Banana slugs are curious creatures, around since the dinosaurs, and possessed of 27,000

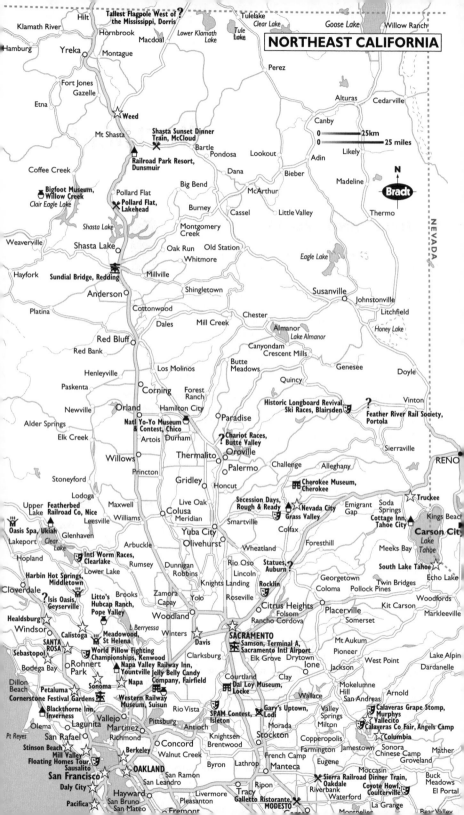

teeth-like things with which they eat their weight every day. Because they trail slime and have tentacles that move independently, they can see in two directions at once, which makes the race vaguely interesting. The slugs are returned to their forest homes afterward.

> **Banana Slug Derby** takes place at the Prairie Creek Redwoods State Park in Orick on the third Saturday in August. Contact the Prairie Creek Redwoods State Park; ✆ 707 464 6101 ext 5301; www.parks.ca.gov /?page_id=415. Directions: 25 miles south of Crescent City on Hwy 101. Take the Newton B Drury Scenic Parkway exit and follow the signs.

The coveted Tahoe Cup is won by one of two sternwheelers, California's *Tahoe Queen* or Nevada's *M S Dixie*, which race against each other each year at the **Great Lake Tahoe Sternwheeler Race**. The only authentic sternwheeler race west of the Mississippi, the event attracts thousands of spectators to the southern shores of the lake as well as hundreds of participants dressed in period costumes. A flotilla of boats follows the sternwheelers, acting as unofficial escorts. The California–Nevada border serves as the start and finish line for the 6-mile course.

> **Great Lake Tahoe Sternwheeler Race** takes place on Labor Day just off shore at the Edgewood Tahoe Golf Course. Contact Virtual Tahoe; ✆ 800 210 3459; www.virtualtahoe.com. The race starts at 11am. Directions: the Edgewood Tahoe Golf Course is on Stateline, north of South Lake Tahoe.

There just has to be a good story behind a feisty town named **Rough and Ready**. The town originally took its name from a mining company named after President Zachary Taylor, or 'Old Rough and Ready' as he was known. But the real story began in April 1850 when the population of 3,000 miners, gunslingers, and honky-tonk women seceded from the union to protest a mining tax and the prevailing state of the town's lawlessness. By forming the Great Republic of Rough and Ready they became a free and independent republic, maintaining their rebellious independence until a burst of patriotism on July 4 found them rescinding their secession. Now, on the last Sunday of every June the town (pop 1,500) remembers their quirky claim to fame with **Secession Days**, including the Secession Days Play, a melodrama performed in the center of town. Funky and funny, the off-key play ends with a spirited rendition of *God Bless America* followed by a volley of fake gunshots. As always, the proclamation from 1850 is read: 'Whereas, we the people, hereby establish a peaceful independent republic in the State of California. Furthermore, we declare because it be God's will to perpetuity, we cease to be reduced to seeing our property and lives being taken over by those not of us, but those against us. Therefore, we the people of the township of Rough and Ready deem it necessary and prudent to withdraw from the territory of California and from these United States of America to form peacefully, if we can, and forcibly, if we must, the Great Republic of Rough and Ready.'

> **Rough and Ready Secession Days** takes place in Rough and Ready on the last Sunday in June. Contact the Rough and Ready Chamber of Commerce, PO Box 801, Rough and Ready, CA 95975; ✆ 530 272 4320; www.roughandreadychamber.com. Directions: Rough and Ready is west of Grass Valley off Hwy 20.

Even the spectators are encouraged to dress in 1870s' clothing when watching skiers race in the **Historic Longboard Revival Series Ski Races**. Early longboard skis, nicknamed 'Norwegian Snowshoes', were carved from a single piece of wood and ranged in length from nine to 14 feet. They came with a 6ft center stick that had to be placed between the legs, used for braking and steering by leaning on it. (Today the manufacturer dubs them Soprano Sticks.) To race, contestants must wear leather boots and serious historic attire. Only authentic, handmade wax, called dope, can be used to speed the skis along. Prizes are given for the best crashes as well as the best costumes and race times.

> **Historic Longboard Revival Series Ski Races** takes place at Plumas Eureka Ski Bowl, in Plumas Eureka State Park with heats in January, February and the finals in March. Contact the Eastern Plumas Chamber of Commerce, 8989 Hwy 89, Blairsden, CA 96103; ☎ 800 995 6057; www.easternplumaschamber.com. Directions: the Longboard races take place in the ski area of the Plumas Eureka State Park, 5 miles west of Blairsden on County Road A-14.

The Old Sacramento historical district is transformed into a scene from the 1850s during Old Town's **Gold Rush Days**, complete with dirt-covered streets, horse and buggy carriages, covered wagons, Pony Express re-enactments and Wild West shootouts. Cars are banned in favor of horses and visitors walk the dusty streets and boardwalks just as the pioneers did 150 years ago. Living history characters roam the street in costume and you never know when you'll come upon a street drama unfolding before you.

> **Gold Rush Days** takes place in the old Sacramento Historical District, in Sacramento in September. Contact the Sacramento CVB; ☎ 800 292 2334; www.sacramentocvb.org. Directions: on I-5, take the J St exit and follow the signs to the old Sacramento Historical District.

Veggies take center stage at the **Placer Farm & Barn Festival**, an event that combines farm tours, agricultural artists and entertainment. The main activity is **AGROart**, a competition where individuals and groups create sculptures made of fruits and vegetables. The results are both impressive and funny and you'll be astounded at the carvings and sculptures that can be created out of supermarket produce. The festival also takes to the road for a self-guided tour of working farms where you can interact with farm animals and enjoy the modern and vintage barns they inhabit.

> **Placer Farm & Barn Festival** takes place in Sierra College Quad, Rocklin, in October. The farm tour is restricted to 300 vehicles. Contact the Placer Farm & Barn Festival; ☎ 530 885 5670; www.placerfarmandbarnfestival.com. Directions: from I-80 W take Rocklin Rd and turn right to the college. From I-80 E take the Sierra College Blvd/Rocklin Rd exit and turn east. Take a right on Rocklin Rd, and Sierra College will be on the right.

The delta town of Isleton holds the Del Rio **SPAM Contest** every winter to honor not just the pink potted pork product, but its label as well. Seems that only SPAM labels stayed attached to their mother ships when all other kinds of cans lost their identification during the floods of 1996. There's a SPAM cooking contest, SPAM costumes, a SPAM eating contest (no hands and if you throw up, you're disqualified), a SPAM sing-along and a SPAM carving contest. Past recipes included Spamaghetti, Spamoni, and Spam Wonton Soup. Past carvings include the *Titanic* with its sour cream-covered iceberg. In the USA, a can of SPAM is consumed every 3.6 seconds.

SPAM Contest takes place in Isleton in February. Contact the Isleton Chamber of Commerce, PO Box 758, Isleton, CA 95641; ✆ 916 777 5880; www.isletoncoc.org.

PECULIAR PURSUITS

If running a real diesel locomotive is on your list of things to do before you die, then the **Feather River Rail Society** has a deal you probably can't resist. You and up to three of your friends can rent such a vintage locomotive and operate it, under close supervision, of course, on the museum grounds. Your adventure can be on a switch engine, a road locomotive, or a combination of both in a double session. Income from this **Run-A-Locomotive** program helps fund the restoration of other vintage train equipment.

Feather River Rail Society PO Box 608, 700 Western Pacific Way, Portola, CA 96122; ✆ 530 832 4131; www.wplives.org/FRRS_Home/frrs_home.html. Rentals are available from mid April to mid November and are subject to weather. Reservations are required. Directions: from CA-70, take the Portola exit and turn south onto Gulling St. Turn right onto Pacific, then right onto Western Pacific Way.

Almost every Sunday from December through February you can attend the **Butte Valley Chariot Races**. Way up in this far northeastern corner of California, the racers, mostly ranchers, gather to compete against one another in up to a dozen heats per race day. Racing in the winter, when they're not as busy working as during other seasons, these loyal, committed fans of the hobby huddle around 50-gallon fire drums, warming their hands and chatting congenially between races. The chariots are mostly rudimentary with a homemade quality about them, but the horses are superb animals, passionately trained all year for the sport.

Butte Valley Chariot Races happen at Macdoel Downs in Butte Valley on Sundays from December to February. Contact the Butte Valley Chariot Racing Association; ✆ 530 397 3711; www.cot.net/~orecal/drivethr/chariot1.html. Directions: take Hwy 97 one quarter mile north of MacDoel to Sheep Mountain Rd and follow the signs.

Perhaps the most memorable experience in this region of the state can be found at the **Living Memorial Sculpture Garden**, a powerful and haunting tribute to veterans of all wars created by Dennis Smith who formed the sculptures as a way of healing from his own Vietnam War experience. Each of the ten larger-than-life-size metal sculptures depict the passions of war, portraying themes such as *Those Left Behind*, *POW-MIA*, *The Nurses*, *The Refugees*, and *Coming Home*. With Mt Shasta as a powerful backdrop, this outdoor garden and labyrinth is planted with 58,000 pine trees, one for every American soldier lost in the conflict. The setting is one of stark beauty and spirituality and should not be missed.

Living Memorial Sculpture Garden PO Box 301, Weed, CA 96094; www.livingmemorialsculpturegarden.org. Directions: the LMSG is on the west side of Hwy 97, just under a mile north of country road A12.

While you're up in that remote neck of the woods, the tiny town of Dorris, population 886, has a flagpole so high that a quarter of the town's residents would have to stand on one another's shoulders to reach the top. It's the **Tallest**

Flagpole West of the Mississippi. The Dorris Lion Club built it as a fundraiser and the flag it flies is an enormous 30ft x 60ft.

> The **Tallest Flagpole West of the Mississippi** Dorris, CA. Contact the Butte Valley Chamber of Commerce, 304 S Main St, Dorris, CA 96023; ℂ 530 397 3711; www.buttevalleychamber.com.

Dentist Ken Fox always had a passion for sculpting but it wasn't until he was in his forties that he began indulging in shaping more than teeth. Beginning with a colossal statue he called the *Amazon Archer*, a 120 ton, 42ft-high nude woman he built in the parking lot of his dental building, he followed up with an Amazon Warrior, again nude, followed by a giant Chinese coolie pushing a wheelbarrow, a tribute to the Chinese laborers who settled the area. The **Auburn Statues**, as they're called, weren't all that popular when Fox starting constructing them in the 60s; in fact, the school district routed buses away from his building so the kids wouldn't have to see the naked ladies. But now the town has embraced their strange claim to fame and various Fox statues can be seen at three locations in Auburn. Contact the chamber and they'll fax you a map.

> **Auburn Statues** Auburn. Contact the Auburn Chamber of commerce, 601 Lincoln Way, Auburn, CA 95603; ℂ 530 885 5616; www.auburnchamber.net. Directions: The Chinese coolie statue is at the Auburn Chamber office, 601 Lincoln Way (at the corner of Elm and Lincoln). The Claude Chana statue is at the Maple St exit from I-80, and the Amazonian Warrior and Amazonian Archer statues are at the artist's dental office on Auburn Ravine Road at the corner of Palm Ave.

MUSEUMS AND COLLECTIONS

The **World Famous Asphalt Museum** is the peculiar passion of associate professor Scott Gordon who houses the strange collection in his office in the engineering building at Sacramento State University. Hidden behind a folding screen, the four 'story' (shelf) collection has a huge web presence compared to its actual physical size. Gordon used to drive a lot and, envious of other's museums, began collecting chunks of asphalt from the roads he traveled. Understandably the museum drew few visitors until he opened it on the web. Now he gets contributions from all over the world, storing them behind the screen. You can visit the museum during the professor's office hours.

> **World Famous Asphalt Museum** Office of Scott Gordon, California State University, 6000 J St, Sacramento, CA 95819; ℂ 916 278 7946; www.ecs.csus.edu/~gordonvs/ asphalt/asphalt.html. *Open during office hours.*

The **National Yo-Yo Museum** is home to yo-yos from the 1920s to the present and the enthusiastic staff can take you through the history of the toy, demonstrating their own considerable skills along the way. It's also home to the world's largest yo-yo, dubbed Big Yo, a 256lb, 50-inch diameter model that actually works as long as it's hoisted and played by a crane

operator. In 2004 they celebrated Big Yo's 25th birthday by playing it at the **National Yo-Yo Contest** held each October. Every Saturday the museum sponsors a bring-your-own-yo-yo practice session from noon to 2pm in the alley behind the store. Two to three hundred of the best yo-yo players in the country end up at the museum for league finals each year, competing in a variety of string and looping tricks. This is an ever-evolving skill as yo-yo technology transforms the sport.

> **National Yo-Yo Museum** is located in the rear of Bird in the Hand, 320 Broadway, Chico, CA 95928; ✆ 530 893 0545; www.nationalyoyo.org; chicotoymusuem.com. National Yo-Yo Contest is held the first Saturday in October. The Museum is on Broadway between W 3rd and W 4th St.

Dedicated rail buffs from the Bay Area Electric Railroad Association are responsible for the **Western Railway Museum** where you'll see a nostalgic collection of electric railway cars in the display barn being restored by volunteers. The visitor center tells the story of electric railroading from 1890–1960 and you can take a quaint train trip through the hills around the museum.

> **Western Railway Museum** 5848 State Hwy 12, Suisun, CA 94585; ✆ 707 374 2978; www.wrm.org. *Open Sat and Sun 10.30am–5pm, and Wed–Sun 10.30am–5pm between Memorial Day and Labor Day.* Directions: on CA-12, midway between Suisun-Fairfield and Rio Vista.

QUIRKYVILLES

Locke, a Sacramento delta 'town', makes for a short but memorable stop. Founded in 1915 after a fire destroyed the Chinese section of adjoining Walnut Grove, the town was laid out, built, and inhabited entirely by the Chinese. By the 40s Locke was at its peak with 1,500 residents, herb shops, fish markets, gambling halls, brothels, and its own one-room schoolhouse. Not quite a ghost town, Locke today has around 75 residents and a smattering of shops and restaurants amid the shabby and abandoned buildings.

> **Locke** Contact the Dai Loy Museum, Locke; ✆ 916 776 1661; www.locketown.com. Directions: on I-5, exit at Walnut Grove–Thornton Rd and follow the signs to Walnut Grove. Locke is half a mile north of Walnut Grove.

Most ghost towns just fall into ruin, decaying until no-one is left. But in **Cherokee** around a dozen folks still live among the ruins of this former Gold Rush town, maintaining a museum open only on weekends. They celebrate their most exciting holiday every September – **President Hayes Days** – to commemorate his visit there in 1880. In its heyday the town, home of the most famous hydraulic gold mine in the world, had a population of more than 1,000.

> **Cherokee** Contact the Cherokee Museum, 4226 Cherokee Rd, Cherokee, CA 95965; ✆ 530 533 1849; www.rockincherokee.com. Directions: on CA-70, turn onto Cherokee Rd 12 miles north of Oroville.

TOURS

Merging theater and standup comedy, Old Sacramento's **Hysterical Walk** is an entertaining romp that makes fun of the more eccentric elements of California's history. More like a stroll than a walk, the tour is led by talented comics, performing in character and costume, who weave historical truth in with tall tales.

And some of the tales get mighty tall indeed, enhanced by historical characters being 'channeled' through the guides as well as interactive games and melodramas as a way of personalizing historical situations. Ambling through the district with guides like Cindy Speakman as Myrtle T Handpickle, you'll not only laugh yourself silly, you'll pick up a bit of history as well. Come Halloween they add ghostly walks, holding séances and channeling murderers.

> **Hysterical Walks** start at the Rio City Café, 1110 Front St, Sacramento. Contact Hysterical Walks; ☎ 916 441 2527; www.hystericalwalks.com. Walks are scheduled for Fri and Sat at 7pm and 8.30pm. Groups require a reservation.

It takes just seconds to eat one, but a week to make, trivia you'll learn at the **Jelly Belly Candy Company** tour. During the 40-minute experience you'll be on olfactory overload, surrounded by the sweet smells of chocolate and fruit as you watch the process of Jelly Belly candy making. After the tour you can sample the results or have lunch at the café where you can order Jelly Belly-shaped pizza and hamburgers.

> **Jelly Belly Candy Company** One Jelly Belly Lane, Fairfield, CA 94533; ☎ 800 953 5592; www.jellybelly.com. Factory tours operate daily 09am–4pm (except holidays). Directions: from I-80 in Fairfield, take the Hwy 12 exit, turn onto Abernathy Rd, then left onto Courage Dr, left onto North Watney Way and left onto Jelly Belly Lane.

ODD SHOPPING

An array of delightfully strange characters are strung up throughout **Tanglewood Forest**, an enchanting shop in downtown Nevada City run by doll artist Marci Wolfe. Shopping in her world of fairies, gnomes, Tree Elves, Brumbles, gentle witches and kind wizards is a charming experience as the creatures dangle and dance all around you. In this storybook landscape each of her characters is sculpted with original hands, faces, and various other body parts, then clothed and airbrushed until they take on distinct personalities.

> **Tanglewood Forest** 311 Commercial St, Nevada City, CA 95959; ☎ 800 854 2521; www.tanglewoodforest.com. Directions: on CA-49 in Nevada City, take the Broad St exit and go west. Turn right onto Union Alley, then left on Commercial St.

QUIRKY CUISINE

It's one thing to dine in an elegant old railcar but it's even better if the cars are moving, especially if the scenery is as memorable as the meal. The **Shasta Sunset Dinner Train**, an experience enhanced with linens, fine china, polished silver and crystal, run on various schedules from April through December from downtown McCloud near Mt Shasta for the three-hour, four-course meal. Originally built for the Illinois Central in 1916, the restored mahogany and brass dining cars run over the historic McCloud Railway known for its steep grades, sharp curves, and infamous switchbacks. The line also runs open-air excursions during summer afternoons.

> **Shasta Sunset Dinner Train** 328 Main St, McCloud, CA 96057; ☎ 800 733 2141; www.shastasunset.com. The train runs from April 27 to December 27 on a varying schedule – see the website for details. Reservations required. Directions: on I-5, take the McCloud/Reno exit

and travel east 10 miles on Hwy 89, turning left on Colombero Ave. Follow Colombero into town, crossing the tracks, and turn right on Main St to reach the station.

A meal at the **Squeeze In**, aptly named because it's just ten feet wide, takes some time, not because the service is slow (it isn't), but because it takes a while to read the menu and the walls. The place offers a staggering 57 types of omelets, all named for local Truckee characters, most of whom created the omelet ingredients themselves. With names like Saint Sue, Buckin' Buster, Trippy Thomas and Terrible Tim-Tommy, it can't help but make you fantasize about their originators. After you've ordered it's time to read the walls covered with decades of graffiti.

Squeeze In 10060 Donner Pass Rd, Truckee, CA 96160; ☎ 530 587 9814; fax: 530 587 2439. Directions: on I-80 in Truckee, take the Donner Pass Rd exit towards Truckee. Squeeze In is on Donner Pass Rd between Spring St and Bridge St.

While you're on Donner Pass Road, stop in at **Bud's Sporting Goods and Fountain** for coffee and dessert. Their sign claims 'Ice-cream, worms, and guns since 1948'. Started by a man who loved fishing and ice-cream, you'll find an old-fashioned soda fountain right in there along with live bait, fishing, poles, hunting equipment, and paintball guns. They make sodas and ice-cream floats the old-fashioned way.

Bud's Sporting Goods and Fountain 10043 Donner Pass Rd, Truckee, CA 96191; ☎ 530 587 3177. Directions: see above.

Pollard Flat ain't nothin' but a pit stop off Highway 5 but it's an entertaining one, especially if you have to use the bathroom. The restaurant walls are covered with political sentiments, flags are everywhere, and pithy sayings abound, like those on a server's shirt: 'If a man speaks in the forest, and no woman can hear, is he still wrong?' A mannequin propped in the bathtub has an unusual reaction if you snap her picture.

Pollard Flat Contact Pollard Flat USA, 24235 Eagles Roost Rd, Lakehead, CA 96051; ☎ 530 238 2534. Directions: on I-5, take exit 712.

ROOMS WITH A SKEW

If you're looking for a tranquil respite, California style, try **The Expanding Light** where you can do as much meditation and yoga as you want without having to sign up for any kind of structured workshop. Set on 800 acres of pine forest in the Sierra foothills, the 'personal retreat' option gives you a choice of double rooms with shared baths or individual cabins with a communal bathhouse. They also offer spiritual lifestyle coaching, holistic health techniques and massage, and holiday retreats.

The Expanding Light 14618 Tyler Foote Rd. Nevada City, CA 95959; ☎ 800 346 5350; www.expandinglight.org. Directions: on Hwy 49 north of Nevada City, take the Malakoff Diggins exit, then turn right onto Tyler

Foote Rd. Drive for about 4.7 miles on Tyler Foote until you see the large 'Ananda Village' sign, turn left onto Ananda Way. Then turn left again at the first fork in the road. Follow the signs up the hill to The Expanding Light.

Stewart Mineral Springs, a sacred healing retreat in the shadow of Mount Shasta, offers some additional ways to unwind. While drop-in visitors can enjoy the mineral baths, your overnight stay in a Native American tepee might include a purification sweat lodge ceremony.

Stewart Mineral Springs 4617 Stewart Springs Rd, Weed, CA 96094; ✆ 530 938 2222; www.stewartmineralsprings.com. Directions: on I-5 north of Weed, take the Edgwood exit and drive west. Follow Stewart Springs Rd 4 miles to the entrance.

Each of the 15 theme rooms at the **Fantasy Inn** has its own Jacuzzi spa along with mood lighting, beds on lighted pedestals, and 'intriguing' mirror treatments to enhance the romantic experience. Leaving nothing to chance, the inn offers extensive wedding packages, complete down to hair and make-up services, transportation options like a horse and buggy or limo, and an on-site lingerie boutique. The rooms themselves are lavish, varying in theme, including a tropical treehouse, an Arabian tent in a desert oasis, a Western fantasy, Graceland, and Marie Antoinette.

Fantasy Inn 3696 Lake Tahoe Blvd, South Lake Tahoe, CA 96150; ✆ 800 367 7736; www.fantasy-inn.com. Directions: the Fantasy Inn is on Lake Tahoe Blvd (US50) between Ski Run Blvd and Wildwood Ave.

If you like your kitsch quaint, head for the **Cottage Inn** at Lake Tahoe. Built in 1938 in 'Old Tahoe' style, the knotty-pine theme rooms, thankfully equipped with updated plumbing, pay homage to various themes. With names like Old Fishing Hole and Stagecoach Stop, you get the idea. The just-opened Bear Lodge, though, features five new theme rooms done up more extensively in themes ranging from the romantic southwestern Dreamcatcher to the Sailaway and Happy Trails.

Cottage Inn Box 66, Tahoe City, CA 96145; ✆ 800 581 4073; www.thecottageinn.com. Directions: the Cottage Inn is on Hwy 89 north of Sunnyside.

Some of the guests at the **Swan-Levine House** celebrate their birthdays by spending the night in the very room where they were born, the white-tiled surgical suite in the former hospital turned B & B. Now painted pink and furnished with white wicker furnishings, the suite's bathroom still contains the old scrub sinks accessorized with an assortment of old bedpans and other hospital equipment. Elsewhere in the rambling three-story inn are rooms converted from prior patient wards and nurse's quarters, Owners Howard Levine and Margaret Warner Swan have been renovating the historic building for three decades, filling it with an eclectic mix of antiques, 40s' and 50s' collectibles, art from their printmaking studio, and art from other artists. Guests have the option to learn printmaking during their stay.

Swan-Levine House 328 South Church St, Grass Valley, CA 95945; ✆ 530 272 1873; www.swanlevinehouse.com. Directions: Swan-Levine house is in South Church St between Walsh and Temby St.

The Banana Bike (©Terry Axelson) and the Guitar Cycle (©Ray Nelson), two of California's more imaginative alternative forms of transportation (HB)

'Bats in the Belfry'
'Gourd of the Rings' and
'Pandamorium' pedal the
kinetic sculptures
over the sand
dunes at
Ferndale's Kinetic
Sculpture Race (BE)

The **Delta King Hotel** floats a retired 285ft sternwheeler with 44 staterooms and a view of either the Sacramento River or Old Town Sacramento depending on whether your room is port or starboard. Built in 1927, the ship left the dock each night as a speakeasy during the prohibition era, providing drinking, jazz, and gambling for sensation-starved patrons. After World War II the *Delta King* was drafted into the navy, serving on San Francisco Bay as a floating barracks, troop transport, and hospital ship. After being sunk for a year-and-a-half in the mid 80s, she was resurrected and towed to Old Town for restoration.

> **Delta King Hotel** 1000 Front St, Old Sacramento, CA 95814; ✆ 800 825 5464; www.deltaking.com. Directions: the Delta King is located on the Sacramento River at the foot of K St in Old Sacramento.

The **Railroad Park Resort & Caboose Motel** is a charming cluster of restored cabooses, plus one honeymoon boxcar, which have been refurbished into comfortable, if quirky, quarters. The restaurant and lounge is also built inside antique railroad cars. The motel is open year around; the restaurant weekends only April through November.

> **Railroad Park Resort** 100 Railroad Park Rd, Dunsmuir, CA 96025; ✆ 530 235 4440; www.rrpark.com. Directions: on Hwy 5 north of Redding, leave at exit 728, then turn onto Railroad Park Rd, heading northwest. The resort is less than a mile along this road.

ATTRACTIONS

Once just a pit stop on the way to Oregon, little Redding has made a big splash in the pond of architectural wonders with the opening of the pedestrian-only **Sundial Bridge** designed by renowned architect Santiago Calatrava. So named because its 217ft-high pylon acts as a sundial, casting timely shadows on the plaza beside the Sacramento River, the bridge satisfies even the most rabid of California environmentalists, a situation almost unheard of in this litigiously green state. Designed not to interfere with sensitive salmon spawning grounds, the bridge is anchored on the shores rather than in the river and the surface is translucent glass so that light can pass through it to reach the water's surface. Almost entirely financed by a private foundation, Redding is now the little town that could.

> **Sundial Bridge** Contact the Redding Convention and Visitors Bureau, 777 Auditorium Dr, Redding, CA 96001; ✆ 530 225 4103; www.visitredding.com. Directions: on I-5 near Eureka, take the Eureka exit. Go 1 mile west to exit 1/Park Marina Dr. Right at top of the off-ramp – stay right, but merge to the left-hand lane to the northeast Convention Center parking lot.

Historic Old Sacramento fills their event calendar with a variety of amusing activities. Halloween brings Spookmotive train rides along with Ghost Tours, eerie evening walks that explore Sacramento's haunted heritage. At Easter, living history re-enactors display their Easter finery in a traditional promenade. New Year's Eve has a fine Sky Concert Fireworks show and in February they put on 'Love and Passion in the Gold Fields', a play based on the adventure and romance of a printer's apprentice turned 49er and the beloved lady he left back home.

> **Historic Old Sacramento** Contact the Sacramento CVB; ✆ 800 292 2334; www.oldsacramento.com. Directions: on I-5, take the J St exit and follow the signs to the Old Sacramento Historical District.

JUST PLAIN WEIRD

The Sacramento International Airport commissioned sculptor Brian Goggin to create a 'provocative' sculpture for their new terminal expansion. The result, part of the city's Art in Public Places program, is titled **Samson** and consists of 800 pieces of luggage attached to the perimeter of two existing columns. Airport baggage carts appear to support the teetering loads of old suitcases that extend all the way up to the ceiling of the terminal. Even though the suitcases are securely anchored to the columns by hidden bracing, the structures appear tipsy, as if they're about to topple from their excessive loads. The work is both startling and engaging.

> **Samson** Terminal A, Sacramento International Airport, Sacramento, CA 95815; ✆ 916 922 4789; www.sacairports.org. Directions: on I-5, take exit 528 and follow the signs.

Holey Cow. At UC Davis the dairy herd contains half a dozen fistulated cows that, basically, are donor cows with accessible holes in their sides so that veterinarians can transfer ruminating juices to other cows that have trouble producing their own. Every year at **Davis Picnic Day** one of these cows is on display with their hole and Tupperware-style plastic closure. Visitors can line up and take a turn sticking their arm in the cow and feeling the inside of the cow's rumen as it digests grass. How weird is that?

> **Davis Picnic Day** happens in April at the UC Davis Campus. Contact Picnic Day Office, 343 Memorial Union, One Shields Ave, Davis, CA 95616; ✆ 530 752 6320; www.picnicday.ucdavis.edu. Directions: on I-80 south of Sacramento, take the UC Davis exit onto Old Davis Rd to the campus.

Oh-so-environmentally correct **Davis** takes its frogs very seriously, so seriously that they spent $14,000 to build a **Toad Tunnel** so the little darlings wouldn't get squished by traffic when their seasonal migration path was disrupted by a new roadway. The mayor, backed by legions of pro-frog advocates, prevailed upon the city to spend the money to install a 12-inch diameter metal tube under the new roadway so the creatures could continue to find the way to their promised land. Unfortunately the toads ignored their new tunnel because there's no longer any habitat awaiting them on the other side. Despite local efforts to entice them back with their own 'hotel' on the other side, they seem to have abandoned their old stomping grounds, perhaps moving on to a community with less time on their hands.

> **Davis Toad Tunnel** Contact the Davis C & VB, 130 G St, Davis, CA; ✆ 530 297 1900; www.davisvisitor.com. Directions: from I-80 at Davis, exit Richards Blvd going east. From Richards/Cowell, turn left onto PoleLine/Lillard. Turn right onto Fifth St, then immediate right into the Post Office parking lot, where you can park when visiting the Tunnel.

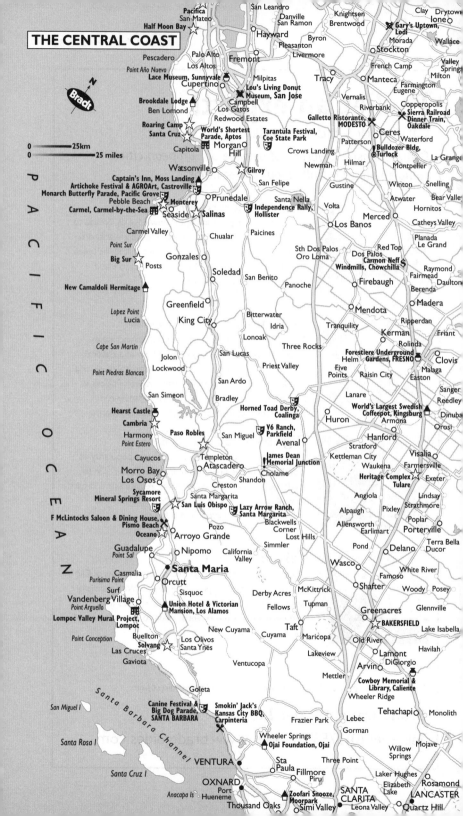

The Central Coast

FESTIVALS AND EVENTS

The **Roaring Camp Railroad** in Felton offers a number of novel ways to enjoy their historic steam and beach train journeys, running creative theme events like their October **Halloween Ghost Train**. For this event the six-mile redwood forest route is transformed into the *Legend of Sleepy Hollow*, with riders urging Ichabod Crane to 'Run, Ichabod, Run!' as he flees the Headless Horseman. Fall also offers the scarecrow and pumpkin-carving run, with visitors getting to carve a pumpkin or make their own scarecrow at special stations around the depot. At Easter you can join the Extraordinary Hunt when children search for candy and toys at the top of Bear Mountain. September offers the Great Train Robbery with lawmen and desperados dueling it out atop the mountain. May brings one of the largest Civil War encampments in the western US with mock military battles and belching cannons while trains circle the meadow camp. November is Mountain Man Rendezvous time when 1840s' trappers and traders gather to trade goods, replenish supplies and demonstrate their frontier skills. You're welcome to wander through their Old West and Native America encampments. Finally, December brings the best way to see Santa as the Christmas Holiday Train, with Santa, carolers and hot cider, rolls through a forest illuminated with thousands of lights.

> **Roaring Camp Railroad** PO Box G-1, Felton, CA 95018; ☎ 831 335 4484; www.roaringcamp.com. Directions: on Hwy 880 in Scotts Valley, take the Mt Hermon Rd exit and drive northwest 3.5 miles to Felton. Mt Hermon Rd ends at Graham Hill Rd. Turn left on Graham Hill Rd and drive half a mile to Roaring Camp (on the right).

For music that's a cut above the rest, check out the **Musical Saw Festival** held the second weekend of every August. The world's greatest saw players come out of the woodwork to join other acoustic musicians in a variety of performances, including bluegrass, country, folk, gospel, blues, classical, and even show tunes (but don't expect heavy metal!). There's a saw-off competition that draws one to two dozen of the planet's finest players, a Chorus of the Saws that unites up to 50 playing in unison, and a musical saw workshop for those who want to sharpen their skills. According to Morgan Cowin, a past festival champion and president of the International Musical Saw Association,' the saw is the only true musical instrument that will be OK after stirring a fire.' In fact, he often warms up by holding his saw over the flames.

> **Musical Saw Festival** happens in Roaring Camp in August. Contact the International Musical Saw Players Association; ☎ 415 459 7722; www.sawplayers.org

If you didn't get to see the frogs jump in Calaveras County, the annual **Horned Toad Derby** in Coalinga will give you a taste of frog racing. This event pits frogs with names like 'Toadtanic' and 'Toadquila' against their Kermit challengers while humans compete in fire-fighter water-fights. The toads are captured in the Coalinga Hills with permits since they're a protected species. Very PC, very California.

> **Horned Toad Derby** is held annually in May. Contact Coalinga Chamber, 380 Coalinga Plaza, Coalinga, CA 93210; ☎ 800 854 3885 or ☎ 559 935 2948; www.coalingachamber.com

It's all about noise and power at the annual **Pacific Coast Dream Machines** show. If it's motorized, mechanical, and (preferably) massive, it qualifies for display at this showcase of 2,000 machines from the 20th and 21st centuries. The sheer number of driving, flying and working machines, all hissing and roaring, has guys flocking to this event. Auto buffs show up with their muscle cars and low riders, aviators with their home-builts and classics, collectors with their gas- and steam-powered farm equipment, and garage inventors with the object of their passion. Spread out over hundreds of acres at the airport, the show also includes vintage engines like those powering old washing machines and lawnmowers. The Tractor Pull is a crowd favorite with roaring contenders in tractors and trucks trying to out-pull one another in competitions involving up to 15 tons.

> **Pacific Coast Dream Machines** festival takes place in April at the Half Moon Bay Airport. Contact Miramar Events, PO Box 27, 708 The Alameda, El Granada, CA 94018; ☎ 650 726 2328; www.miramarevents.com/dreammachines. Directions: the Half Moon Bay Airport is alongside Hwy 1, north of Half Moon Bay.

Garlic fans, 125,000 of them annually, consider the **Gilroy Garlic Festival** a breath of fresh air. This decades-old festival keeps this small farming town on the map with its garlic ambassador, Belle of the Bulb Pageant, gourmet garlic alley, and gourmet garlic cook-off. Festival-goers consume two tons of fresh garlic during the three-day event.

> **Gilroy Garlic Festival** takes place in July in the Christmas Hill Park in Gilroy. Contact the Gilroy Garlic Festival Association Inc, PO Box 2311, 7473 Monterey St, Gilroy, CA 95020; ☎ 408 842 1625; www.gilroygarlicfestival.com. Directions: on Hwy 101 at Gilroy, follow the signs.

More than 250,000 people show up at the **Half Moon Bay Pumpkin Festival**, an event famous for gargantuan pumpkins, pumpkin-carving competitions, and the never-ending search for Charlie Brown's Great Pumpkin. The biggest event is the weigh-off, a highly anticipated and stressful moment that can dash an entire year's worth of hope. In 2003 six pumpkins weighed in at over 1,000lb each; in 2004 the winner was an enormous 1,229lb, taking home prize money of $6,145 ($5 a pound). There's also an award given for the most beautiful pumpkin specimen. Look for a scarecrow contest, a haunted house, a pumpkin parade, pie-eating contests, and demonstrations by world-class pumpkin carvers working on pumpkins that can be as big as a small car. Children can enter their own carving contests.

Half Moon Bay Pumpkin Festival takes place on Main St, Half Moon Bay in October. Contact Miramar Events, PO Box 27, 708 The Alameda, El Granada, CA 94018; ✆ 650 726 9652; www.miramarevents.com/pumpkinfest. Directions: on Hwy 1 in Half Moon Bay, follow the signs to the parking area.

It just doesn't get much cuter than the **Monarch Butterfly Parade**, held annually since 1939 to celebrate the return of up to 40,000 Monarch butterflies to their winter sanctuary in Pacific Grove. All the elementary-school kids in town participate, marching by grade and classroom, in costumes that parents, teachers, and kids have labored over for weeks. Kindergartners, dressed as butterflies, always lead the procession followed by a promenade of those in grades 1–6, most dressed as some kind of butterfly friend such as a caterpillar, flower, or tree. Fourth graders always dress as figures from California history. The parade has been going on for so long that grandparents can remember marching in it themselves. This one ranks really high on the 'aww' meter. The best time to view the monarchs is from Thanksgiving through early March. They attach themselves to trees in huge clusters, folding back their wings and looking like clumps of dead leaves during chilly or damp weather.

Monarch Butterfly Parade takes place in Pacific Grove in October. Contact the Pacific Grove Chamber of Commerce, PO Box 167, Pacific Grove, CA 93950; ✆ 800 656 6650or ✆ 831 373 3304; www.pacificgrove.org. Directions: on Hwy 1 south of Monterey, take the Del Monte Ave exit and head west.

The town of Pacifica celebrates the one week each year when the weather is most likely to be sunny with the **Pacific Coast Fog Fest**. Thirty-five tons of sand is spread in a vacant lot and a world-champion sandcastle builder spends up to a week creating a masterpiece that lasts as long as the weather holds. There's also a pea-soup cooking competition and the life-sized Mer-Person contest where non-profit groups create their vision of what a Mer-Person would look like. The winner is selected by a people's-choice vote.

Pacific Coast Fog Fest takes place on Palmetto Ave in Pacifica in September. Contact Fog Fest, PO Box 846, Pacifica, CA 94044; ✆ 650 355 8200; www.pacificcoastfogfest.com. Directions: on Hwy1, take the Oceana Blvd exit and follow signs to parking.

Aging bikers flock to the **Hollister Independence Rally**, a nostalgic Harley event that memorializes the hell-raising days of bikers past. Only now, instead of riding into town and causing trouble, the Harley enthusiasts, average age 45, ride in with their credit cards, contributing a chunk to the local economy during the three-day event. In addition to bike games like the slow race, the weenie bite, and the joust, they honor the art of tattooing in a contest that rewards the best in design from skulls to flames to full-body art. The arm wrestling contest draws a big crowd as does the Wall of Death stunt show. Vendors line the streets selling everything the affluent biker could possibly need or want.

Hollister Independence Rally takes place in Hollister in July. Contact the HIRC, 334 Fifth St, Hollister, CA 95023; ☏ 831 634 0777; www.hollisterrally.com. Directions: Hollister is on Hwy 25, southeast of Gilroy.

All artichokes grown in the USA are grown in California and Castroville's claim to fame is its status as the 'Artichoke Capitol of the World'. Every year the town holds its famous **Artichoke Festival**, the highlight of which is the **AGROArt** contest, a quirky, three-dimensional fruit and vegetable artwork competition. Open to individuals as well as teams of professionals, grown-ups, and students, contestants enter an arena toting their produce and supplies at 10am, with judging taking place four hours later. All sculptures must be at least 60% fresh produce, 10% artichokes, and hearty enough to stay on display for two days. Wood, wire, glue, tape, and plastic may be used to hold the produce in place. The prizes are significant, totaling $5,000 in cash for the first- and second- place winners. Past entries include a fire-eating dragon, a crocodile, and a snake crawling through grass made of artichoke leaves.

AGROArt takes place at the **Artichoke Festival** in May in Castroville. Contact Castroville Festivals, PO Box 1041, Castroville, CA 95012; ☏ 831 633 2465; www.artichoke-festival.org. Directions: on Hwy 1 north of Monterey, take the Castroville exit (Hwy 183). Then follow the signs to parking areas.

What do you do with hundreds of thousands of begonia flowers about to be thrown away? At the homespun **Begonia Festival** they begin with a hat-decorating contest, then float dozens of decorated barges down Soquel Creek to the lagoon during the Nautical Parade. They've been doing this for more than five decades as the region is headquarters for most of the world's begonia bulb production. It turns out that begonia blossoms are at their most spectacular just before the bulbs are harvested and millions of flowers would otherwise go to waste if not picked for the festival. The floats can get quite elaborate. Past entries include a replica of St John's Episcopal Church and a caboose complete with a RR crossing and puffs of blossom 'smoke'. You can view the floats being constructed prior to the event.

Begonia Festival takes place over Labor Day weekend in Capitola. Contact the Begonia Festival; ☏ 831 476 3566; www.begoniafestival.com. Directions: Capitola is off Hwy 1, east of Santa Cruz. The festival offers free parking at the Crossroads Center parking lot and a free shuttle service. For the Crossroads Center, take the Bay St exit on Hwy 1 and head south.

They're big, they're hairy, and most people are so afraid of them they'd never dream of seeking them out, let alone going to a festival in their honor. Yet the **Tarantula Festival** and Fall Barbeque draws hundreds of spider fans eager to learn more about the misunderstood creatures. You can watch them mate and buy crafts made from the critters. Contrary to myth, these are non-aggressive, fragile creatures that get a bum rap, failing to live up to their fearsome movie reputations. Their sting is no worse than that of a bee or wasp and they consume harmful pests like cockroaches, flies, and vermin. Some people like to keep them as house pets.

Tarantula Festival takes place in October in Coe Park in Morgan Hill. Contact the Henry W Coe State Park, 9000 East Dunne Ave, Morgan Hill, CA 95037; ✆ 408 779 2728; www.coepark.org. Directions: on Hwy 101 south of San Jose, take the East Dunne Ave exit and head east. After 3 miles, take the right turn at the Y onto East Dunne Ave.

You know it must be the first Saturday in June when you're surrounded by thousands of dressed-up dogs. The **Big Dog Parade and Canine Festival**, an annual fundraising event for the Big Dog Foundation, is a Santa Barbara tradition with costumes, floats, and marching bands celebrating man's best friend. Honoring service dogs, rescue dogs, and just plain mutts, the event brings out the best in everyone, dogs and owners alike.

Big Dog Parade and Canine Festival takes place in Santa Barbara in June. Contact the Big Dog Foundation, 121 Gray Ave, Santa Barbara, CA 93101; ✆ 800 9 BIG DOGS; www.bigdogs.com/bigdogclub/ bdfoundation.asp

PECULIAR PURSUITS

The Wild West, California style, offers some unique opportunities for family bonding. For starters, there's the thrice-yearly **Mother–Daughter Cowgirl Bootcamp**, a three-night 'laid-back adventure retreat' offering plenty of wrangler training supplemented by in-room fireside massage. Fly-fishing, line dancing, barrel racing and lasso lessons fill the days along with golf and tennis. How California is that?? But there are no phones or televisions at the Alisal Guest Ranch and Resort, hosts of the event.

Mother–Daughter Cowgirl Bootcamp Contact the Alisal Resort, 1054 Alisal Rd, Solvang, CA 93463; ✆ 805 688 6411; www.alisal.com. Directions: on Hwy 246 in Solvang (northwest of Santa Barbara), turn south onto Alisal Rd.

Indulge your inner dude by joining one of the spring or fall **Cattle Drives** at the **Lazy Arrow** or the **V6 Ranch**. While you can pretend to reprise Billy Crystal's role in the *City Slickers* movie, your hosts are far more congenial than the crusty Curly, rewarding your hard work with hearty food, fireside entertainment, and downright luxurious camping accommodations. You'll spend a good five or six hours a day in the saddle (and feel the results!), really learning the ropes from wranglers who are surprisingly patient with greenhorns of all skill levels.

Lazy Arrow Ranch 9330 Camatta Creek Rd, Santa Margarita, CA 93453; ✆ 805 238 7324; www.lazyarrow.com. Cost $950. Directions: on Hwy 101, take the CA-58 exit and head east towards Santa Margarita. After around 60 miles, turn Left on Camatta Creek Rd.

V6 Ranch 70403 Parkfield Rd, Parkfield, CA 93451; ✆ 805 463 2323; www.parkfield.com/v6.htm

You can take advantage of a real California experience by soaking in one of the redwood hot tubs dotted all over the wooded hillside at the **Sycamore Mineral Springs Resort**. These private outdoor spas, canopied by sycamore and oak trees, are bubbling with natural healing mineral waters. You can also enjoy a massage before or after your soak, and then recover with a healthy meal in their restaurant.

If you're in need of serious renewal, they offer retreat packages that include lodging, yoga, counseling, and time in their labyrinth and meditation garden.

> **Sycamore Mineral Springs Resort** 1215 Avila Beach Dr, San Luis Obispo, CA; ☎ 805 595 7302; www.sycamoresprings.com. Directions: on Hwy 101 in San Louis Obispo, take the Avila Beach Dr exit and follow as road curves to the west. Sycamore Mineral Springs Resort is located 1 mile down on the left-hand side.

MUSEUMS AND COLLECTIONS

It's hard to imagine spending $200,000 on an object that keeps the papers on your desk from blowing away, but after a visit to the **Paperweight Museum** you'll have a better understanding of the incredible skill and craftsmanship that goes into making these decorative glass orbs. Not to be confused with their tacky cousins the snow globes, paperweights represent the most difficult aspects of glassmaking, requiring tiny, intricate scenes to be encased inside a dome. The process is so delicate that only one in three makes it to the final stage.

> **Paperweight Museum** L H Selman Ltd Gallery of Fine Glass, 23 Locust St, Santa Cruz, CA 95060; ☎ 800 538 0766; www.theglassgallery.com. Directions: the Museum is in the Selman gallery on Locust St between Cedar St and Pacific Ave.

There's probably nothing that the docents at the **Lace Museum** don't know about lace and its history. Located in an unassuming strip mall, this extensive collection is enthusiastically maintained by volunteers of the museum's non-profit guild, a group dedicated not just to preserving the art of lace making, but of demonstrating that everyone is capable of making something worthy of being handed down to the next generation. You'll see both manmade laces and laces that nature makes – like spider webs, insect wings and lace wood – as well as human-hair jewelry and sculptures.

> **Lace Museum** 552 S Murphy Ave, Sunnyvale, CA 94086; ☎ 408 730 4695; www.thelacemuseum.org. *Open Tue–Sat 11am–4pm.* Directions: the museum is on S Murphy Ave between El Camino Real and Olive Ave.

ECCENTRIC ENVIRONMENTS

Hearst Castle is what happens when eccentricity and money meet a big, big ego. Millions of words have been written about this opulent estate of 165 rooms (90,000 square feet, 41 fireplaces, 61 bathrooms, 56 bedrooms, 19 sitting rooms, and 127 acres of gardens) and no trip to the central California coast would be complete without experiencing this extraordinary display of wealth. According to legend, Hearst said to famous architect Julia Morgan in 1919: 'Miss Morgan, we are tired of camping out in the open at the ranch in San Simeon and I would like to build a little something.'

The castle and grounds are so huge that tours are broken down into five separate experiences. Tour One is an overview recommended for first-time visitors and includes the *National Geographic* movie about the building of the castle. Tours Two and Three take in additional areas of the main house as well as the guest quarters. Tour Four concentrates on the grounds and gardens while Tour Five is a special Evening Tour that gives you the experience of visiting the castle at night as one of Hearst's guests. Available only in the Spring and Fall, the Evening Tour features docents dressed in period costume and a newsreel of the castle's heyday in the 30s.

Hearst Castle 750 Hearst Castle Rd, San Simeon, CA 93452; ℄ 805 927 2020; www.hearstcastle.org. Reservations for the tours are strongly recommended. Directions: Hearst Castle is on Hwy 1, north of Cambria and San Louis Obispo.

Known to his neighbors as Captain Nitt Witt or Dr Tinkerpaw, recluse Art Beal spent 51 years constructing a different kind of castle from that of his famous neighbor, William Randolph Hearst. **Nitt Witt Ridge**, as it's called, was Art's 'castle on a hill', his 'Poor Man's Hearst Castle', three tiers of salvaged materials lovingly assembled by the former garbage collector who worked for the town of Cambria. Using only hand tools and whatever he could scavenge, his castle is constructed of artfully arranged junk, mostly cans, car parts, abalone shells, TV antennas, driftwood, and local rocks. It's an intricate network of terraced gardens, stone arches and buildings. He never threw anything away and the house still displays his clothing and personal effects as if he still lived there. You can just drive by or, to arrange a tour, call Michael and Stacey O'Malley who recently bought the property and are in the process of restoring it.

Nitt Witt Ridge 881 Hill Crest Dr, Cambria, CA 93428; ℄ 805 927 2690. Reservations are required. Directions: on Hwy 1 in Cambria (north of San Louis Obispo), take the Cambria Dr exit and head northeast onto Main St. Turn Left onto Cornwall St, then left onto Hillcrest Dr.

QUIRKYVILLES

With 61 murals, Lompoc is one of America's premier mural cities. Devised as a way to enhance the local economy, the **Lompoc Valley Mural Project** uses art to attract tourism. The huge murals are painted on the sides of buildings, each a different style and theme. Some trick the eye as in the trompe l'oeil depiction of a three-story mansion. Others illustrate Lompoc's claim to fame as the Flower Seed Capitol of the World while still others pay tribute to the town's historic events and people. Each September the town sponsors the Mural-in-a-Day project in which a team of artists and painters add yet another to their already impressive collection.

Lompoc Valley Mural Project. Pick up a free map for a self-guided tour or arrange for guided group tours at the Chamber of Commerce, 111 S I St, Lompoc, CA 93436; ℄ 800 240 0999; www.store.yahoo.com/lompoc/.

Santa Cruz: the very name conjures up images of bikinis, boardwalks, and surfers, a place that represents the very essence of funky-style beach life. Only in Santa Cruz will you find the Compassion Flower Inn, a hemp-themed 'bed, bud, and breakfast' that caters to medical marijuana users. Only in Santa Cruz does Santa arrive each year on a surfboard and only in Santa Cruz are you in the country's first 'nuclear-free zone'. Nearly everything in town exudes a free-spirited aura and a disinclination to conform to anyone's standards.

Fun and funky, the town caters to the weird. Dogs have no trouble finding a masseuse to tend to their tired paws. The University of California at Santa Cruz has a mascot, the banana slug of all things. During the holidays the skeleton of a giant blue whale that washed ashore in 1979 is displayed at the marine lab, outlined with 900ft of rope lights. The legendary Giant Dipper, a classic wooden roller coaster, got an 80th birthday party in its honor, having carried 50 million riders during that time. There's a museum, the **Santa Cruz Surfing Museum**, dedicated just to surfing legends. Once a year the **Santa Cruz Follies**, performed by people (well) over the age of 50, perform a two-hour variety show, the culmination of a year of rigorous song-and-dance training. In nearby Aptos they hold the **World's Shortest Parade** every Independence Day when practically the whole town turns out, humans and animals alike, in costume to parade along the two-block route.

Santa Cruz Contact the Santa Cruz County Conference & Visitors Bureau, 1211 Ocean St, Santa Cruz, CA; ✆ 831 429 7281; www.santacruz.org. Directions: Santa Cruz is on Hwy 1, north of Monterey and south of San Francisco.

Santa Cruz Follies takes place in September at the Santa Cruz Civic Auditorium. Contact SCO Inc, 222 Market St, Santa Cruz, CA 95060; ✆ 831 423 6640; www.baymoon.com/~follies/follies.html

World's Shortest Parade takes place on July 4 in Aptos, on Soquel Dr. Contact the Aptos Chamber of Commerce, 7605A Old Dominion Court, Aptos, CA 95003; ✆ 831 688 1467; www.aptoschamber.com. Parking is limited.

Carmel is an incredibly picturesque village, famous for its past mayor, Clint Eastwood, and for its ordinance banning high-heeled shoes. The reason for the 1959 law is simple: the streets are cobblestone or brick, the many ancient trees have roots protruding in the walkways, and the city got tired of trip-and-fall lawsuits. Anyone spotted wearing the offending shoes will be reminded of the ordinance, but their credit card will still be accepted in the shops even if they are scofflaws. You can actually go into city hall and request a permit to wear high heels. Clint Eastwood ran on a platform that he would allow ice-cream to be sold on the streets again.

Carmel Contact Carmel California Visitor and Information Center, San Carlos between 5th and 6th, Carmel-by-the-Sea, CA 93921; ✆ 800 550 4333 or ✆ 831 624 2522; www.carmelcalifornia.org. Directions: Carmel is near Hwy 1 south of Monterey.

You can get a sugar high just looking at **Solvang**. It's impossibly cute and you'll get a rush just breathing in the aroma of its numerous pancake restaurants and pastry shops. This quaint little tourist village, founded in 1911 by Danish educators and farmers, looks just like old-world Denmark with its thatch and copper roofs, windmills, horse-drawn carriages, cobblestone sidewalks, gas lamps, and flower-lined streets. Gift shops galore sell everything from European collectibles to handcrafts to chocolate and some of the shopkeepers even wear Danish costumes. Architecturally, the town evolved from its farming roots as Danish carpenters and artisans migrated west, ultimately creating the fairy-tale village that exists today. Just outside the village is the **Quicksilver Miniature Horse Farm**, another picturesque stop where you can see several dozen of the miniature foals that are born each spring.

Solvang www.solvangca.com. Directions: take Hwy 246 off Hwy 101 at Buellton.

Quicksilver Miniature Horse Farm 1555 Alamo Pintado Rd, Solvang, CA; ✆ 805 686 4002.

TOURS

The whole family can experience what it was like to cross the desert on a **Covered Wagon Tour**, led by naturalist guides eager to share their knowledge of desert survival and Indian history. The two-hour trip ends with dinner around a campfire. After a few hours in a covered wagon, the kids should develop a new appreciation for the SUV with AC and DVD.

Covered Wagon Tour PO Box 1106, La Quinta, CA 92253; ☎ 800 367 2161; www.coveredwagontours.com. Reservations required.

It's the ultimate joyride in the ultimate of vehicles, a wild adventure through the Grand Canyon of sand dunes on an **Oceana Dunes Humvee Tour** with **Pacific Adventure Tours**. You start out sedately enough, traveling along the state's only beach highway at 15mph, learning about the ecology of the ten square miles of dune area and taking in the small city of tents, campers, and ATV rental shacks that take up residence on the dunes each summer. Then, suddenly, you're thrusting upward, screeching over 30ft-high dunes, careening sideways along dune walls, and wondering why this seemed like such a good idea five minutes earlier. But, as you crest the dune's ridges and take in the vast, undulating landscape, you'll be overwhelmed with the beauty of it all. Tours are available with varying degrees of adventure, including a mild one for seniors and for those with sensitive constitutions all the way up to extreme for those determined to prove they could take on The Terminator. The tours leave from the **Rock 'N Roll Diner**, a pair of 1948 rail cars converted into a 50s' theme restaurant.

Oceana Dunes Humvee Tour Contact Pacific Adventure Tours, PO Box 336, Oceano, CA 93445; ☎ 805 481 9330; www.pacificadventuretours.com. Tours Depart from the **Rock 'N Roll Diner**, 1300 Railroad St, Oceano, CA, 7 days a week. Cost $20–48. Reservations required.

If you've ever wondered what some of those weird vegetables are that you see in your supermarket, Evan Oakes from **Ag Venture Tours** can probably tell you. His specialty is agriculture tours and he's well aware that Californian's fondness for the strange and unusual extends to their shopping carts. From Evan you'll learn how brocolinni (a cross between broccoli and kale) got its start and why arugula is so difficult to grow and so expensive to buy. An agricultural scientist for the University of California Co-operative Extension office in Salinas, he's been researching vegetables and wine-grape production for more than a decade. Besides the veggie tour, he also offers a kid-friendly animal farm tour and various wine tours, including one on horseback.

Ag Venture Tours PO Box 2634, Monterey, CA 93942; ☎ 831 643 WINE or ☎ 888 643 WINE; www.whps.com/agtours

For a novel way to see the Monterey area, take the **Monterey Movie Tour**, a three-hour, 32-mile motorcoach ride past the locations where 200 scenes from TV and movies have been filmed. During the tour you watch the scenes that match the locations you're passing on on-board TVs. Interest in visiting film sites is so popular that the county film commission recently published a map that lists the location of 190 film scenes shot in the region including *Play Misty for Me*, *Mutiny on the Bounty*, and *From Here to Eternity*. At one stop you can frolic near the spot where Troy and Sandra filmed a sandy love scene in *A Summer Place*.

Monterey Movie Tour Contact Monterey Bay Scenic Tours, 2 Serrano Way, Monterey, CA 93940; ☎ 800 343 6437; www.montereymovietours.com. Reservations required. Tours depart from the Monterey Convention Center, 1 Portola Plaza.

ODD SHOPPING

Carmon Neff is unofficially known as the 'Windmill King' and, seeing as he's been building them for 30 years, the title is a fitting tribute to one of the country's pre-eminent windmill craftsmen. The yard of his shop, at the intersection of Robertson Boulevard and Road 15, displays 15 to 20 of his creations at any given time. Mostly he sells them to cattle ranchers, but you can buy his most popular windmill, a 12ft high, 4ft-diameter model, for $800.

> **Carmon Neff Windmills** Robertson Blvd and Road 15, in Chowchilla, CA. He also represents Aermotor Windmills down the street at 14371 Road 15, Chowchilla, CA; ✆ 559 665 3379. Directions: on CA-152 southwest of Chowchilla (southwest of Yosemite), take the Robertson Blvd exit and drive 2 miles to the northeast.

Featuring an amazing selection of military miniatures, toy soldiers, and historical chess sets, the **Soldier Gallery** is one of just two dozen of such stores in the country. This combination gallery, hobby shop and bookshop will fascinate anyone with a passion for history and its wars. No conflict is too obscure for their book collection with titles like *Clive of India's Finest Hour*, the *Zulu 1879*, or the *Boer in Natal*. The chess sets are captivating, among them King Arthur's Fantasy, Pirates versus the British Navy, Justice versus Evil, the Crusades, the Battle of Troy, and Robin Hood and his Merry Men. There are models, dioramas, puzzles, military action figures and vehicles like armored cars and tanks, and specialized collections like those from Russia and China. One such is the Streets of Old Hong Kong, complete with miniature figures of a barber and his customer, a dentist and his patient, a tea merchant, and a shopper being carried in a sedan chair.

> **Soldier Gallery** 789 Main St, Cambria, CA 93428; ✆ 805 927 3804; www.soldiergallery.com. Directions: the Store is on Main St in Cambria, between Arlington and Sheffield St.

Peter Zobian describes his **Vintage Automobilia** shop as a passion run amok. He's been buying and selling vintage automobiles and related antiques for more than 50 years and his collection of aviation and automobile memorabilia, toys, models, and car parts is displayed at this little store tucked away in a corner of Cambria. With things like headlamps, pressed steel and tin toys, and event badges, he describes his inventory as 'rare and unique to just plain neat old stuff'. He has an especially extensive collection of old car magazines and dealer brochures from the 20s through the 50s.

> **Vintage Automobilia** 604 Main, Cambria, CA 93428; ✆ 805 927 7800; www.vintage-automobilia.com

You've probably never seen a stranger, or more entertaining assemblage of goods than you'll find at **Oceano Nursery**. This place is wild, so wild that dinosaurs roam the grounds. So do elephants, giraffes and sharks, huge scrap-metal creatures that sometimes spout water as bizarre garden fountains. These rusted creations share space not just with trees and plants, but with stuff like architectural fragments, wagon wheels, woodcarvings, recycled glass rocks, whimsical sculptures, funky ceramics, aquarium supplies and taxidermy fish in this rambling junk yard/antique store/gift shop/nursery. This is pack-rat heaven, the place to buy signs that say things like 'Still Plays With Boats' and the perfect place to stock up on stuff that will make people say, 'Where on earth did you get *that?*'. They also propagate many of their own plant specimens so even the greenery is unique.

> **Oceano Nursery** 1311 Paso Robles St, Oceano, CA 93445; ✆ 805 489
> 4456; fax: 805 773 0017. Directions: the nursery is located on Hwy 1 in
> Oceano, south of San Luis Obispo.

QUIRKY CUISINE
A room off to the side of Lou's Donut Shop holds a most unexpected surprise: **Lou's Living Donut Museum**, a shrine to American military heroes filled with photos and memorabilia honoring those who served in World War II. Every Saturday veterans of that war gather to be interviewed and to have their stories videotaped for posterity. The place is famous for its donuts – they come with their holes reattached.

> **Lou's Living Donut Museum** 387 Delmas Ave, San Jose, CA 95126;
> ✆ 408 295 5887. Directions: the museum is just off Hwy 87 at the
> junction of Hwy 87 and Hwy 280.

Talk about farm fresh! There are two organizations in the region offering an elegant, innovative way to bring you face to face with the source of your food: **Field Dinners**, literally meals served up right where your food is grown. **Outstanding in the Field** and **Culinary Santa Cruz** both organize a variety of in-field dinners during the growing and harvest season, bringing together featured chefs with local farmers and other producers such as wine-, cheese-, and bread-makers. Host farmers provide the land and long banquet tables, laid with linen and accruements worthy of a magazine cover, are the setting for the multi-course meal. Aproned waiters serve what will likely be the freshest food you've ever tasted. A hundred or more people make reservations for each dinner.

> **Field Dinners** happen in various locations during the year.
> www.outstandinginthefield.com and www.culinarysantacruz.com.
> Reservations are required.

You don't normally think of fast food joints as worthy of a visit just for the view, but the Taco Bell on Pacifica State Beach, also referred to as **Taco Bell Beach**, sits right on the edge of the sand and is famous for its walk-thru window. It seems that surfers are reluctant to leave their boards on the beach long enough to go inside.

> **Taco Bell Beach** 5200 Coast Hwy, Pacifica, CA 94044; ✆ 650 355 4210;
> www.tacobell.com. Surfboard not required. Directions: the Taco Bell is
> on the Coast Hwy (Hwy 1) at the south end of the beach in Pacifica.

Ask for a refill on your glass of water at **F McLintocks Saloon and Dining House** and you're in for a big surprise. First, your server tells you to hold your empty glass on top of your head. Then he or she climbs on a chair, blindfolds him or herself with a napkin, raises their water pitcher high (2–3ft above your head) and pours. You do your part by remaining very still; they do theirs by paying attention during the mandatory 'high-water pour' training session. Kids, especially, *love* seeing this performed. This infamous stunt got it started around 15 years ago when a waiter named Hans responded to a dare from a customer. There's a plaque in his honor in the entry as well as thousands of Polaroid photos of folks celebrating their birthdays at the restaurant. This high-energy restaurant is also famous for their fried Turkey Nuts, a surprisingly tasty delicacy. Make reservations as the place is always jam-packed.

> **F McLintocks Saloon and Dining House** 750 Mattie Rd, Shell Beach (Pismo Beach), CA 93449; ✆ 805 773 1892; www.mclintocks.com. Directions: on Hwy 101 in Pismo, take the Shell Beach exit onto Mattie Rd and head southeast (parallel to the highway). Reservations recommended.

A Santa Cruz institution since 1979, the **Saturn Café** is known for its entertainment value and for their left-wing politics. The place is run as a worker's collective with all employees and owners meeting weekly to vote on everything from menu phrases to the brand of tortilla chips they'll serve. The tables are dioramas filled with bits and pieces of life, stuff like ticket stubs, dried-up corsages and old driver's licenses. The walls are painted with wild murals and the wait staff as eclectic as the décor, some with hair and facial jewelry that make it hard not to stare. Wednesday is Wig Out night; wear one and you get 20% off.

> **Saturn Café** 145 Laurel St, Santa Cruz, CA; ✆ 831 429 8505; www.saturncafe.com. *Open Sun–Thu 11.30–3am, Fri–Sat 11.30–4am.* Directions: the café is on Laurel St between Pacifica Ave and Front St.

'If it's not fun, we're not doin' it'. That's Big Bubba's motto, nicely reflected at **Big Bubba's Bad BBQ**. Owner Roger Sharp, known for his BBQ concession stands at fairs across the West, spent three years converting a motorcycle shop into a Western-themed restaurant for families complete with a mechanical bull that can be slowed down for less adventurous riders. Kids love the talking buffalo, the talking cowboy, and the first-come, first-served eat-in jail cells.

> **Big Bubba's Bad BBQ** 1125 24th St, Paso Robles, CA; ✆ 805 238 6272; www.bigbubbasbadbbq.com. Directions: on Hwy 101 in Paso Robles, take the 24th St exit and head west.

Most vintners take their wine tasting very seriously. Not so Claudine and Terry Blackwell, owners of **Clautiere Vineyard**. A visit to this wine-tasting room, the most photographed one in the region, involves not just good wine but plenty of wacky fun as you're encouraged to don outlandish theatrical wigs while sipping. According to Terry, amazing transformations take place when you're wearing a wig, especially these wigs, a dizzying array of personas ranging from Louis XIV to Marge Simpson. 'People became more playful while wearing a wig,' says Terry, 'especially the women'. The winery also puts on 'tastefully raunchy' drag queen events.

> **Clautiere Vineyard** 1340 Penman Springs Rd, Paso Robles, CA 93446; ✆ 805 237 3789; www.clautiere.com. Directions: on CA-46 east of Paso Robles, turn south onto Union Rd, then left onto Penman Springs Rd.

ROOMS WITH A SKEW

Walk with the animals. Talk with the animals. Sleep (practically) with the animals at **Vision Quest Safari B & B.** Your accommodation is an African-style tent bungalow surrounded by big cats, elephants, ostriches, zebras, and monkeys. All these animals are superbly trained creatures, stars of television and movies, working for Wild Things Animal Rentals. In the morning your breakfast might be delivered by an elephant or baboon (accompanied by a trainer, of course). This close encounter of the wild kind also offers several experiences to enhance your

Quirk Alert

While searching for a new flavor to add to his **HotLix** gourmet lollipop business, the sweet, salty taste of tequila crossed Larry Peterman's mind. But what good is tequila without the worm, you ask? That's what Peterman thought as well, and now his tequila lollipops (complete with worm), are the cornerstone of his business. Besides the tequila lollipops you can also buy other bug-centered suckers such as the Crème de Menthe-flavored 'Cricket Lick-Its' ('so good you'll be chirping'), Larvets (BBQ-flavored, cheddar cheese, or Mexican spice; take your pick), and several non-bug-enhanced flavors like margarita, piña colada, and jalapeño.

Not just any bugs that wander in off the street get to become a HotLix. All the insects used in Peterman's candies are raised on-site and are FDA approved. Grown using natural foods like apples and bread, the bugs are guaranteed to be edible, although there's no guarantee that you'll want to eat them when you're confronted with one. Aside from numerous retail customers and a booming internet business, HotLix can also be found at museums, particularly those featuring prehistoric exhibits. Amber InsectNside, a toffee-flavored bar designed to look like fossilized amber complete with crickets and larvae, was inspired by the Smithsonian's National Museum of Natural History's Amber Exhibit.

In addition to growing his business, HotLix's insect aspect has made Peterman something of an expert in edible bug circles. His culinary skills are in demand at entomologist gatherings and television shows, where he's whipped up full-course insect dinners featuring delicacies like Jerusalem crickets ('sliced like a lobster and charbroiled') and chocolate cockroach sculptures. He's also provided universities with edible pests for scientific conventions. When gourmet ice-cream chain Cold Stone Creamery wanted to introduce a Survivor-esque 'flavor' as part of a promotion with the CBS series, they knew just where to turn for their chocolate-covered crickets.

HotLix PO Box 447, Grover Beach, CA 93433; ✆ 1 800 EAT WORM; www.hotlix.com. HotLix candy is also available in many museum stores.

visit. The Pachyderm Package gives you two hours with the elephants – you bathe, walk, ride, socialize, and pose for pictures sitting on their trunks. Walk With The Animals is a four-hour, also hands-on adventure. If you can't stay the night, they offer daily, drop-in public tours.

Vision Quest Safari B & B 400 River Ranch Rd, Salinas, CA 93908; ✆ 800 228 7382or ✆ 831 455 1901; www.wildthingsinc.com. Directions: on Hwy 101 in Salinas, take the Laurel Dr exit and head west on Laurel Dr. Turn left onto Davis Rd, then left on Reservation Rd. Reservation will turn into River Rd.

The **Brookdale Lodge** has two claims to fame. The first is the **Brook Room Restaurant**, built around a natural stream named Clear Creek that runs right through the restaurant. Built in the early 1920s, the restaurant, with its trout-filled brook and sky-lit ceiling, was made famous by Ripley's Believe It or Not. The rustic redwood log and gingerbread terraces overlook 70ft of creek flowing by below. But it's the second claim to fame, as one of the most haunted hotels in America, that keeps a steady stream of ghost hunters coming to the lodge hoping for a sighting of Sarah Logan, the six-year-old niece of the former owner who drowned in the 40s in the dining-room creek. The lobby, the Fireside Room, and room 46 seem to be the most haunted by her presence. Over the years, priests and psychics have been hired to rid the lodge of her ghost but, to date, Sarah still roams the place along with, say the psychics, around four-dozen other spirits. The Lodge was once *the* place to stay in the Santa Cruz mountains but today retains little of its former glory.

Brookdale Lodge 11570 Hwy 9, Brookdale, CA 95007; ☎ 831 338 6433; www.brookdalelodge.com. Directions: the lodge is on Hwy 9 north of Santa Cruz.

Grandmother of kitsch, the **Madonna Inn** in San Luis Obispo has been famous for its décor since opening with just a dozen rooms in 1958. Lovingly built by Alex and Phyllis Madonna, now in their eighties, the décor is heavily influenced by rock, which Alex loves, and by hot pink, which Phyllis adores. Today the inn has 109 theme rooms, all of them so gaudy and so excessively romantic with over-the-top fantasy décor that choosing the most outrageous is quite a challenge.

The Caveman Room is certainly a contender with its boulder walls, rock ceilings and furniture covered in animal skins. Ditto the Jungle Rock Room, where a whole herd of faux zebras must have made the ultimate sacrifice. Then there's the Madonna Suite, a riot of red, pink, rock and crystal. In the Cabin Still room, the still dispenses water instead of whiskey. We're not talking subtle here; this has to be Liberace's idea of heaven on earth. Plumbing at the inn often does weird things with water flowing in places you'd never expect. It streams, cascades, and spirals across rocks and boulders before reaching its destination.

There's enough fake fur and plastic to make Martha Stewart weep. Stop in even if you're not staying to gawk at the public rooms and watch people walking around with their mouths hanging open. There are grape leaves everywhere, carved into wood, woven into carpet, pressed into chandeliers and forged out of iron. Cherubs, roses, and plastic plants covered in Christmas tree lights abound. The men's bathroom usually has as many women as men in there, all snapping pictures of the rock waterfall activated as you approach to take care of business. The structure is huge, more like a walk-in fireplace than a urinal. The Steak House dining room is a riot of pink leather, brass, plastic grapes, yet more cherubs and gigantic floral carpeting to say nothing of the huge stone tree that lights up with fiber-optic blooms. Even some of the cakes in the bakery are pink. Be sure to bring your camera.

Madonna Inn 100 Madonna Rd, San Luis Obispo, CA 93405; ☎ 800 543 9666or ☎ 805 543 3000; www.madonnainn.com. Directions: on Hwy 101 in San Luis Obispo, take the Madonna Rd exit and head southwest.

The **Monterey Bay Aquarium**, among the finest aquariums in the world, offers a novel way to enjoy the exhibits. At their Family Camp-Ins, families with kids under six years of age get to explore the aquarium after hours and then sleep next to their favorite exhibit.

> **Monterey Bay Aquarium** 886 Cannery Row, Monterey, CA 93940;
> ☎ 831 648 4800; www.montereybayaquarium.com. Directions: the
> aquarium is on the west end of Cannery Row in Monterey.

Each of the rooms at the funky-romantic **Deetjen's Big Sur Inn** has a set of journals in which past guests have written their hopes, dreams, fantasies, and histories. Voyeuristically fascinating, they're just one of many reasons to visit this historic inn set in one of California's most beautiful places. Nestled among the coast redwoods, the inn was built by 'Grandpa' Deetjen in the 1930s to provide accommodation for those enamored of the bohemian Big Sur lifestyle. Occasionally using prison labor from a nearby highway project, Grandpa built the rooms and cabins himself, Norway style, giving each a unique name and personality. Quaint, cozy, and rustic, he filled them with funky antiques and trinkets. Meanwhile, the stunningly obese 'Grandma' held court by offering therapy sessions from a bed in the dining room. Today everything is pretty much as Grandma and Grandpa left it, the inn being run by a foundation dedicated to its preservation. Breakfast and dinner are served in the memorabilia-filled restaurant. There are no phones, TVs, or cell-phone reception; just peace and inspiration.

> **Deetjen's Big Sur Inn** 48865 Hwy 1, Big Sur, CA 93920; ☎ 831 667
> 2377; www.deetjens.com. Directions: the inn is located on Hwy 1, 30
> miles south of Carmel.

If any place can be said to offer rooms with a skew, it would have to be **Esalen**. Long the center of California's human potential movement, the **Esalen Institute** is world famous for its breathtaking setting, funky accommodations, and astounding choice of personal exploration and arts workshops. Since you have to sign up for some kind of experiential training or 'personal retreat' in order to stay there, it's probably more accurate to describe the place as a skew with rooms.

When it comes to personal and social transformation, Esalen rests today on its laurels as California's quintessential source of inspiration, a shining jewel in a sea of alternative consciousness. (Location may have something to do with it, perched as it is on some of the most spectacular landscape on the planet.) Ever since its founding in the 60s, some of the finest minds in the world have flocked there to teach workshops ranging from the physical to the philosophical, introducing California, and later the rest of the country, to the concepts of mind-body connections, holistic health practices, and expanding consciousness. In 1989 Russia's Boris Yeltsin came to relax and re-think Soviet–US relations, an event that became known as 'hot tub diplomacy'.

Today they offer a staggering 500 workshops a year. If you want to study massage, mask making, or chanting, Esalen can provide. On a deeper level, you can explore Holistic Sexuality, Psychic and Intuitive Healing, or muster up The Courage to Change. Garden buffs can explore Floral Arts as Spiritual Practice or Gardening for the Soul. Whatever experience you crave, you'll find it in their catalog, a cornucopia of transformative, healing experiences. Some of the programs even offer college or continuing education credit.

You get a choice of accommodations with your workshop, most of which last three, five, or seven days. Standard accommodations are two or three to the room;

bunks house four or more per room. They warn: 'All of our accommodations are shared. You or your room-mate may snore. Please come prepared (nose guards, ear plugs, etc) for this possibility'. They also warn that the facility is 'technologically inconvenient' and clothing optional in the hot springs, bath, massage, and pool areas. You choose for yourself how you'll feel most comfortable, clothed or sans such. Food is included, as is 24-hour use of the bath facilities, the Art Barn, and scheduled movement classes.

Esalen Institute 55000 Hwy 1, Big Sur, CA 93920; ✆ 831 667 3005; www.esalen.org. Directions: the Esalen Institute is located in Esalen off Hwy 1, south of Julia Pfeiffer Burns State Park.

Another skew with rooms (or, rather, yurts, tents and domes) is the **Ojai Foundation's Center for Living Council**, famous for its Ropes Course. A group experience for all ages, the Ropes Course challenges you to overcome personal limitations by navigating a series of rope, log, and cable obstacles, some close to the ground; others high above it. Part of an adventure challenge designed to build confidence, trust, and team spirit, it's really quite an extraordinary experience. Other ways to enjoy the semi-wilderness eco-retreat village include designing an individual retreat, one that could include a solo right of passage, or participating in a 'reverent listening' workshop event.

Ojai Foundation 9739 Ojai-Santa Paula Rd, Ojai, CA 93023; ✆ 805 646 8343; www.ojaifoundation.org. Reservations required. Directions: the foundation is located on Hwy 150, east of Ojai.

If your idea of getting away from it all means total peace and quiet, consider **New Camaldoli Hermitage**, a monastery offering knock-out views along with their skew which, in this case, means NO TALKING. The two-dozen Benedictine monks, who spend their lives here in silent contemplation, provide sanctuary for a handful of 'retreatants' each night. Each of the nine guest rooms are single-occupancy only, enhancing the experience of solitude, and each has a garden overlooking the ocean. The furnishings are spartan – just a cot, a desk, and a table – and you get your monk-prepared food from the communal kitchen. The only exception to the rule of silence is in the bookshop and, of course, when you call for your reservation. Silence must be in great demand as they're usually booked months in advance on summer weekends.

New Camaldoli Hermitage 2475 Hwy 1, Lucia, Big Sur, CA 93920; ✆ 831 667 2456; www.contemplation.com. Reservations required. Directions: on Hwy 1 25 miles south of Big Sur village and three-quarters of a mile south of Lucia Lodge, turn onto the entrance road, on the inland side of the highway which is marked by a sign and a large wooden cross. Follow this road to the top (about 2 miles) and look for the parking sign in front of the bookstore.

You don't need to be a birdwatcher to compete for the title of best birdspotter at the **Captain's Inn at Moss Landing**. This nautical themed B & B is one of the country's top-ten areas for birdwatching, boasting 300 species of birds potentially visible at the inn. Each of the six rooms in the rear building of this delightful inn has an actual boat incorporated into the décor as well as great views of the marsh, river, and sand dunes. The innkeepers provide a birding checklist in each room and challenge guests to beat previous spotting records, one of which was 32 different species, from your bed, without leaving the sheets, and all before breakfast. And if you don't see enough from your bed, the captain will take you on an Elkhorn Slough Safari, a pontoon boat where you get to see yet more birds as well as harbor seals and sea otters. On certain fall Saturday afternoons they offer pie-baking and beer-tasting classes.

Captain's Inn 8122 Moss Landing Rd, Moss Landing, CA 95039; ☎ 831 633 5550; www.captainsinn.com. Directions: on Hwy 1 in Moss Landing (north of Monterey), take the Moss Landing Rd exit and follow the road.

If you like your quarters quirky, you can't beat The **Union Hotel and Victorian Mansion**, the kind of place that just begs your inner child to come out and play. Located in the tiny western town of Los Alamos (pop 1,375), the hotel is a worthy destination in itself, offering not just the best theme rooms this side of the Mississippi, but interactive 'time travel' events as well.

Of the two buildings, the mansion is where you'll find the theme rooms. It has six rooms, five of them themed in astonishing detail and just waiting for you to come inside and play. Each room has a different theme and, in each one, you have to *discover the secret entry to the bathroom* on your own. In some of the rooms, you even have to find the hidden TV, VCR, and refrigerator. All the rooms have huge hot tubs, all are painted with intricate murals enhancing the theme, all have music and movies that match the theme, and all are marvelously, romantically kitschy.

The Fifties' Room is designed like a drive-in movie set. You lay in your Cadillac bed and watch old movies on the room's wall-size screen, turning the neon lights down low and adjusting the volume on an old-fashioned drive-in speaker stand. Even the sink is set into a Cadillac trunk. In the Egyptian room the fantasy is that of a sheikh in his tent and conjures up images of Cleopatra and Rudolph Valentino. Finding the bathroom in this one is a real challenge, but here's a hint: it involves King Tut. Next is the Pirate Room, like an old-fashioned sailing vessel, complete with intricately carved wood, lanterns that sway, and a sound system that mimics waves and seagulls. In the Gypsy Room you're in a forest, sleeping in a caravan wagon and soaking in a hot tub topped by a huge stained-glass canopy. When you turn the lights down in here, the effect is amazing. By the time you get to the Roman Room, it won't surprise you at all to sleep in a chariot and watch Rome burning around you. The bathroom, with its catacomb murals, is especially hard to find. Every room includes breakfast in bed, delivered by dumbwaiter, so you're gently awakened by delicious aromas. These are probably the best executed, most all-encompassing theme rooms in the West, created over a period of ten years in the 80s by eccentric Dick Langdon who achieved such theatrical excellence with the help of some of his Hollywood friends.

Current owner Christine Williams bought the property, which includes the adjoining, impeccably restored **Union Hotel**, after Langdon died and has given it her own special twist. She puts on time-travel events, thrusting you into time periods reflected in the property's history. One such is her Stagecoach Murder Mystery. Dressed as an Old West character, you step off a stagecoach and into the past, playing your part as suspect, victim, or even as murderer. Others are a Prohibition Mystery event and a Christmas Civil War Costume Ball. Usually held the fourth Saturday of each month, each event includes dinner. During the summer she offers overnight camp for grown-ups, a week of old-fashioned, kid-like activities like hikes, horseback riding, croquet, and hayrides, with charades, and ghost stories around the campfire. There's also a hedge maze on the property. Reserve well in advance for the theme rooms.

Union Hotel and Victorian Mansion 362 Bell St, Los Alamos, CA 93440; ☎ 800 230 2744; www.unionhotelvictmansion.com. Directions: on Hwy 101 in Los Alamos, take the CA-135 exit towards Los Alamos. The hotel is on this street between St Joseph St and Drum Canyon Rd.

ATTRACTIONS

Bonfante Gardens, a horticultural-based theme park, is famous for its **circus trees**, often featured in the mid-1900s by Ripley's Believe-It-Or-Not. The trees were created by Axel Erlandson who, motivated by divine inspiration, spent 40 years of his life shaping and grafting the bodies and arms of trees into complex coils and spirals. He formed them into fantastical shapes like arches, hearts, lightning bolts, basket weaves, and rings. After Axel's death in 1964, many of the trees – sycamores, ash, cork, and box elders – died before preservation efforts could take hold. Eventually, 19 of them were bought by park owner Michael Bonfante and then carefully transported 50 miles to the park. The park, with its gentle rides and lush plant life, is geared towards families with young children as well as garden lovers, the result of Michael's desire to create a place that combined fun and education with a focus on landscaping. There are 30 rides and attractions set in this horticultural wonderland of uniquely manicured trees, plants and flowers and the attractions are designed to educate guests about the importance of horticulture in society.

Bonfante Gardens Family Theme Park 3050 Hecker Pass Hwy, Gilroy, CA 95020; ☎ 408 840 7100; www.bonfantegardens.com. Hours vary seasonally. Directions: on Hwy 152 east of Gilroy.

Travelers on Highway 68 can't help but spot the larger-than-life farm workers toiling in the fields at the Outdoor Art Gallery at The Farm. These giant sculptures, a dozen in all, are modeled after actual workers at **The Farm**. Created by local artist and former produce worker John Cerney, they're meant as a tribute to the hard-working people employed in the Salinas Valley farming industry. The four figures near the produce stand depict men packing iceberg lettuce. Further out in the fields you'll see the farmer along with his irrigator, harvesters, and thinners. The Farm itself is an agricultural education center, demonstration farm, produce stand and recreation center all rolled into one, growing 45 of the 120 different crops for which the valley is known. They offer 'meet the farmer' tours, crop tours, and farm-animal encounters. During the summer they have a children's watermelon-eating contest and in the fall they have pumpkin picking, pumpkin races, and hayrides.

The Farm PO Box 247, Salinas, CA 93902; ☎ 831 455 2575; www.thefarm-salinasvalley.com. Free admission, open April to December 22. Directions: on Hwy 68, take the Spreckels Blvd exit and head west.

JUST PLAIN WEIRD

The college town of San Luis Obispo has a truly unique claim to fame: a narrow alleyway whose walls are densely covered on both sides by tens of thousands of pieces of gum, mostly of the bubble variety. **Bubble Gum Alley** got its first blob sometime in the 50s and it became a tradition for students to leave a lasting impression on the town by leaving their wads behind. The city tried several times to clear out the alley, but finally gave up the effort in the 60s. Today they simply clean the sidewalk once a week. If you want to deposit yours way up high, you'll need to stand on someone's shoulders; otherwise, just add it to the globs already there.

Bubble Gum Alley is located in downtown San Luis Obispo, CA. Information: contact San Luis Obispo Chamber of Commerce, 1039 Chorro St, San Luis Obispo, CA 93401; ✆ 805 781 2777; www.visitslo.com. Directions: the alley is on Higuera St, just north of Broad St.

The legend of the immortal actor James Dean lives on, 50 years after the all-too-mortal movie star died after crashing his Porsche into a Ford Coupe at the middle-of-nowhere intersection of Highways 46 and 41 on September 30 1955. Tourists have been coming to the desolate spot ever since and, in 2002, the intersection was officially declared the **James Dean Memorial Junction**. Nearby, in the parking lot of the Jack Ranch Café, is an actual memorial, a stainless-steel and aluminum sculpture placed there several decades ago by a Japanese businessman and ardent fan. Fans gather every year on September 30 to honor their fallen idol, celebrating his life with memories, music, and, of course, cars.

James Dean Memorial Junction is at the junction of Hwys 46 and 41 between Fresno and Paso Robles; www.jamesdeanmemorialjunction.com

The strange rock sculpture that seems to be growing out of the ground off Willow Road at Willow Oaks Park is actually a series of stone couches that seem to sprout organically from the soil. That was the intention of sculptor Brian Goggin who was commissioned to create a piece that would reflect Menlo Park's changing city character. Once an agricultural community, it became a middle-class suburb before morphing into the upscale place it is today. Menlo Park has an ordinance requiring developers of all commercial, industrial and municipal projects costing at least $250,000 to dedicate 1% of construction costs to public art projects and the **Menlo Park Couches** is one result.

Menlo Park Couches is located in Willows Oak Park on Willow Rd in Menlo Park. Contact the Menlo Park Arts Commission, City of Menlo Park, 701 Laurel St, Menlo Park, CA 94025; ✆ 650 330 2200; www.menlopark.org/commissions/com_arts.html. Directions: on Hwy 101 in Menlo Park, take the Willow Rd exit and head south. Willows Oak Park is on the left-hand side of this road.

Los Angeles/ Orange County

FESTIVALS AND EVENTS

Halloween is celebrated in a big way in West Hollywood, so big that almost half a million people attend the festivities. One of the country's biggest street parties, the **Halloween Costume Carnaval** turns a one-mile stretch of Santa Monica Boulevard into California's sixth-largest city for the night. While part of the event's attraction is the star-studded pop entertainment it provides, it's really the costumes that take center stage, with a month of preliminary competitions determining the grand finale on Halloween night when the winners of the best individual, best group and most creative costumes are anointed. Political figures and pop culture are always popular costume themes, so don't be surprised to see people dressed like a Florida voting booth, Martha Stewart, or carbohydrates. Dogs have their say, too at the Doggy Costume Contest and you can compete in an intergenerational Pumpkin Carving Contest. The infamous Drag Races feature La-La land's most beautiful drag queens racing in high heels.

> **Halloween Costume Carnaval West Hollywood** is held annually on or about October 31. Contact the West Hollywood CVB, 8687 Melrose Ave, Suite M-38, West Hollywood, CA 90069; ✆ 800 368 6020; www.visitwesthollywood.com. Directions: the Carnaval takes place on Santa Monica Blvd between Doheny Dr and La Cienga Blvd.

This has to rank as one of the wackiest events to have ever originated by bar bet. **Moon Amtrak** draws thousands of people to a chain-link fence in an industrial part of Laguna Niguel on the second Saturday of every July. They arrive by motorcycle and motorhome, by car and by truck as early as Friday evening and set up for a long, beer-fueled, and downright bizarre 'tail' gate party. Come morning, these otherwise respectable people do something they'd normally never dream of doing – they drop their drawers and 'moon' the two-dozen passenger trains that pass by that day. A giant schedule is posted outside the bar and, at the sound of a train whistle, everyone sprints into position along the fence and moons the astonished passengers. Regulars come prepared, dressing in skirts and elastic-waist pants. Vendors hawk commemorative T-shirts and

104

there's usually someone selling sun block with a 'Moonblock' paste-on label. There are plenty of Amcrack jokes and more cameras than cheeks in evidence.

You'd think a spectacle of this kind would just attract rednecks and the kind of people who express themselves in less than socially adept ways. But, in fact, the Moon Amtrak crowd is much like that you'd find at a combination Harley rally/PTA meeting – that is, you get all kinds, from nurses, doctors and teachers (who may even be bikers themselves) to politically correct California-style rednecks just looking for a good excuse to misbehave. When it gets dark they've been known to moon by flashlight and by lanterns hung on the fence, hundreds of bare bums glowing in the flickering light. The mooning, which has been going on since a bar challenge started it all 25 years ago, draws crowds to both sides of the fence. The trains are booked solid months in advance for moon day. No-one actually sponsors or organizes this event; it just has a life of its own. Amtrak tries to ignore it and the local police simply turn the other cheek (ha!). Best to arrive in the morning as the trains are more likely to slow to a crawl before they get behind schedule. The crowd dwindles substantially by mid afternoon.

Moon Amtrak takes place annually the second Saturday in July across from Mugs Amway Saloon in Laguna Niguel, CA; www.moonamtrak.org. Directions: on I-5 in Orange County, take the Avery Pkwy exit. Turn west at the end of the off-ramp, then north on Camino Capistrano. The train tracks will be on your left, and Mugs Amway Saloon is a mile along this road. Please don't park next to the chain-link fence next to the train tracks. That's where the 'mooning' happens.

The ultimate example of life imitating art has occurred every summer since 1932 at the **Pageant of Masters** in Laguna Beach. Part of the Festival of Arts, the pageant, known as Tableaux Vivants or Living Pictures, is a living re-creation of classical and contemporary art masterpieces, portrayed by real people posing to look exactly like the figures in original works of art. With the audience sitting under the stars in an outdoor amphitheater, scene after scene unfolds, accompanied by music and narration. Giant reproductions of famous works of art, including paintings, carvings and sculpture, are exposed one after the other. Several times during each performance, the lights are turned on as the backdrops and foregrounds are being changed so you see the costumed, made-up volunteer 'actors' take their various spots. As the music begins, the actors freeze and the three-dimensional tableau takes form as an art masterpiece. The volunteers, many of whom have been involved with the pageant since childhood, are chosen based on their size, shape and suitability for the work of art being portrayed. They are required to hold their poses for 90 seconds without moving. Occasionally a pigeon perches on one of the living statues. The evening always closes with a living representation of Leonardo Da Vinci's *The Last Supper*. Behind the scenes it's the scene painters, sculptors, make-up artists, costume and lighting designers who are the real stars. The amphitheater seats upwards of 2,000 and tickets sell out quickly with 250,000 people attending each year. Admission includes the juried art festival itself.

Pageant of Masters is held annually in July and August in Laguna Beach, CA. Contact Pageant of the Masters, 650 Laguna Canyon Rd, Laguna Beach, CA; ☎ 949 494 1145; www.foapom.com. Directions: on I-405 in Costa Mesa, take the CA-73 south exit towards San Diego, then take the Laguna Canyon Rd exit, then turn right onto CA-133 (Laguna Canyon Rd).

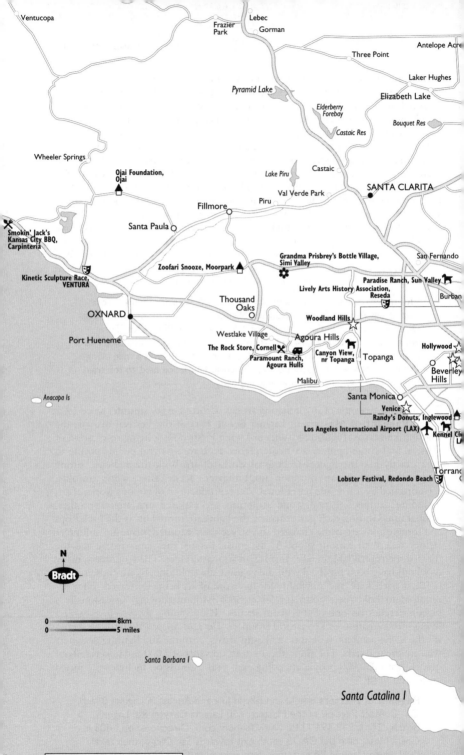

Ventucopa

Frazier Park   Lebec
Gorman

Antelope Acre

Three Point

Laker Hughes

Pyramid Lake

Elizabeth Lake

Elderberry Forebay

Bouquet Res

Castaic Res

Wheeler Springs

Castaic

Lake Piru

SANTA CLARITA

Ojai Foundation, Ojai

Val Verde Park

Fillmore   Piru

San Fernando

Santa Paula

Smokin' Jack's
Kansas City BBQ,
Carpinteria

Grandma Prisbrey's Bottle Village,
Simi Valley

Zoofari Snooze, Moorpark

Paradise Ranch, Sun Valley

Kinetic Sculpture Race,
VENTURA

Lively Arts History Association,
Reseda

Burban

Thousand
Oaks

Woodland Hills

OXNARD

Westlake Village

Agoura Hills

Hollywood

Port Hueneme

The Rock Store, Cornell

Canyon View,
nr Topanga

Topanga

Beverley
Hills

Paramount Ranch,
Agoura Hulls

Malibu

Santa Monica

Anacapa Is

Venice

Randy's Donuts, Inglewood

Los Angeles International Airport (LAX)

Kennel Cl
LA

Torranc

Lobster Festival, Redondo Beach

N

Bradt

0 ———— 8km
0 ———— 5 miles

Santa Barbara I

Santa Catalina I

LOS ANGELES AREA

San Nicolas I

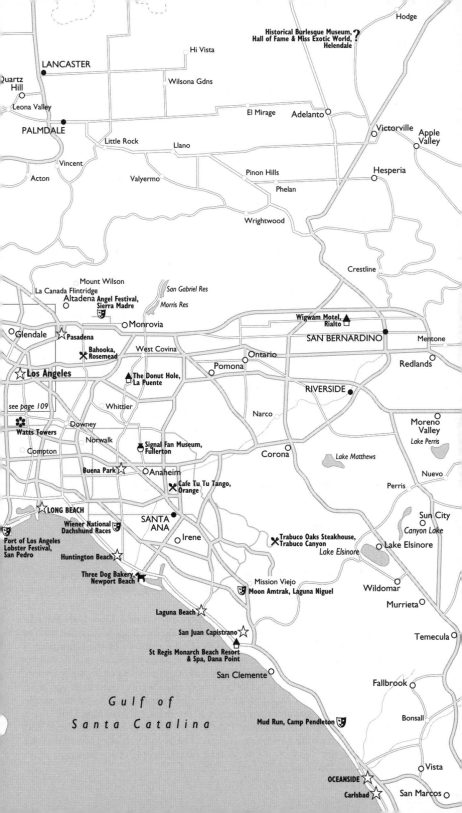

Hodge

Historical Burlesque Museum,
Hall of Fame & Miss Exotic World,
Helendale

LANCASTER

Hi Vista

Quartz
Hill

Wilsona Gdns

Leona Valley

El Mirage   Adelanto

Victorville   Apple
Valley

PALMDALE

Little Rock   Llano

Vincent

Valyermo   Pinon Hills

Hesperia

Acton

Phelan

Wrightwood

Crestline

Mount Wilson   San Gabriel Res

La Canada Flintridge
Altadena Angel Festival,
Sierra Madre   Morris Res

Wigwam Motel,
Rialto

Glendale   Monrovia

SAN BERNARDINO   Mentone

Pasadena

Bahooka,
Rosemead   West Covina   Ontario

Redlands

Los Angeles   Pomona

RIVERSIDE

The Donut Hole,
La Puente

see page 109

Whittier   Narco

Moreno
Valley
Lake Perris

Watts Towers   Downey

Norwalk

Compton   Signal Fan Museum,
Fullerton   Corona   Lake Matthews

Nuevo

Buena Park   Anaheim   Perris   Sun City
Canyon Lake

LONG BEACH   Cafe Tu Tu Tango,
Orange

SANTA
ANA   Trabuco Oaks Steakhouse,
Trabuco Canyon   Lake Elsinore

Wiener National
Dachshund Races

Port of Los Angeles
Lobster Festival,
San Pedro   Irene   Lake Elsinore

Huntington Beach   Wildomar

Three Dog Bakery,
Newport Beach   Mission Viejo   Murrieta
Moon Amtrak, Laguna Niguel

Laguna Beach

San Juan Capistrano   Temecula

St Regis Monarch Beach Resort
& Spa, Dana Point

San Clemente   Fallbrook

Gulf of
Santa Catalina   Bonsall

Mud Run, Camp Pendleton

Vista

OCEANSIDE

Carlsbad   San Marcos

Across the road from the Festival of the Arts and situated in a tranquil eucalyptus grove, the **Sawdust Art Festival** was founded in 1966 as an antidote to stuffy, boring art shows. All of the 200 artists exhibiting have to live in Laguna Beach and create what they sell. Many of them work while you watch and you can see glass-blowing demonstrations at one of the few glass kilns in the country, get your hands really dirty working a potter's wheel at the ceramics booth, or take one of the various painting or printmaking classes.

> **Sawdust Arts Festival** is held in July and August in Laguna Beach. Contact the Sawdust Arts Festival, 735 Laguna Canyon Rd, Laguna Beach, CA 92651; ✆ 949 494 3030; www.sawdustartfestival.org. Hours: 10am–10pm. Directions: as Pageant of Masters above.

San Juan Capistrano is famous as the place the swallows return to nest each year after wintering in Argentina and the town celebrates their usual March 19 return with a week of wacky activities. The Presidents Ball, with its non-stop gaming, kicks off **Swallows Week** with a dance where everyone dresses in Western, Spanish, Mexican or early California costume. The townsfolk then stay dressed up for the rest of the week, especially on Hoos'gow Day when anyone not dressed in Western wear risks being arrested and tossed in the hoos'gow (a portable jail) that roams around the town. Any clean-shaven man risks the same fate, so stubble is the order of the day. Jail sentences are short for those who make bail by purchasing a fundraising novelty to help defray the cost of the Swallows Day Parade, the country's largest non-motorized parade. The Hairiest Man Cowboy and Soiled Dove contests take place at the **Swallows Inn**, the town's legendary cowboy/biker/just plain folk saloon known for their Monday night $10 steak dinners and for their Western and swing dance bands. The winner of the Soiled Dove competition is the one most convincingly portraying an old Western dance-hall saloon girl who's been up all night 'entertaining'. The Hairiest Man Cowboy competitors start clean shaven in January and grow wild facial hair for two months prior to the contest.

> **Swallows Week** takes place in March in San Juan Capistrano. Contact the Mission San Juan Capistrano, PO Box 697, San Juan Capistrano, CA 92693; ✆ 949 234 1300 ext 315; www.missionsjc.com. Directions: events take place in various locations through the town. See the website for details.

> **Swallows Inn** 31786 Camino Capistrano, San Juan Capistrano, CA 92675; ✆ 949 493 3188; www.swallowsinn.com. Directions: the inn is at the junction of Camino Capistrano and Ortega Hwy, just off I-5.

Around 1,500 marchers make up the outrageously satirical **Doo Dah Parade**. Unlike the structured Tournament of Roses Parade that it spoofs, anyone with an appreciation of irony can march in the Doo Dah, organized by the Unorganizers Unofficial Committee. There are no judges, no sponsors, no commercials and not a serious face in the crowd. Each year they anoint a queen chosen in public tryouts; in 1997 it was the deceased Lily Hodge, whose ashes were carried in an urn along the parade route by her husband who claimed Lily had always loved the parade. The Doo Dah has spawned such legends as the Briefcase Marching Drill Team, the Hibachi Marching Grill Team, and the Invisible Man Marching Band. With marchers like Linoleum Bonaparte, Confused Dogs in Drag, the Howdy Krishnas and Elvirus & the Vaccines, it's no wonder 40,000 people cram the streets to see the spectacle, a Pasadena tradition since 1976.

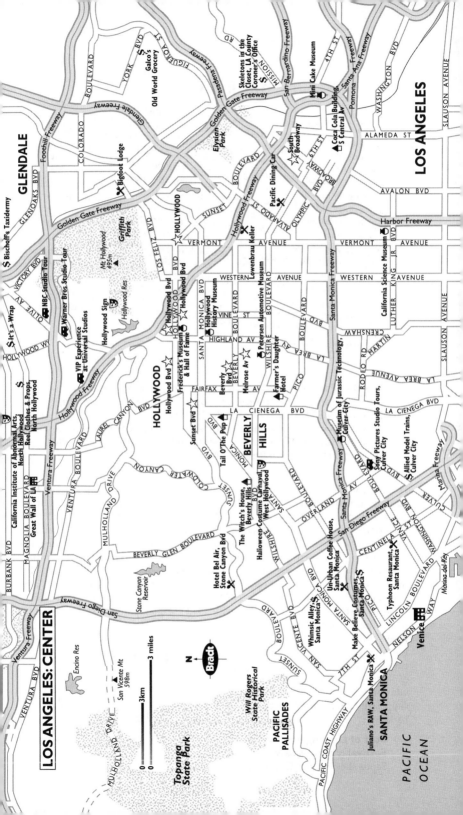

Quirk Alert

Cities across California host **Hair Wars** from time to time, a musical touring production in which African-American hairstylists showcase their most outrageous, most over-the-top hairstyles in a three-hour runway extravaganza. Gathering their own models, choosing their own music and costumes, and choreographing their own routines, hundreds of stylists perform, vying for the honor of not just being the most memorable 'hair entertainer', but of being discovered for videos, magazines, television, movies and billboards. They prepare for months, often spending thousands of dollars on their presentations. How over the top can their creations get? Well, they use a lot more than styling gel, including foam, glue, and chicken wire. Consider the windshield made of blue hair, complete with working windshield wipers. Or the hairycoptor, a do from which a whirling, remote-controlled, hair-draped toy helicopter emerged. Or the beehive hairdo that concealed a live snake. Even the clothing can be made of hair, such as the full-length skirt made of braided synthetic hair trimmed with a teased fringe of human hair. There's no specific website for this so just search 'Hair Wars' to find out more.

Doo Dah Parade is held annually in November. Contact Pasadena Convention and Visitors Bureau, 171 South Los Robles Ave, Pasadena, CA 91101; ☎ 800 307 7977 or ☎ 626 795 9311; www.pasadenadoodahparade.com. Directions: the parade begins at the corner of Holly and Raymond, goes south on Raymond to Colorado Blvd, and west on Colorado to Pasadena Ave.

How do you call a lobster? Hint: it doesn't involve a cell phone. At the **Port of Los Angeles Lobster Festival**, you gather at the shore, face the ocean, flail your arms about and shout, chant, rant and rave. This is a lot easier for the 12-and-under set that compete for a prize computer, but there's nothing to stop you from making a fool of yourself if you wish, unless, of course, you consider your pride. In the old days grown fishermen opened the lobster season by performing this ritual; whether this improved the catch is anyone's guess. If you'd rather not do the hootin' and hollerin' bit, you can opt to dress up your pet as a lobster – or as any seafood item – and enter the Lobster Dog Pet Parade. If your pet can't, or won't, wear the costume, then build a float with a kid's wagon, put your stubborn pet in it, and drag it along the parade route.

If all else fails, dress yourself as a lobster and carry your pet. The parade is based on the legendary exploits of Bob the Lobster Dog who hung out on the docks and supposedly guided in the fleet by barking.

Port of Los Angeles Lobster Festival is held annually in September in Ports O'Call Village,

Quirk Alert

Wearing historically accurate clothing and behaving in a manner befitting specific time periods, members of the **Lively Arts History Association** hold vintage dress balls with themes like a Jane Austen Evening, a Scarlet Pimpernel Ball, Gatsby Night, a Speakeasy Soirée, the 1929 Crash, and the Statehood Ball. At each event most attendees dress according to the ball's era and behave according to the rules of etiquette for that particular time. A page on their website, the Gentleman's Page, covers how a proper gentleman would have comported himself during the 19th century, including his behavior and his attire. The dances are open to anyone interested in living history and you don't need a costume to attend. But you do need to dress formally. Most of the events are held in the Pasadena area.

Lively Arts History Association 7341 Etiwanda Ave, Reseda, CA 91335; www.lahacal.org. Events happen at various times and locations through the year. See website for details.

San Pedro, CA; ☎ 310 366 6472; www.lobsterfest.com. Directions: the festival is held in ports O'Call Village, at the end of Hwy 110. Free parking and a festival shuttle are offered at Miner and E 22nd St.

Redondo Beach has its annual **Lobster Festival**, too, a zany three-day feast and fest with attendees wearing lobster costumes, grass skirts, Hawaiian shirts and bikinis. They're never short of high school athletes to compete in the Clam Linguini Eating Contest.

Lobster Festival is held annually in September in Redondo Beach, CA. Contact Redondo Beach Visitors Bureau, 200 N Pacific Coast Hwy, Redondo Beach, CA; ☎ 310 376 6911 or ☎ 310 374 7373; www.lobsterfestival.com. Directions: at the Seaside Lagoon in Redondo Beach.

People powered and bizarre, kinetic sculptures are ludicrous vehicles designed just for the fun of racing them against other equally absurd contraptions. Made from all matter of machine scrap, gears, old bicycles and floatation devices, those in the day-long **Kinetic Sculpture Race at Ventura** start with a noisy launch into the harbor, a timed race along a water course and along a sand bar, and end with a race around an oval grass track and a trip through a gooey mud pit. The prizes are as offbeat as the vehicles and their drivers, with awards for the snappiest dresser, the best bribe, the most mediocre, the crankiest, and the one that leaves the best skid marks. The public can serve as Kinetic Kops – enforcing race rules and collecting bribes to ignore them – or as judges for those with a keen eye for mechanical details and a highly developed sense of humor.

Kinetic Sculpture Race at Ventura is held annually in September. Contact the Kinetic Sculpture Race; ☎ 805 652 0000; www.kineticrace.com. Directions: the race takes place on land and in the water at Ventura Harbor, starting near the Four Points Sheraton.

On Hwy 101 in Ventura, take the Seaward Ave exit and turn left on E
Harbor Blvd, then right on Schooner Dr. Parking is available next to
the hotel.

It's hardly the Kentucky Derby of the dog world, but the **Wiener National
Dachshund Races** bring in a crowd just as dedicated to the outcome. During each
heat, two- to three-dozen of the stubby-legged pooches are supposed to race 20
yards but, in reality, these distractible dogs find the sights, sounds, and smells along
the route far more interesting. The real show is in watching their owners beg,
plead, and cajole their pets along the course, using everything from bratwurst to
laser lights, tennis balls to treats. More than 600 wiener owners are involved,
bringing their dogs from time to time to compete in the monthly races. The
biggest attendance, though, is at the annual Oktoberfest race where the dogs
compete in their own costume contests and the winning pooches get to ride with
the mayor in the Oktoberfest Parade.

> **Wiener National Dachshund Races** are held annually in Old World
> Village in Huntington Beach in October. Contact the Old World Village,
> 7561 Center Ave, Huntington Beach, CA 92647; ✆ 714 898 5111;
> www.oldworldvillage.net. The races start at 2pm. Directions: on Hwy
> 405 in San Diego, take the Beach Blvd exit towards Huntington Beach,
> then an immediate right onto Center Ave.

It might seem strange that the owner of the world's largest bunny collection is also
the organizer of the **Angel Festival**, but Candace Frazee believes strongly in both
angels and rabbits. She started the first Angel Festival in 1993 to bring people
together to share angelic thoughts. Today the festival draws angel lovers from all
religions, faiths and philosophies to talk about angels, buy angelic art and crafts,
sing angelic songs, dance angelic dances and attend angelic lectures. Awards are
given honoring angels, living or dead, who display angelic behavior. A free book is
given to anyone named 'Angel' and a $5 coupon to anyone who comes dressed as
an angel. Devils Food cake isn't on the menu; only Angel Food.

> **Angel Festival** is held annually in Sierra Madre in October. Contact the
> Angel Festival, PO 273, Pasadena, CA 91102; ✆ 626 794 4458;
> www.theangelfestival.com. Directions: the festival takes place at
> Memorial Park, 222 W Sierra Madre Blvd, Sierra Madre.

The world's largest street-painting festival, **Absolut Chalk** brings about 600 artists
from virtually every walk of life to an area two blocks long in Pasadena where they
create chalk murals on the pavement using 25,000 sticks of pastel chalk. Besides
seeing the work of invited 'madonnari', the Italian word for street painter, the
public is invited to try their hand as well by painting their own murals at
Chalkland, a special area for kids and families. At the conclusion of the event the
artists themselves select the most outstanding murals.

> **Absolut Chalk** is held annually in June in Pasadena. Contact The
> Lightbringer Project, 64 N Raymond Ave, Pasadena, CA 91103; ✆ 626
> 440 7379; www.absolutchalk.com. Registration is required to participate,
> but attending is free. Directions: the festival is held in the Paseo Colorado
> shopping village on Colorado Blvd off I-210 in Pasadena. Take the
> Colorado Blvd exit and turn left onto Colorado Blvd. The shopping
> village is on the south side.

Above Sculptor Clayton Bailey with his robot family near Port Costa (JF)

Below Clowns enthrall passengers and spread laughter on a San Francisco rapid-transit train (MD)

Left Santa shares a political message with tourists at San Francisco's Fisherman's Wharf (MD)

Below Californians go way overboard when it comes to boarding their pets at Paradise Ranch in Los Angeles (PR)

All you need is a swimsuit and a certain lack of good judgement to join the 100 or so swimmers who meet every New Year's Day for the **Huntington Beach Pier Polar Plunge**. While the water isn't nearly as cold (temperatures in the 40s and 50s) as that endured by polar bear cubs on the east coast, this is plenty cold for Southern Californians accustomed to balmy temperatures. Donate $10 to charity and you'll get a certificate proving you did it; $20 gets you a commemorative beach towel.

> **Huntington Beach Pier Polar Plunge** takes place annually in Huntington Beach Pier, behind Duke's on New Year's Day. Contact the Huntington Beach CVB, 301 Main St, Suite 208, Huntington Beach, CA 92648; ☎ 714 969 3492; www.hbvisit.com/events/index.html. The plunge takes place at 9am. Directions: Duke's is at 317 Pacific Coast Hwy.

PECULIAR PURSUITS

Open only for shows put on by talent too strange to perform elsewhere, the **California Institute of Abnormal Arts** 'raises the bar on bizarre' according to the *LA Times*. This nightclub/theater/performance space supports underground music, puppetry, magic, and film that is just too weird to get any respect from the mainstream Los Angeles entertainment world. With its sideshow décor of bright yellows and reds, the space features a collection of sideshow exhibits and memorabilia such as two-headed babies and the real remains of a famous French clown. The club provides a venue for acts like the Circus Jerkus, America's Most Bipolar Circus, and The Girlie Freak Show with its comedic erotic dancers performing death-defying stunts.

> **California Institute of Abnormal Arts** 11334 Burbank Blvd, North Hollywood, CA 91601; ☎ 818 506 6353; www.ciabnormalarts.com. Directions: the Institute is on Burbank Blvd between Tujunga Ave and Bakmar Ave.

There's no place like Hollywood for celebrating itself and they do it well with two quirky icons: the **Walk of Fame** and the **Hollywood Sign**. Celebrating its 80th birthday in 2003, the sign was a former real-estate billboard that read 'Hollywoodland' until 1949 when it lost its last four wooden letters to become an advertisement for the newly blossoming town. The most infamous tale the sign can tell is that of the suicide of a young actress in 1932 who leapt to her death from the top of the 'H'. When the Pope visited in 1978, pranksters changed it to read 'Holywood' and in the 70s it briefly read 'Hollyweed' to protest anti-marijuana legislation. By the time it reached middle age at 50, the 'D' had fallen down and both 'O's had disintegrated. A fund raising campaign resulted in the erection of a brand new metal sign.

The **Walk of Fame** got its start in 1960 with 2,500 sidewalk star spaces dedicated to honoring not just movie actors, but those from television and the theater as well. Look below a celebrity's name within their star for a symbol that will tell you in which category they're being honored: a motion picture camera for movie actors and directors; a TV set for television stars and producers; a phonograph record for singers, songwriters and recording artists; a radio microphone for radio-broadcast artists, and theater masks for stage performers. Lassie, Rin-Tin-Tin, and Big Bird have stars, as does Thomas Edison who invented motion pictures. Robert Redford and Clint Eastwood don't have stars, having somehow eluded the judge's favor all these years. Every month there's an unveiling ceremony as new stars are dedicated

Quirk Alert

Pranksters with an agenda, members of the **Los Angeles Cacophony Society** perpetrate their mischief in pretty outrageous ways, counting on the public's gullibility and outrage to kick in before they realize they've been taken. For example, they set themselves up at the rest stop of the Los Angeles Marathon offering donuts, beer, cigarettes, chips, cheeseburgers and lap dances. To their credit, they did bring chairs.

The **LA Cacophony Society** www.la.cacophony.org. Their motto: You may already be a member.

and the star has to be there in person for the event. Often, they bring along their star friends and the public is welcome to attend the unveiling. (You can get a list of upcoming unveiling ceremonies online.)

The **Walk of Fame** covers both sides of Hollywood Blvd from Gower to La Brea, and both sides of Vine St from Yucca to Sunset; www.seeing-stars.com/Calendar/index.shtml#WalkOfFame, or call the Chamber of Commerce's automated hot line to hear about the next celebrity scheduled for a star event: ☎ 323 469 8311.

Hollywood Sign The best viewpoints and photo-ops for the sign are on levels 2 through 5 above the main courtyard at the Hollywood & Highland Center at the corner of Hollywood Blvd and Highland.

MUSEUMS AND COLLECTIONS

You won't know quite what to make of the **Museum of Jurassic Technology** in Culver City, which seems to be precisely what the museum is all about. As you wander through the labyrinth of impeccably displayed exhibits, you won't be alone as you stare quizzically and ponder the sanity of what you're observing. This is a very, very strange place where, according to curator David Wilson, confusion can lead to a very creative state of mind; so creative, in fact, that you could end up believing that eating a mouse on toast can cure bedwetting. It's a place where literature, dreams, and science collide, a place to be fascinated by the inexplicable. The museum's exhibits aren't necessarily what they seem to be and they ask questions that don't necessarily beg to be answered. The more you see, the less you understand. It's not that you have to suspend belief, just that you have to give up the notion of certainty. You'll see spore-inhaling ants, incredibly detailed peach pit carvings, inventive theories on the nature of oblivion and bats that can seemingly fly through solid objects. You can't quite be sure exactly what is fact and what is fiction, which is the fun of it all. David recently received a MacArthur genius grant for his work here, so just go with the flow.

Museum of Jurassic Technology 9341 Venice Blvd, Culver City, CA 90232; ☎ 310 836 6131; www.mjt.org. Open Thu 2–8pm; Fri–Sun 12 noon–6pm; closed Thanksgiving, Christmas, Easter, 1st Thu in May. Directions: on I-10, take the Robertson exit and go south. Turn tight onto Venice Blvd. The museum is located just east of the intersection of Bagley Ave and Venice Blvd on the north side of the street.

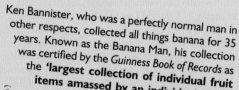

Quirk Alert

Ken Bannister, who was a perfectly normal man in other respects, collected all things banana for 35 years. Known as the Banana Man, his collection was certified by the Guinness Book of Records as the **'largest collection of individual fruit items amassed by an individual in the world'**. His obsession began in 1972 when he started handing out 'smiley' banana stickers at conventions to promote his non-banana business. Banana Man took off from there and he began to develop the persona, even dressing in Gumby-like banana outfits from time to time and appearing on dozens of TV shows, including Jay Leno's Tonite Show. At his Banana Museum in Altadena, Ken arranged his 17,000-item collection in sections: hard items, food and drink items, notions, clothing, soft items and wall items. From an 8ft yellow banana couch to banana body spray to banana lamps, Ken had it all in his densely crowded museum. He was the Top Banana of the International Banana Club with 8,500 members in 17 countries. If you sent him a banana item, you got a banana merit; collect enough merits and you'd earn a Banana Degree. (FYI: The record for fast banana eating stands at 12 bananas in two minutes.) As of spring 2005 Ken has the entire collection up for sale.

Ken Bannister's Banana Collection www.bananaclub.com.

Sci-fi fans idolize Forrest Ackerman, the man who coined the phrase 'sci-fi', who acted in dozens of early science-fiction films, and who amassed a huge collection of sci-fi film memorabilia. Fans make the pilgrimage to the elderly man's home, known as the **Ackermansion**, on Saturday mornings when 'Forry', as he prefers to be called, holds one of his open houses. His bungalow is stuffed to overflowing with memorabilia, posters, props and pictures, genuine things like Bela Lugosi's ring, Dracula's cape, and the original brontosaurus that ate the soldiers in the 1933 *King Kong* film. Forry is known as a gracious host, eager to share stories of his days in the Hollywood spotlight.

Ackermansion Forrest Ackerman, 4511 Russell Ave, Hollywood, CA 90027; ☏ 323 MOON FAN. Please call to confirm tour arrangements and to get directions. Tours are conducted most Saturdays from 11am–12 noon.

Almost every baby boomer can remember sneaking illicit peeks as teenagers into the shop windows of Frederick's lingerie stores. At the **Frederick's of Hollywood Lingerie Museum and Celebrity Lingerie Hall of Fame** you'll see the 'software' that made Mr Frederick famous and the underwear of the famous who wore his sexy creations. His motto was 'Don't dream it . . . live it', and he not only gave folks plenty to dream about, he made it easy to buy the paraphernalia from which fantasies are made. Above the retail store is the museum, with undies of the rich and famous: Ethel Merman's girdle, Mae West's marabou negligee, Tom Hanks's boxer shorts, Susan Sarandon's garter belt, and one of Madonna's infamous bustiers. It isn't difficult to imagine Cher, Loni Anderson, Joan Collins and Robert Redford in their unmentionables on display, either. Phyllis Diller left instructions – her bra is embroidered with the words 'this side up'. From mementos of Hollywood's golden girls to underwear from every cast member of Beverly Hills 90210, the museum reinforces the image of Hollywood as a romantic and glamorous place. The museum is the site of Frederick's very first store.

Frederick's of Hollywood Lingerie Museum and Celebrity Lingerie Hall of Fame 6608 Hollywood Blvd, Hollywood, CA; ✆ 323 466 8506; www.seeing-stars.com/Museums/Fredericks.shtml. Free admission. Open daily 10am–9pm; Fri 10am–6pm; Sat & Sun 12 noon–5pm.

It's an odd, odd world inside the **Hollywood History Museum**, home of Jayne Mansfield's white picket fence, Russell Crowe's *Gladiator* costume, and Hannibal Lecter's entire jail cell set, complete with straightjacket and head muzzle, from *Silence of the Lambs*. Opened in 2003 in the historic Art Deco Max Factor building, the eclectic 2,800-item collection belongs to Donelle Dadigan, a Los Angeles real estate developer who spent ten years relentlessly pursuing her vision of a museum that would let people see the real Hollywood. There are four floors of exhibits containing thousands of items, including Tommy Lee Jones's *Men in Black* suit, Rudy Vallee's megaphone, Elvis Presley's bathrobe, fake eyelashes belonging to Joan Crawford, a life-size model of a dead-looking actress, and plaster life masks of the faces of Clark Gable and Humphrey Bogart. You can rent the gruesome *Silence of the Lambs* cell block for special events.

Hollywood History Museum 1660 N Highland Ave, Hollywood, CA; ✆ 323 464 7776; www.seeing-stars.com/Museums/ HollywoodHistoryMuseum.shtml. Open Thu–Sun 10am–5pm.

The **California Science Museum** is more like an amusement park than a conventional museum, merging science and learning in a playful way through more than 100 interactive exhibits. You can build a giant archway, then test it to see how it would hold up in an earthquake. Or flight-test a spaceship you've designed yourself or take a thermal portrait of yourself. Visit Tess, the anatomically correct 50ft-tall transparent human and watch her react with animation, animatronics, and special effects. Plus you can test your nerves by riding the High Wire Bicycle 43ft up in the air.

California Science Museum 700 State Dr, Los Angeles, CA 90037; ✆ 323 SCIENCE; www.californiasciencecenter.org. Directions: on Hwy 110 (Harbor Freeway) in LA, take the Exposition Blvd exit, then to Flower St. Turn left on Flower to Figueroa St. Enter Exposition Park half a block on the right (39th St), and follow Guest Parking signs to the parking structure.

Cake decorators have more than just conventions and a Hall of Fame to call their own. They have the Cake Lady and her **Mini Cake Museum**, both located in – of all places – a retirement home. Frances Kuyper, a famous cake decorator and TV personality for all things cake, used to have the museum in her home. But after her husband died, she moved the whole kit and caboodle with her into the retirement home. All 150 Styrofoam and perma-ice cakes made the move, although some of them got a bit squished in the process, hence the 'mini' part. They showcase the various techniques she used to make her a cake-decorating diva. She also has a collection of 500 books on the subject and offers tours and demonstrations right there on the premises. Frances was best known for her air-brushed portrait cakes, including ones of Archie Bunker, Carol Burnett, Dinah Shore, Carol Channing and President Ronald Reagan.

Mini Cake Museum Hollenbeck Home, 573 South Boyle Ave, Los Angeles, CA 90033; ✆ 323 263 6195 or ✆ 323 780 3810; www.hollenbeckhome.com/minicakemuseum.html. Tours are by appointment only.

Like most outsider artists in the mid 1900s, John Ehn, aka the **Old Trapper**, had a vision he couldn't ignore, so he populated his motel property with a gaggle of concrete-sculpted cowboys, cowgirls, gunslingers, miners, dance-hall girls and Indians, throwing in a Boot Hill graveyard for good measure. Obsessed with the Wild West theme, he filled his Old Trapper Lodge with Western memorabilia and covered the face of the building with tools. After his death his family had to sell the property and Pierce College decided to adopt the sculptures, displaying them on the grounds in Cleveland Park behind the Animal Sciences building.

Old Trapper sculptures are on the campus of Pierce College, 6201 Winnetka Ave, Woodland Hills, CA 91371; ✆ 818 719 6401; www.piercecollege.edu. Directions: on Hwy 101 east of Hidden Hills, take the Winnetka Ave exit and head north. Turn left onto the campus grounds on Brahama Dr, then left onto Stadium Way and left onto El Ranco Dr. Cleveland Park is on the right side of this road.

Some eccentrics, infused with the unshakable belief that their way is the right way, manage to attract huge followings. Logically located in the Hollywood land of make believe, the **L Ron Hubbard Life Exhibition** canonizes the guru who started the religion of Scientology. You can't just browse the 30 or so displays honoring the man who supposedly was proficient in several dozen fields, though. You have to take a tour of the high-tech exhibition that dramatizes not only his stories and accomplishments, but also the pearls of wisdom he uttered on his way to riches. According to the exhibit, Mr Hubbard was – among other things – a master mariner, a police officer, a photographer, an artist, a naval intelligence officer, a daredevil pilot, an explorer, a horticulturist, and a science-fiction writer. By the time you finish the highly dramatized, two-hour tour, the only thing you'll be certain of is his marketing skill. The Church also has a Celebrity Center International in Hollywood, one of 12 worldwide that recognizes the importance of celebrity artists to society. In L Ron's words, 'A culture is only as great as its dreams and its dreams are dreamed by artists.'

L Ron Hubbard Life Exhibition 6331 Hollywood Blvd, Los Angeles, CA; ✆ 323 960 3511; www.lronhubbardprofile.org/exhib.htm. *Open Fri and Sat 10am–11.30pm.* Located in the Hollywood Guaranty Building at the corner of Ivar and Hollywood Blvd.

The **Ripley's Believe It or Not Museum** in Hollywood features a human-hair bikini; a replica of a half-ton man who weighed 1,069lb when he died at the age of 32; art made from dryer lint; a fur-covered trout used in a hoax; and hand-painted potato chips. There's also a sculpture of the Golden Gate Bridge made by toothpick artist Steve Backman who spent two-and-a-half years creating the 13ft sculpture from 30,000 toothpicks. The Buena Park museum has a rooster with a 15ft-tail, an eight-legged pig, a two-headed calf and a *Last Supper* scene made entirely of toasted bread.

> **Ripley's Believe It or Not Museum** 6780 Hollywood Blvd, Hollywood, CA 90028; ☏ 323 466 6335; www.ripleys.com. *Open Sun–Thu 10am–10pm; Fri and Sat 10am–11.30pm.* Directions: the museum is at the corner of Hollywood Blvd and Highland Ave.

> **Ripley's Believe It or Not Museum** 7850 Beach Blvd, Buena Park, CA 90620; ☏ 714 522 1155; www.ripleysbuenapark.com. *Open Mon–Fri 11am–5pm; Sat and Sun 10am–6pm.* The museum is 1 block north of Knotts Berry Farm.

The **Guinness World Records Museum** tells the story of a man who, in 1900, walked on his hands from Vienna to Paris, a distance of 871 miles. He averaged 1.58mph and completed the journey in 55 ten-hour 'walking' sessions. It also tells of a woman with 20in-long fingernails, a VW Bug with 18 students crammed inside, and a frozen cricket spitting record of 32.5ft. Thousands of world records are brought to life here in vivid displays that help you really experience the bizarre lengths to which people will go to become a Guinness record holder.

> **Guinness World Records Museum** 6764 Hollywood Blvd, Hollywood, CA; ☏ 323 463 6433; www.guinnessattractions.com. *Open 10am–12 midnight.* Directions: the museum is located on Hollywood Blvd, between N Highland Ave and N Las Palmas Ave.

If anyone were going to open a museum devoted to erotica, Hollywood would be a logical location. Honoring the long-neglected stars of adult entertainment, the **Erotic Museum** strives to educate the public about human sexuality through entertaining exhibits of erotic pictures, movies, diagrams, paintings and interactive multi-media experiences. Sex and Technology explores the evolution of adult toys while Sex and the Muse presents sex through the eyes of painters and photographers. Films from various eras, such as the only stag film thought to be made by Marilyn Monroe, are presented in the projection room.

> **Erotic Museum** 6741 Hollywood Blvd, Hollywood, CA 90028; ☏ 323 463 7684; www.theeroticmuseum.com. Admission $12.95. Adults only. *Open Sun–Thu 12 noon–9pm, Sat and Sun 12 noon–12 midnight.* Directions: the museum is on Hollywood Blvd between McCadden and Las Palmas.

Steve Lubanski and Candace Frazee give each other at least one bunny-related gift every day. And they've been doing so since 1992 which explains how they've amassed, according to Guinness, the 'world's largest bunny collection'. Some days they may exchange four or five bunnies, explaining their accumulation of 19,000 and counting. They're avid collectors, acquiring Rose Parade float bunnies and a rare Elvis Parsley bunny. The **Bunny Museum** is in their home, although it's hard to find a place for humans amid the overflowing displays in each room. Even the hallways are filled with big-eared critters in every conceivable form. The TV room houses the stuffed collection, but you need to look hard to find the screen. The rest of the rooms house more of the collection, all neatly categorized by type and name. Bugs Bunnies live in the garage because they're just too common to get special treatment. Wander out to the backyard and you'll find still more bunnies. Ditto the front yard with the huge rabbit sculpted from a giant shrub. Six live rabbits have free run of the house and one, dearly departed Shoney Bunny, is 'mounted' in a glass case.

Bunny Museum 1933 Jefferson Dr, Pasadena, CA 91104; ✆ 626 798 8848; www.thebunnymuseum.com. Open by appointment only. Directions: the museum is on Jefferson Dr, a block north of E Washington Blvd in Pasadena.

John Rietveld is fascinated by traffic signals, so much so that he's collected in excess of 80 traffic signals and 600 road signs, displaying them at his private **Signalfan Museum of Traffic Control**. Dedicated to the preservation of historical traffic-control devices, John has been indulging his passion for the subject since childhood when he would make play traffic lights out of cardboard and draw roadways with chalk on the sidewalks. His collection, mostly of American signals, goes as far back as the 30s. As for his road signs, they're all legally retired signs; nothing is stolen. The oldest one is an AAA 1920s' directional sign leading to San Diego. It's really something to see the signals in his garden all lit up and in working order.

Signalfan Museum of Traffic Control Fullerton, CA; www.signalfan.com. To visit, email John at signalfan@signalfan.com and request an appointment or give him a call at ✆ 714 296 7216. The museum is in his home and garden not far from Disneyland.

Perfectly capturing one of America's greatest obsessions, the **Petersen Automotive Museum** in Los Angeles is dedicated to the influence of the automobile on American life. This is much more than a car museum; it's a visual road map back to the past, exploring the influence the automobile had on American culture and lives. Displayed in theme settings, there are hundreds of classic cars, trucks, sports cars, and motorcycles that showcase Americans' love affair with their wheels. The museum has special theme shows such as Hollywood Star Cars, Art Cars, Monster Trucks, the Low Rider Tradition, and the World's Fastest cars.

Petersen Automotive Museum 6060 Wilshire, Los Angeles, CA; ✆ 323 830 CARS; www.petersen.org. *Open Tue–Sun 10am–6pm*. Directions: the museum is at the corner of Wilshire Blvd and Fairfax Ave.

Corky Carroll, known as the best surfer in the world in 1968, was the first person to be paid to surf. His story, and that of other legends like Linda Benson, the first female championship surfer and Anette Funicello's double in the *Beach Party* films, is portrayed at the **International Surfing Museum in Huntington Beach**. Heart of the Southern California surf scene, this cozy, volunteer-run museum is crammed with memorabilia from the sport's beginnings in the 20s, through its heyday in the 50s and 60s, and up to the present. Each year the museum hosts the Surfing Walk of Fame induction ceremonies and they have high hopes of raising enough money to build a museum worthy of the sport and its impact on the culture of the beach region.

> **International Surfing Museum** 411 Olive Ave, Huntington Beach, CA 92648; ✆ 714 960 3483; www.surfingmuseum.org. *Open summer 12 noon–5pm, Sun 9am–6pm.* Directions: the museum is on Olive Ave, between 4th and 5th St, 2 blocks from the Pacific Coast Hwy (Hwy 1) and the pier.

ECCENTRIC ENVIRONMENTS

Love of garbage motivated a 60-year-old woman to spend the last 25 years of her life transforming her third-of-an-acre lot into **Grandma Prisbrey's Bottle Village** in Simi Valley. Using hundreds of thousands of bottles and objects scavenged from the dump, she built 13 now-decaying structures to house her varied collections along with sculptures, shrines, wishing wells and walkways. Television tubes form a fence; walkways glisten with broken shards of glass and pottery. A spooky doll-head shrine has discarded heads perched on top of tall poles, while a birdbath is embedded with car headlights. The pencil house held her collection of 17,000 pencils; there's also a house made of shells and a shrine made of horseshoes. The Leaning Tower of Bottle Village and an Intravenous Feeding Tube Fire Screen give you some idea of the lengths to which Grandma would go to express her quirky sense of humor. While alive she delighted in giving you the 25-cent tour, peppering her commentary with anecdotes, then playing the piano and singing risqué songs to you in the meditation room. She died in 1988 after living a tragic life that probably led to her strange obsession. She married her first husband when she was just 15 – and he was 52 – and had seven children by him, six of whom having died during her lifetime. She also lost another husband, a fiancée, and all but one of her siblings.

> **Grandma Prisbrey's Bottle Village** PBVC, PO Box 1412, Simi Valley, CA 93062; ✆ 805 584 0572; www.echomatic.home.mindspring.com/bv/. Visits are by appointment only.

Smack dab in the middle of the Watts district, scene of the explosive civil rights riots of 1965, Simon Rodia's **Watts Towers** rise, a monumental work of folk art that took the Italian immigrant 33 years to construct. Intended as a tribute to his adopted country, the enormous structure includes three towers (the tallest of which is 99ft high), a gazebo, patios, birdbaths, spires and a structure he called the Ship of Marco Polo. The steel sculptures are covered with mortar and embedded with tens of thousands of pieces of tile, pottery, cooking utensils, linoleum, seashells and glass, and 7-up and Milk of Magnesia bottles (Simon especially liked the green and deep-blue bottle colors). Working from 1921 to 1954, Simon labored alone, using only simple tile-setter's tools and a window washer's belt and buckle to scale the heights. The giant towers dwarfed his tiny house. When he decided he was finished, he sold the place for a pittance and simply walked away. While his efforts weren't always appreciated by his neighbors, or by the city, today Watts Towers is renowned worldwide and has been decreed the smallest state park (0.11 acres) in California. The Watts Towers Art Center displays rotating folk art exhibits of the work of local 'outsider' artists and gives tours of the towers on weekends.

Watts Towers Towers and Art Center, 1727 E 1765 East 107th St, Los
Angeles, CA 90002; ✆ 213 847 4646; www.trywatts.com. Tours
approximately every half-hour on Fri 11am–2.30pm, Sat
10.30am–2.30pm, Sun 12 noon–3pm. Directions: on I-105 in LA, take the
Wilmington Ave exit and head north on Wilmington Ave. Turn left on E
108th St, then right onto Willowboork Ave and right onto E 107th St.

QUIRKYVILLE

While a case could be made that all of Los Angeles and Orange counties could be
called a Quirkyville, the line has to be drawn somewhere and **Venice** is just
screaming out for the honor. In the two or three hours it takes to walk from one
end of the one-mile-long Venice Beach Boardwalk to the other, you'll experience
a range of peculiar behavior unrivaled elsewhere in the state, or, for that matter, in
the whole country. Surfers, rollerbladers, sidewalk psychics, tattoo artists, rappers,
body builders, street performers, street people, and the homeless, representing a
wide variety of race and ethnicities, populate the boardwalk along with the densely
packed shops selling everything from the most trite of tourist trinkets to books,
music, and tattoos. Sidewalk vendors line the beach side of the boardwalk, selling
their arts and crafts as well as their services as fortune tellers, tarot-card readers,
and masseuses. A variety of ethnic and beach-fare restaurants abound for when you
need a breather from all the craziness going on around you. It's an unintentional
carnival born of opportunity and a strange evolution of social conditions.

Venice has a long history of stubborn weirdness, getting its start a hundred
years ago when an eccentric named Abbot Kinney built the place to mimic the real
Venice, complete with manmade canals, gondolas, and a kitschy amusement pier.
By mid century most of the canals had been drained and filled and the amusements
long since gone, and the town became a mecca for artists, musicians, beats, hippies,
and anyone else seeking freedom of expression. The area also attracted the
homeless, conflicting with an explosive rise in property values along the beach and
remaining canals. Today the politics revolve around the rights of the homeless and
renters versus the rights of property owners, with half the town wanting to stay
rooted in rootlessness and the other half striving for respectability. There's also a
long-standing feud between the rights of shops owners versus the rights of the
unlicensed vendors on the beach.

Meanwhile, life goes on as usual on the Boardwalk with its never-ending parade
of the bizarre. The Sandman may be tirelessly making his awesome sand
masterpieces, only to see them washed away time and again. The anti-circumcision
guy may be making his point, and political speakers and 'living' statues will be
setting up their stumps. Psychics set up their props, hoping their auras attract
customers for tarot card, astrology or palm readings. Incense is in the air, as is
inflammatory and (often) unsubstantiated political and religious rhetoric. But the
heart of the Venice scene is **Muscle Beach**, the top tourist attraction in the area.
There the buff and the beautiful show off their bodies, their six-packs glistening in
the sun as they perform body sculpting and muscle-building feats on the vast array
of equipment installed near the ocean. This is testosterone central where body-
beautiful boy toys are made.

Spend another few hours wandering along Abbot Kinney Boulevard and Main
Street and you come upon a fine assortment of eccentric stores selling delightfully
daft merchandise either to tourists or to their strange clientele. Almost bereft of
chain stores (Venetians hate cookie-cutter formula retail), the street is filled with
trendy clothing and funky furnishings boutiques. At **Audrey's Good Vibrations**
you can get your charkas tested for free and strengthen your emotional and

spiritual well-being while stocking up on organic oils, elixirs and flower essences to rid yourself of negativity and restore karmic balance. In 2001, **Abbot's Habit**, a congenial neighborhood coffee house and hangout, staged a Midsummer's Nude Dream in which a dozen men and women performed poetry and music while nude, setting the stage for their now twice-yearly nude poetry readings. At **Perry's Beach Café** you can rent bikes and roller-blades, gawking and gliding with the sea of similarly equipped. Perry's also offers guided tours where you can learn about what you're seeing while getting your exercise and trying to look cool.

Set designers frequently browse stores in Venice looking to rent scene-setting furnishings. **Obsolete** showcases industrial and folk art that emphasizes body parts, including an extensive display of anatomical mannequins and charts, land art (the study of signs), and human head sculptures and carvings. **Urban Country** has a large selection of antique American flags, carnival antiques (including shooting-gallery targets), and circus folk art. **Surfing Cowboys** is all about vintage beach and Hawaiiana culture with enough Tiki, rattan, and mid-century modern to recreate your own 50s' rec room. Vintage skateboards, surfboards, posters and pottery supply the accessories. The **Perfect Piece** focuses on vintage metal from the industrial age between the two world wars, making innovative furnishings out of old stuff like dental carts, trash cans and surgical tables. Everything here is pretty much one of a kind. The modernist, Palm Springs aesthetic is alive and well at **Chicken Little**, a store featuring vintage mid-century furniture, lighting, tchotchkes (knick-knacks), men's ties, smoking memorabilia, and neon signs. Operating hours vary at all these stores, especially when the surf's up.

Obsolete 222 Main St, Venice, CA 90291; ✆ 310 399 0024; www.obsoleteinc.com. *Open Wed–Mon 11am–6pm.*

Urban Country 218 Main St, Venice, CA 90291; ✆ 310 315 1927; www.urbancountryantiques.com

Surfing Cowboys 1624 Abbot Kinney Blvd, Venice, CA 90291; ✆ 310 450 4891; www.surfingcowboys.com. *Open Sun–Wed 10am–6pm-ish, Thu–Sat 10am–8pm-ish.*

Perfect Piece 1216 Abbot Kinney Blvd, Venice, CA 90291; ✆ 310 581 1002; www.perfectpiece.com. *Open Wed–Sun 2–6pm, or by appointment.*

Chicken Little 1323 Abbot Kinney Blvd, Venice, CA 90291; ✆ 310 581 1676. *Open daily 12 noon–6pm.*

Audrey's Good Vibrations 1204 Abbot Kinney Blvd, Venice, CA 90291; ✆ 310 664 1180; www.energyheals.com. Directions: the store is on Abbot Kinney Blvd between Aragorn Ct and Cadiz Ct.

Abbot's Habit 1401 Abbot Kinney Blvd, Venice, CA 90291; ✆ 310 399 1171. Directions: the bakery is on Abbot Kinney Blvd between California Ave and Milwood Ave.

Perry's Beach Café & Rentals at various locations along the beach & bike path; ✆ 310 372 3138; www.perryscafe.com

TOURS

Considered one of the country's most imaginative public art projects, the Los Angeles Metro totally integrates art and sculpture into its stations and bus stops. Required by law to spend 0.5% of their construction budget on public art, they've done so wisely, collaborating with the architects, artists, and neighborhoods involved in new or remodeled transportation projects. The results, which you can tour with the **Metro Art Docent Council**, go far beyond just hanging artwork or setting sculpture. Your senses of sight, sound and touch get involved with installations involving bird sounds, a wishing well, a 30ft hand throwing a 'paper' airplane, concrete living-room furniture, an interactive space museum, kinetic sculptures, imaginary conversations, and 10,000 thought-provoking questions stenciled on a wall. More than 250 artists are involved in the ongoing project.

Metro Art Docent Council ✆ 213 922 4ART; www.metro.net/about_us/metroart/default.htm. Tours are held monthly on the first Saturday and Sunday of every month. On Saturdays the tours begin at 10am in front of the Metro pylon at Hollywood & Highland Aves. Sunday tours begin at 10am in front of the information booth inside historic Union Station on Alameda Ave. Just show up; no reservations required. Custom tours arranged for groups of 15 or more.

Being taken around town by tour guide Anne Block has been likened to being shown around by Auntie Mame. Vivacious, hip and audacious, Anne will pick you up in her gold Caddy and show you the 'real' LA, demystifying a city that many people find alien and intimidating. She takes you beyond the standard tour-bus dreams-come-true rap, concentrating on the eclectic, offbeat and outrageous cultural aspects that real people who live here experience. Specializing in the 'gloriously unusual', she calls her business **'Take My Mother★Please'** since so many of her clients hire her to take their relatives around so they don't have to. Anne delights in finding the madcap, offbeat soul of the place she truly loves, exploring the ever-changing pop culture that makes Los Angeles so fluid and fascinating. After a day with this 50-something woman, you'll see the city in a whole new light and perhaps even understand the quirky essence of one of the most eccentric places on earth. She began her tour business after escorting the famous comedienne Lily Tomlin to a film festival in Berlin. Anne's tours are totally customized depending upon your interests. Some of her clients' favorites include a beauty day on the Sunset Strip, the *LA Confidential* tour and the *Pretty Woman* tour based on the famous movie.

Take My Mother★Please Tours ('or any other VIP) Tours PO Box 35219, Los Angeles, CA 90034; ✆ 323 737 2200; www.takemymotherplease.com

While not technically a tour, a visit to the **Great Wall Of Los Angeles** involves walking alongside a mural that is half a mile long and 13ft high. It also involves history as its panels depict how ethnic groups influenced the development of the state from pre-history times through the 50s. Located on the walls of a flood-control channel, the world's longest mural is the work of 400 artists who labored for five summers creating the piece, completing it in 1983. The panels are both poignant and humorous, making their social comments in a subtle way. For example, one panel traces the evolution of Hispanics from Aztec warriors to the gardeners of today. The same organization responsible for the original mural, The Social and Public Art Resource Center (SPARC), is planning to restore and extend the mural, adding scenes from the 60s to the present.

Great Wall Of Los Angeles contact SPARC, 685 Venice Blvd, Venice, CA 90291; ✆ 310 822 9560; www.sparcmurals.org. Directions: the mural is in a flood control canal alongside Coldwater Canyon Ave. On the

Quirk Alert

If any place in the country were going to need a service called **MarriageToGo.Com**, it would have to be Los Angeles. This mobile marriage licensing service takes the wait out, meaning you can propose and then have the license in your pressed-for-time hands within a few hours. Not only that, they'll also perform short-notice and theme weddings. Among their specialties are historic themes like Victorian, Shakespearean and Gothic as are contemporary ones like Dr Suess or Harry Potter. They'll even perform weddings on roller-coasters or while you're skydiving.

Ventura Freeway between I-405 and I-170, take the Coldwater Canyon Ave exit and head north.

Taking advantage of the **VIP Experience at Universal Studios** provides a more intimate and authentic look at the studio than does the regular studio tram tour. Known as 'The Entertainment Capital of the Entertainment Capital', the studio itself covers 420 acres, most of which is off-limits to visitors. The VIP Experience gets you off the tram and behind the scenes: into sound stages, prop warehouses, and production facilities and on the sets of shows in production. You get a close-up look of the *Psycho* house and the Bates Motel. After the tour your pass vaults you to the head of the line for all rides and attractions plus gives you access to a special VIP lounge. Celebrities themselves take this tour, prompting the studio to produce a booklet on how to behave around them titled, *A Visitor's Guide to Celebrity Etiquette: How To Keep Hollywood A Fabulous Place For Celebrities.*

VIP Experience at Universal Studios Universal Studios Hollywood, 100 Universal City Plaza, Universal City, CA 91608; ✆ 800 UNIVERSAL; www.themeparks.universalstudios.com.

A visit to Tinseltown wouldn't be complete without at least one studio tour. After all, some mighty strange things go on during the making of movies. Besides Universal Studios, which is more like a theme park, several movie and television studios hope you'll visit to see what they're up to although none of these tours offers the authentic experience that you'll get at Universal's VIP Experience. The **Warner Bros** tour is the most interesting of the bunch. Every tour is somewhat different. You get to see functioning set and costume departments, studio sets, outdoor sets and, possibly, celebrities at work. The on-site museum has real Oscars and lots of film memorabilia from every Warner Bros film ever made.

Warner Bros Studio Tour 4301 West Olive, Burbank, CA; ✆ 818 846 1403; www.studio-tour.com. Tours depart every half hour between 9am and 4pm; photo ID required. Directions: the tours depart from gate 3 of the studio lot, on West Olive south of Hwy 134.

The only commercial TV station offering tours, **NBC Studios** gives a simple, if canned, behind-the-scenes walking tour that includes the studio where the *Tonite Show* is filmed as well as costume and prop warehouses. While you walk past the make-up and wardrobe department, you don't actually get to see them or go inside.

But you do get to see examples of special effects and sit where the audience sits to see Jay Leno.

NBC Studios Tours 3000 West Alameda Ave, Burbank, CA 91523;
✆ 818 840 3537; www.nbc.com. Directions: the studio is on West
Alameda Ave, between Bob Hope Dr and N California St.

Sony Pictures Studio is the home of *Jeopardy!* and *Wheel of Fortune*, two of the most successful game shows in history. The two-hour walking tour is a realistic look at the inner workings of this studio, formerly the MGM Studios. Depending on which facilities are in use, you may see actual production sets, how musical scoring and recording is done, and how sets and background murals get made. On the *Jeopardy!* set you get to sit in the audience seats. Because it's a working studio you do stand a chance of seeing actors at work.

Sony Pictures Studio Tours 10202 West Washington Blvd, Culver
City, CA 90232; ✆ 323 520 TOUR;
www.sonypicturesstudios.com/tours.html. Directions: tours depart from
the Sony Pictures Plaza on West Washington Blvd Parking is on Madison
Ave.

Many of the movies you thought were filmed in locations overseas or in the American West were actually filmed on ranches belonging to the studios, properties located within 35 miles of Hollywood and thus considered 'in town' from a union-wage standpoint. (Out-of-town wages cost the studios considerably more.) **Paramount Ranch**, located on 2,700 acres in the hills above Malibu, has, at one time or another, hosted replicas of European villages, early San Francisco, and, especially, Old West towns. The ranch was primarily used from the 20s through the 40s and more than 100 movies, most of them Westerns, were filmed there. Today you can visit the ranch, now part of the National Park Service, and stroll the streets of the remaining Western town, imagining what it was like when John Wayne and James Garner walked those very same streets dispatching bad guys. Filming still takes place at the ranch. HBO filmed portions of *Carnivale* there and the *X-Files* shot their 2001 season finale there too.

Paramount Ranch Paramount Ranch Rd (off Cornell Rd), Agoura Hills,
CA; ✆ 818 597 9192; www.seeing-stars.com/Studios/
ParamountRanch.shtml. Directions: on the Ventura Freeway in Agoura
Hills, take the Kanan Rd exit then turn south. Turn left (southeast) on
Cornell Rd and take it up about 2.5 miles to Paramount Ranch Rd. Turn
right (west) and follow the road into the ranch.

Architecturally speaking, Los Angeles has always built fascinating and innovative structures. Whether it's the Capitol Records Tower Building, built to look like a stack of records, or the Art Deco hotels and theaters, or the stunningly eccentric Walt Disney Concert Hall, **Architecture Tours LA** explains their significance and history in one of half a dozen tours of the area. While riding around in a 1962 Cadillac, architectural historian Laura Massino explains how the valley's receptiveness to avant-garde architecture played a role in shaping the city's persona.

Architecture Tours LA PO Box 93134, Los Angeles, CA 90093; ✆ 323
464 7868; www.architecturetoursla.com. Tours depart from various
locations: see website for details.

Quirk Alert

Angelyne (www.angelyne.com) is representative of those 'only in LA' stories. Back in 1984 she was promoting her rock band by putting up posters along the Sunset Strip. On a whim, she put up a billboard of herself that showed only her buxom blonde bombshell image along with her first name. The billboard became the talk of the town and, almost overnight, she became famous – not for anything she did, but for simply being on billboards. Hundreds of billboards, bus-stop panels, and murals later, she's become a quirky icon of Hollywood. The Angelyne phenomena resulted in television and magazine interviews, radio shows, personal appearances and film cameos all over the world. The billboards run not just in LA, but also in New York, Washington DC, England, and Europe. Her persona is famous: an aging bombshell, extra big on top with an extra tiny waist, and driving a pink corvette. Picture Barbie at 50 and counting. Her fan club has 20,000 members, her logo merchandise is sold all over the world, and spotting Angelyne (in person or in her car) is an obsession with many, requiring proof – sort of like claiming you've seen Bigfoot. There's even a website for addicted Angelyne spotters. On her own website she'll 'escort' you around the city, showing you the secrets of Hollywood and some of her own very special secret places as well. Her fame is quite an achievement considering it started out as a figment of her own imagination. She ran (and lost) for mayor of Hollywood.

Bonding through shopping is a concept every woman is familiar with. Pair it with a tour of LA's famous fashion district and you have the making of an ideal day, at least if you love shopping. **Urban Shopping Adventures**, the only authorized tour provider for the district, offers a number of ways to get inside the wholesale showrooms that supply much of the country with up-to-the-minute fashions and accessories. The most popular is a two- to three-hour walking tour that covers your main shopping interests in the four main market buildings. For those with both taste and money, there's a custom concierge adventure involving a limousine and concierge guides to the more exclusive showrooms.

Urban Shopping Adventures 117 West Ninth St, Suite 511, Los Angeles, CA 90015; ✆ 213 683 9715; www.urbanshoppingadventures.com

ODD SHOPPING

It was bound to happen sooner or later. Harry Potter can now feel at home in California, shopping in **Whimsic Alley**, a re-creation of the mystical London Street where the famous wizard buys his school supplies. The alley, designed by a Hollywood set designer, is a bit like a theme park, selling items you won't find at Wal-Mart. For example you can buy 20 styles of magic wands, although you have to be prepared to supply your own magic. The HP Wizard Store has more Harry Potter items than any store in the world, including student house scarves and ties, spell and potions kits, unicorn droppings, and a limited-edition statue of Dobby the Elf. But it isn't only Harry who's honored in the alley. You can also buy Nightmare Before Christmas products, Marge & Homer Simpson merchandise, and other whimsical souvenirs.

Whimsic Alley located at 2717 Wilshire Blvd in Santa Monica, CA 90403; ✆ 310 453 2370; www.hpwizardstore.com. Halfway between the 405 and the beach.

It's one thing to sell vintage clothes, but what about selling just vintage shoes, just from the 20s–70s, and never worn to boot? The **Re-Mix Shoe Company** sells such shoes for both men and women, shoes like genuine white bucks, saddle shoes, 50s and 60s flats, and wing tips as well as swing dance and 40s' wedgie styles. They also sell a line of reproductions. The experience is almost like shopping in a museum.

The **Re-Mix Shoe Company** 7605 Beverly Blvd, Los Angeles, CA 90036; ✆ 888 254 1813; www.remixvintageshoes.com. *Open Mon–Sat 12 noon–7pm, Sun 12 noon–6pm.* At the corner of Beverly Blvd and Curson Ave.

If you can't find your favorite beverage from the past (and present) at **Galco's Old World Grocery**, then it just plain doesn't exist, at least at the moment. This one-stop shop for pop has the country's largest selection of specialty sodas under one roof, including microbrews, imported, and original old-time sodas. The store looks unimposing from the outside, but inside, with its 70s-era décor, you'll find 450 different varieties of sodas from rare old-timers like Nehi and Moxie to hot new brands hoping to hit the big time. They also sell dozens of old fashioned, 'school-store' candies, bottled waters, and hundreds of brands of beer. Owner John Nese believes in drinking sodas from long-neck bottles, not from cans, and in finding bottlers to recreate old recipes. He's almost single-handedly revitalized a downtrodden industry, encouraging independent small bottlers to produce specialty sodas the old-fashioned way, producing tastes that can bring back a flood of memories 40 years later.

Galco's Old World Grocery 5702 York Blvd, Los Angeles, CA 90042; ✆ 323 255 7115; www.sodapopstop.com. *Open Mon–Sat 9am–6.30pm, Sun 9am–4pm.* Directions: the store is on York Blvd, between N Ave 57 and Milwaukee Ave.

Nick Metropolis never met a fad he didn't like. Known as the King of Collectable Furniture, his corner warehouse and open-air showplace is crammed with furniture so large, so hideous, and so wonderful that you just have to slam on the brakes and take a look. Laughing your way through the clutter, you'll encounter paintings on velvet, iron light fixtures with plastic flowers, leopard-print sofas, and enormous plastic 'hand' chairs that will leave you gasping in both horror and delight. A local artist makes Marilyn, Elvis and Beatle-themed decoupaged tables and dressers. If it's atmosphere you're looking for, you'll find it here among stuff so tacky, so kitsch and so odd that Hollywood set decorators shop here for pieces that are likely available nowhere else on the planet. (They do a big business in prop rentals.) While you can find some well-designed examples from each era from the 40s through the 80s, the inventory skews mostly to things so bad, they're good.

Nick Metropolis Collectible 100 S La Brea Ave, Los Angeles, CA; ✆ 323 934 3700; www.nickmetropolis.com. *Open daily 10am–7pm.* Directions: the store is on S La Brea Ave between 1st and 2nd St.

Located right on trendy Melrose Avenue, deco-inspired **Off the Wall Antiques and Weird Stuff** has been called 'the best free 15 minutes in Los Angeles'. With an inventory that specializes in the wonderful-but-strange, you might find a rotating shoe display stand; a neon theatre marquis clock; a 40s' football radio; a Toast-o-lator, a deco toaster that moved your bread from one end of a conveyer belt to the other; a prehistoric cave bear skeleton; an American Airlines Flagship Service silverware set; and vintage bobble heads. They also deal in Airstream trailers, Wurlitzer jukeboxes, giant restaurant and gasoline signs, and sofas and beds made from Cadillacs.

> **Off the Wall Antiques and Weird Stuff** 7325 Melrose Ave, Los
> Angeles, CA; ✆ 323 930 1185; www.offthewallantiques.com. *Open
> Mon–Sat 11am–6pm*. Directions: the store is on Melrose Ave, between N
> Fuller Ave and N Poinsettia Pl.

Chic-A-Boom, also on Melrose, is an ephemera lover's dream, a mecca for memorabilia of the printed kind usually tossed out after its intended use. From calendars to postcards, from posters to magazines, from advertising signs to Sears and Wards catalogs from the 30s through the 70s, this place encapsulates American fashion, political and advertising history. There are piles and piles of magazines (75-plus titles), shelves of mid-century toys and games, and bins of movie materials, buttons, and signs, all lovingly maintained by owners Chris and Paul Scharfman whose passion for their subject knows no boundaries.

> **Chic-A-Boom** 6817 Melrose Ave, Los Angeles, CA; ✆ 323 931 7441.
> *Open Mon–Sat 1–6pm*. Directions: the store is on Melrose Ave between
> N Orange Dr and N Mansfield Ave.

The largest train store ever built, **Allied Model Trains** is a whopping 12,000 square feet, featuring LA's Union Station, a Bavarian village, and an Old West town in miniature, all bustling with trains and activity. With models of virtually every size and make, and all the accessories and building supplies you'd ever need to build your own model village, this store is a haven for train enthusiasts, including celebrities like Bruce Springsteen and Rosanne.

> **Allied Model Trains** 4411 Sepulveda Blvd, Culver City, CA 90230;
> ✆ 310 313 9353; www.alliedmodeltrains.com. *Open Mon–Sat 10am–6pm*.
> Directions: the store is on Sepulveda Blvd, between Barman Ave and
> Braddock Dr.

Thinking of her customers as cast members looking for parts, Ruth Talley at **Make Believe Costumes** is more than just a rental clerk. If you come in looking for a costume, she'll have you go through a stylebook, looking for your inner 'make believe' personality to make itself known. Are you scary? Happy? Scrappy? Sexy? Once she figures out your pretend persona, she'll customize your costume, pulling from her huge selection of props, wigs, masks, and accessories. She'll even help you with your make up, assisted by her staff, mostly actors themselves. There's a retail store in the front of the shop.

> **Make Believe Costumes** 3240 Pico Blvd, Santa Monica, CA 90405; ✆ 310
> 396 6785; www.makebelieve.to. *Open Mon–Sat 10am–6pm, Sun 11am–6pm*.
> Directions: the store is on Pico Blvd between 32nd and 33rd St.

One of the largest costume suppliers in the country, **Hollywood Toys and Costumes** was voted best costume store by *Los Angeles Magazine*. It's no wonder considering the staggering range of ways they can transform you. Besides the costumes themselves, there are 16 different kinds of mustaches, from executive to Fu Manchu to El Macho, beards ranging from rabbi long to bushy wide, and two-dozen styles of teeth, including metal mouth, Bubba, geek and geezer. Naturally they've got all the stage blood, body parts and make-up you'd need to complete the look. There's an endless selection of hats, including pimp 'n ho and religious styles, and a fine selection of human hair and fake wigs. Leotards, ears and tails, feather boas, or wings, this place can make any fantasy seem real.

Hollywood Toys and Costumes 6600 Hollywood Blvd, Hollywood, CA 90028; ℃ 323 464 4444; www.hollywoodtoys.com. *Open Mon–Sat 9.30am–7pm, Sun 10.30am–7pm.* Directions: the store is on Hollywood Blvd between N Cherokee Blvd and Schrader Blvd.

Only in LA could you shop where the witch doctors do – at **Farmacia Million Dollar Botanicas** at the corner of Third and Broadway in downtown LA. This place is, hands down, the most bizarre shopping experience you can have and still be legal. The merchandise is based on various beliefs that herbs, candles, love potions, amulets, spells, powders, saints and rosaries can influence health and happiness. A bewildering array of air fresheners, liquids and oils claim to offer peace and protection, health and wealth, love and luck and spiritual cleansing. Take Dr Buzzard's Court Case Bath and Floor Wash, for example, a liquid to be used when mercy is needed and when you want the scales of justice to tip in your favor. If you're going to court, pour it in your bath; if it's your business that's being judged, pour it in the water used to wash your firm's floors. The Black Destroyer is a powerful oil that 'destroys curses, hatred, resentments, envies and any evil intention towards you or your home'. Powdered iguana foot offers protection while burning candles in the shape of certain male and female body parts will inflame the passions of your intended. A mysterious powder called Tied Up and Nailed pictures an unfortunate man bound in ropes and nailed to the floor. It's meant to assure that a business deal you really want will, indeed, happen. They're working on a website so you can see the bizarre inventory for yourself. It's no wonder they do such a booming repeat business. For every purchase there's someone out there who's going to have to shop for an antidote. It's unlikely you'll ever see a sale on spell-breakers.

Farmacia Million Dollar Botanicas 301 S Broadway (corner of 3rd and Broadway), Los Angeles, CA 90013; ℃ 213 687 3688. Directions: the store is on Broadway between 3rd and 4th.

If you just have to take a piece of Hollywood back home, you'll find a fine selection of Hollywood's kitschiest and tackiest at **Hollywood Souvenirs**. Fancy Paris Hilton or Austin Powers standing at the foot of your bed? They've got dozens of life-size cardboard cut-out personalities – from celebrities to politicos, from sports to super heroes to animated cartoon figures – just ready to ship to your bedside. Want to throw a Tinseltown theme party? They've got all the props, including clapperboard slates, street signs, directors' chairs, and customizable Walk of Fame stars. Add the freeway signs, posters, license plates, mugs, caps, and fake celebrity drivers' licenses and you've still just scratched the surface. Besides, don't you just *have* to have a Surf's Up! Betty Boop beach towel as a memento of your visit?

Hollywood Souvenirs 6800 Hollywood Blvd, Hollywood, CA 90028; ℃ 323 962 8510; www.hollywoodsouvenirs.com. Directions: the store is at the corner of Hollywood Blvd and N Highland Ave.

Soap Plant/Wacko is an outlandish place that sells strange, weird and fun things like inflatable palm trees, white-trash refrigerator magnets (for your front porch refrigerator), head bobbers, lava lamps, a voice changer, and books like *101 Uses for Tampon Applicators.* The store is crammed with whimsical cookie jars, salt and pepper shakers, tiki ware, lunch boxes, greeting cards, beaded curtains, and teapots for sale; there's enough kitsch to keep you busy for several hours. Owner Billy Shire just buys anything that appeals to him, commenting that 'bad taste is timeless.' The soap selection is huge, including 'Wash away Your Worries' and 'Total Bitch'. Billy is also responsible for the art gallery, **La Luz de Jesus**, upstairs of the shop that displays post-pop, outsider, religious, and sometimes deviant art and sculpture. He's been dubbed the 'Peggy Guggenheim of Lowbrow'.

Soap Plant/Wacko 4633 Hollywood Blvd, Hollywood, CA; ☏ 323 663 0122; www.soapplant.com. *Open Mon–Wed 11am–7pm, Thu–Sat 11am–12 midnight, Sun 12 noon–6pm.* Directions: the store is on Hollywood Blvd between N Vermont Ave, and Maubert Ave.

'Part of you thinks it's in poor taste, part of you wants an X-Large'. That's the slogan at **Skeletons in the Closet**, an improbable gift shop in the Los Angeles Coroner's Office. The shop, squeezed into a second-floor office, sells hats, mugs, clothing, toe tags, beach towels, mouse pads, key chains, magnets and more, all carrying the Coroner's name along with a cute body-outline logo. The 'body bag' garment bag is especially apropos and the body-shaped post-it notes and undertaker boxer shorts are a hoot. The idea for the shop came about quite by accident. Employees often had souvenir items made for company events like conferences and sporting competitions. Friends and relatives clamored for a chance to buy these unique items so a tiny 'shop' was set up in a janitor's closet. The rest is history. The shop is so popular they expanded to yet another office and set up a mail-order website. The funds raised support the Youthful Drunk Driver Visitation Program. They're dying for your business.

Skeletons in the Closet Los Angeles County Coroner's Office, 1104 N Mission Rd, 2nd Floor, Los Angeles, CA 90033; ☏ 323 343 0760; www.lacoroner.com. *Open Mon–Fri 8am–4.30pm.*

If you're looking for a classy, but still weird, souvenir of southern California, the **Library Foundation of Los Angeles** sells a 100% silk **San Andreas Fault Tie** showing a map of the region with the fault line running through it.

Library Foundation of Los Angeles 630 West Fifth St, Los Angeles, CA 90071; ☏ 213 228 7509; www.lfla.org. Directions: the store is on West Fifth St between S Flower St and S Grand Ave.

Bischoffs Taxidermy is more than just a place to have your trophy mounted. This is taxidermy Hollywood style, where the deerly departed – and all other species as well – are preserved for roles in movies and television. Prop rental for the entertainment industry and events account for 80% of their business and, if they don't have it in their huge inventory, they'll fabricate whatever animal or body part you need. They specialize in animatronics, creating realistic-looking animals and puppets, like those in *Cat in the Hat, Stuart Little II* and *The Ring*, that move as if they were alive. Need a donkey head man or a man-eating bunny? Bischoffs can create it. You can shop by category for such items as Dead Look

Quirk Alert

Liz Taylor has hers; Michael Jordan has his. So do just plain folk who visit the **House of Creative Scentualization** where, during an hour-and-a-half-long session, your memories, emotions and desires are translated into a fragrance created for you and you alone. Sarah Horowitz-Thran, a perfumer since 1989, consults with you about your favorite things, like your most memorable vacation, happiest childhood memories, and favorite fabrics and colors, and then mixes your essence from her inventory of oils gathered from all over the globe. It's expensive to go in person, but much less so online.

House of Creative Scentualization 〠 888 799 2060; www.creativescent.com. See website for details.

and Roadkill, Paws, Claws, & Tails, Rugs & Hides, Livestock, and Antlers, Skulls, and Bones. Loving pet preservation is another of their specialties.

Bischoffs Taxidermy 54 E Magnolia, Burbank, CA 91502; 〠 818 843 7561; www.bischoffs.net. Directions: the store is on E Magnolia, near the junction of E Magnolia and N 1st St.

It's A Wrap sells clothes right off actor's backs. One of just a handful of places in the world where you can buy stage-set wardrobes, they carry clothing from the movie, television and fashion industries. New shipments arrive daily as productions wrap and the stock can change hour by hour. The front showroom is filled with contemporary clothing for men, women, and children; the back showroom has vintage and costume pieces. The neat thing about shopping here is the embellishments you might find on the clothes – added details that improve the look or the quality of the piece – that were added by the show's costume designers. Plus it's a hoot to buy clothing worn during a violent scene since it may be embellished with 'bullet' holes, knife cuts and/or movie blood. Everything is clean, in pristine condition, and with its history intact. Prices are way below retail except when the actor who wore the item is in great demand. Then the clothing becomes a collectible.

It's A Wrap 3315 West Magnolia Blvd, Burbank, CA 91505; 〠 818 567 7366; www.movieclothes.com. *Open Mon–Fri 11am–8pm, Sat and Sun 11am–6pm.* Directions: the store is on West Magnolia, between N Lima St and N California St.

If it's seen on the screen, **Reel Clothes & Props** might also have it. They carry merchandise from hundreds of films like *Spiderman* and *Fifty First Dates* as well as celebrity clothing like Jennifer Lopez's Miu Miu shoes worn in *Enough*, Delta Burke's silk coat from *Designing Women* and the Harley Davidson boots worn by the singer Pink in *Charlie's Angels 2*.

Reel Clothes & Props 5525 Cahuenga Blvd, North Hollywood, CA 91601; 〠 818 508 7762; www.reelclothes.com. *Open Mon–Sat 10am–6pm.* Directions: the store is on Cahuenga Blvd between Burbank Blvd and Cumpston St.

ODD SHOPPING DISTRICTS

There are several districts worth wandering if you're looking for out-of-the-ordinary shopping experiences. **Melrose Avenue** between Fairfax and La Brea is one of the area's most avant-garde streets of shops and shoppers. Funky and bizarre, most of the boutiques on the street display designs well in advance of their becoming trends and the youthful hip, with their cutting-edge hair and piercings, are out prowling for clothes and accessories to keep them that way. Just the windows alone could keep you entertained, but it's the shoppers who are likely to get most of your attention. There are plenty of restaurants when you need a break. **Rodeo Drive in Beverly Hills**, between Santa Monica Boulevard, Wilshire Boulevard and Crescent Drive, is the total opposite of Melrose where you'll find the most surgically enhanced shoppers in the world shopping on the most expensive street in the world. Meanwhile, the **Third Street Promenade** between Broadway and Wilshire is more like a street fair than a shopping district, an only-in-LA smorgasbord of street performers, chain stores, boutiques, outdoor stalls, book and gift stores, movie theaters and restaurants that stay open until the wee hours.

There's something to offend everyone, especially those from the 'red' states, at **Y-Que** (pronounced 'Ekay' and Spanish for 'so what?'), a shop specializing in T-shirts that make a political statement. Whatever your point of view on politics, religion, sex, and celebrity wrong-doing, you're likely to find just the tasteless, inflammatory, yet clever shirt that perfectly expresses how you feel and that will probably never be worn past your backyard fence.

> **Y-Que Trading Post** 1770 North Vermont Ave, Hollywood, CA 90027;
> ✆ 323 664 0021; www.yque.com. *Open daily 12 noon–8pm.* Directions:
> the store is on North Vermont Ave between Melbourne Ave and
> Kingswell Ave.

PET PURSUITS

Southern Californians indulge their dogs, often to excess. They have their own bakeries, spas, day camps, overnight camps, boutiques, beauty pageants, hotels, limos and even canine party and wedding planners.

Each spring New Leash on Life Animal Rescue puts on a fundraiser, the **Nuts for Mutts Dog Show** and Pet Fair. Common, everyday dogs compete in categories such as Fastest Eater, Best Kisser, Most Physically Challenged and Best Dancer, their owners hoping to win the coveted Best of Show award. Purebred dogs aren't allowed to compete – only mixed breeds can show off their skills. (This being California, the purebreds are probably organizing an anti-discrimination protest as you read this.) *Animal Planet* always films this event to air on their cable television network.

> **Nuts for Mutts Dog Show** takes place in March at the Shepard Stadium
> at Pierce College. Contact Nuts for Mutts; ✆ 818 710 9898;
> www.nutsformutts.com

It's not enough that **Paradise Ranch** offers day camp, overnight camp and bed buddies for pampered pooches. They go way beyond that, picking up and delivering your dog in style in the Mutt Cab, an air-conditioned Mercedes.

Overnights can be spent cage-free in luxurious, hotel-like quarters with human bed buddies so they won't have to sleep alone. Daytime activities include grooming and, for those whose social skills need it, behavioral improvement. Not just any old dog is welcome at the ranch either. They need to be evaluated for suitability, just like applying to a country club.

Paradise Ranch 10268 La Tuna Canyon Rd, Sun Valley, CA 91352; ℃ 818 768 8708; www.paradiseranch.net. *Office hours Mon–Sat 8.30am–6pm.* Directions: on I-5 north of Burbank, take the Penrose St exit and head east on Penrose St. Turn left on Sunland Blvd and right on La Tuna Canyon Rd.

Canyon View is a training ranch for dogs located high up in Topanga Canyon. A visiting doggie's daily routine is much like a human would expect from a spa: stretching, sniffing, breakfast, swimming, lunch followed by a nap, then more play time followed by evening cookies. (Well, perhaps you'd skip the sniffing part.) Besides boarding, the ranch provides obedience training appropriate to the dog's lifestyle and personality, behavioral problem solving (the dog's, not yours), socialization training and pet taxi service. You can tour the facility by appointment.

Canyon View 1558 Will Geer Rd, Topanga, CA 90290; ℃ 310 455 7897; www.canyonviewdogs.com. *Office hours Mon–Fri 8.30am–5pm.* Directions: on Hwy 101 in Hidden Hills, take the CA-27 (Ventura Blvd) exit and head south. Make a hard right turn on Hillside Dr, then right onto Will Geer Rd.

Featured in the movie *Legally Blonde II*, the dog clothes designed by the **Fifi and Romeo Boutique** are for small dogs needing to keep up with the Rovers. Trendy and hip, everything is designed by Yana Syrkin, a long-time people-costume designer. The store, all pink stripes, polka dots and designer mannequins, sells hand-knitted sweaters, fur-trimmed wool coats, scarves, hats and bedding made just for small dogs. Some items have human pieces, too, if you feel the need to co-ordinate. You can also pick up a tote in which to carry your pooch so they won't get their paws muddy during the harsh LA winters. The label got its start when Yana made a cashmere sweater for her ailing Chihuahua 'Yoda'.

Fifi and Romeo Boutique 7782 Beverly Blvd, Los Angeles, CA 90036; ℃ 323 857 7215; www.fifiandromeo.com. Directions: the store is on Beverly Blvd between N Poinsettia Pl and N Alta Vista Blvd.

There they were, pooch and pooch-ess, all dressed up in their formal best and ready to be wed at **Hollywood Hounds**, a canine boutique and spa. *People Magazine* even covered the wedding. Offering ceremonies like 'Muttrimonies' and 'Bark Mitzvahs', and services like doggie massages and pawdicures, Hollywood Hounds can also fit Fido with a biker jacket or a leopard raincoat for those outings in the back of the Hummer. Naturally there's a photographer on hand to take your mutt's portrait or videotape the proceedings.

Hollywood Hounds 8218 Sunset Blvd, Los Angeles, CA 90046; ℃ 323 650 5551; www.hollywoodhounds.com. Directions: the store is on Sunset Blvd between Crescent Heights and Sweetzer.

An antidote for the kennel, the **Kennel Club LAX** is a home away from home for pets whose owners want to keep them close by until the last possible minute. Agility

Quirk Alert

Think about it, have you ever seen an empty seat at any televised gala event? That's because of seat fillers, people hired specifically to take the place of a star that has to go potty or to fill a theater with a full audience. If you have what it takes, mainly the requisite rear end, the right body shape and the right demographic, you, too can become a **seat filler** (www.seatfiller.com). After applying with a resumé, photo and letter explaining why you want to fill seats, the company notifies you when they have an appropriate seat for your age and body type, specifying exactly what type of clothing you should wear; ie 'very hip upper-scale club wear, no logos. 'If you get really good at your job, you could even be promoted to talent escort. You need to live in the area since seats are filled on short notice and there is no compensation other than a good time.

Seat fillers www.seatfiller.com.

training, the newest 'in' sport for dogs, is a popular choice from the menu of activities, as is the weight-reduction program for those who just can't keep their kibble intake under control. And when you get back home a mellow Fido will greet you, teeth brushed and all fluff dried from a massage, manicure, and hot oil treatment at the spa. The boarding options – for both cats and dogs – include theme cottages with TV, VCR and attendants who will sleep with your pet overnight.

Kennel Club LAX 5325 W 102nd St, Los Angeles, CA 90045; ✆ 310 338 9166; www.kennelclublax.com. Directions: the kennel is on 102nd St, a block from LAX.

Three Dog Bakery, with three locations, makes food for pets that's fit for humans. Every package has the nutrition label right on the box, just like human food does, and every recipe uses human ingredients. Tourists who stumble in are shocked when they discover the place isn't a human bakery. They'll even offer you samples of the Lick 'N Crunch oreo cookie to sample for yourself. It's made from carob and vanilla.

Three Dog Bakery 6333 West 3rd St #710, Los Angeles, CA 90036; ✆ 323 935 7512; in the LA Farmers' market. Additional locations at 924 Avocado Ave, Newport Beach, CA 92660; ✆ 949 760 3647 and 24 Smith Alley, Old Pasadena, CA; ✆ 626 440 0443.

Lunch at the beach doesn't have to mean leaving your dog at home. At **Dog Beach** dogs of any size and shape are welcome to frolic off-leash in the sand or romp at the dog park where little dogs and big dogs have their own play areas to keep things amicable. When you get hungry, the **Park Bench Café** is ready, so pet-friendly that they have a Canine Cuisine menu that includes Bow-Wow-Chicken and Rover Easy eggs.

Dog Beach Contact the Preservation Society of Huntington Dog Beach; www.dogbeach.org. Located between Seapoint and Golden West Sts along the Pacific Coast Hwy, 2 miles north of the Huntington Beach pier.

Very Quirky Alert

Hard Art was a phallic replicating service – no kidding – located in LA. (Where else would it be?) They made two kinds of products. The first was a phallic art sculpture, such as a wall plaque, a jar, or an incense burner, produced from a mould of the client's family jewels. The second was a dildo, life-size or 'enhanced'. The client could go into the studio for a hands-on replicating session or start the process elsewhere and continue by mail.

Park Bench Café 17732 Golden West St, Huntington Beach, CA 92647; ☎ 714 842 0775; www.parkbenchcafe.com. *Open Tue–Fri 7.30am–2pm, Sat and Sun 7.30am–3pm.* Directions: the café is in Huntington Central Park, on Golden West St between Slater and Talbert Ave.

QUIRKY CUISINE

With seven times as many tiki drinks on the menu as there are seats at the bar, the **Tiki-Ti** has been a quirky Hollywood stop since the early 60s. Opened by Ray Buhen back at the start of the tropical drink craze, the bar is run today by Mike and Mike, his son and grandson, who keep the recipes for the 80-plus exotic cocktail drinks secret by doing all the bartending themselves. And because they have no employees, it's one of the few places in the state where you can smoke and drink at the same time. The bar's long history is evident on the wall and ceilings, covered as they are with placards signed and dated by the regulars, and by shelves overloaded with kitschy tropical souvenirs donated by customers.

Tiki-Ti 4427 Sunset Blvd, Los Angeles, CA 90027; ☎ 323 669 9381; www.tiki-ti.com. *Open Wed–Sat 6pm–1am.* The bar also closes for three weeks every three months: see website for details.

Come by the **Rock Store** any weekend day and you'll see bikes, sometimes hundreds of them, parked in shiny rows around the most popular biker hangout in the state. Located in the hills between Malibu and the valley, the Rock Store is a bar and burger hangout along some of the area's most inviting biker highways. More than just a pit stop, though, it's a place where vintage and modern bikers come to show off their prized possessions, strutting in their leathers amid the shiny chrome, powerful engines, and testosterone. Notable bike enthusiasts like Jay Leno and Peter Fonda sometimes frequent the scene.

The Rock Store 30354 Mulholland Hwy, Cornell, CA 91301; ☎ 818 889 1311; www.rock-store.com. *Open Sat–Sun only.* Directions: on Hwy 101 east of Thousand Oaks, take the Kanan Rd exit, and head south. Turn left on Sierra Creek Rd, and right onto Mulholland Hwy.

Talk about starving artists! You never know who will be on hand to entertain you during your meal – and thus earn theirs – at **Café Tu Tu Tango**. This theme restaurant is designed like an artist's loft in Barcelona, only here fine art and performance artists work while you're dining on selections from the appetizers-only menu. The décor is upscale artist-garret and all the artwork is for sale. You may see salsa-dancing stilt walkers, tarot-card readers, belly dancers, strolling musicians, singers, and, of course, artists working at their easels. Some of the dancers may even ask you to join in. Their service motto is: 'You don't have to cut off your ear to get attention here'. One of half a dozen in this unique chain, each restaurant has its own local artists and entertainers working for their supper.

Café Tu Tu Tango 20 City Blvd, Orange, CA 92868; ☎ 714 769 2222 and 1000 Universal City Dr #H-101, Universal City, CA 91608; ☎ 818 769 2222; www.cafetututango.com

The last place you'd expect to find take-out barbeque is in an auto-repair shop, but that's exactly where you'll find **Smokin' Jack's Kansas City BBQ**, the result of a dream, literally. Owner Bob Krauss woke up one morning after seeing himself in a dream fixin' barbeque in a Kansas City restaurant. But this was Burbank and he owned an auto-repair shop. Undaunted, he installed a tiny kitchen in the shop and started experimenting with various sauces. Soon his customers were wondering where that smell was coming from and soon Bob was selling barbeque, right there by the parts catalog and the motorcycles.

Smokin' Jack's Kansas City BBQ 3807 Santa Claus Lane, Carpinteria, CA 93013; ☎ 805 566 6602; www.smokinjacks.com. *Open Tue–Thu 5–9pm, Fri 5–10pm, Sat and Sun 11am–10pm.* Directions: on Hwy 101 north of Carpinteria, take the Santa Claus Lane exit and head south.

Only a dinner/theater called **Medieval Times** could have a reservations phone number that boasts 888-WE-JOUST. And joust they do during a two-and-a-half-hour dinner and tournament show that takes place inside an 11th-century-European-style castle. Telling the story of a Princess's love for a gallant knight, the show is filled with medieval pageantry, treachery and battles all the while a four-course meal is being served by wenches. In the end, of course, truth and honor triumph over evil and the spectacle ends with a rousing finale. The knight performers, all of whom have 400 hours of training before achieving knighthood, use weapons like the lance, mace, sword and bola to vanquish their enemies, all the while riding on Andalusian stallions bred for the show by the Medieval Times Ranch in Texas.

Medieval Times 7662 Beach Blvd, Buena Park, CA 90620; ☎ 888-WE-JOUST; www.medievaltimes.com. Directions: the restaurant is 1 block from Berry Knots farm. On I-5 in Buena Park, take the Hwy 91 exit and head east. Then take the Beach Blvd exit and head south.

Dining at **Lowenbrau Keller** is like eating in a combination Bavarian museum and gift shop. Kitschy medieval is everywhere, from the armored knight that heads the main table to the mounted boar's head to the giant cast-iron chandeliers. The oak dining tables are massive and animal trophies and rows of beer steins crowd the walls. Throw in stuffed owls, giant art reproductions, mannequins in suits of armor, and Greek cupid statues and you have enough schmaltz to keep you in schnitzel for a long time.

Lowenbrau Keller 3211 Beverly Blvd, Los Angeles, CA 90057; ☎ 213 382 5723. Directions: the restaurant is on Beverly Blvd between S Dillon St and S Vendome St.

It takes a moment for your eyes to adjust after walking into **Bahooka**, but once they do, you'll find yourself surrounded by 105 aquariums set into practically every available foot of wall space in this restaurant, a cross between the Tiki Room and Pirates of the Caribbean at Disneyland. To say that Bahooka has a nautical/desert island theme is an understatement. Besides the fish tanks, the bamboo walls and ceilings hold hundreds of lanterns plus parrot lamps, timbers, boats, signs, blowfish and ship parts. The bar top itself is a bubbling turtle tank. A landmark rib destination since the 60s, the place is a soothing, peaceful and intimate experience, probably due to the oldies' surf music playing quietly in the background and to the 50 varieties of fish swimming peacefully around in all those illuminated tanks. The long-term staff has a relationship with all the fish, claiming they have distinct personalities, especially Rufas, the 34lb, 29-year-old Pacu (a member of the piranha family) that snatches raw carrots with a fearsome and audible chomp. (Rufas had a bit part in the movie *Fear and Loathing in Las Vegas*.) A full-time keeper cares for the fish and there's a backup generator to keep the aquariums humming in case of a power failure.

Bahooka 4501 N Rosemead Blvd, Rosemead, CA 91770; ℄ 626 285 1241; www.bahooka.com. *Open Mon–Thu 11.30am–9pm, Fri 11.30am–11pm, Sat 12 noon–11pm, Sun 12.00 noon–9pm.* Directions: on Hwy 210 in Pasadena, take the Rosemead Blvd South (CA-19) exit and head south.

The **Trabuco Oaks Steakhouse** is the perfect place to get rid of that hideous tie you got last Christmas. If you show up overdressed to this legendarily casual restaurant, as President Richard Nixon once did, you'll soon find your tie hanging among the 9,000 that have been cut off unsuspecting diners over the years. The ties are everywhere, hanging densely (after being flameproofed) on the ceilings and walls and creating a quiet, if funky, ambiance as a result. Starting life in the 60s as a snack bar for campers, this rustic roadhouse has become a favorite carnivore destination. Look for the giant oak tree growing through the roof from the center of the dining room and the extensive collection of Jim Beam whiskey bottles in the lobby.

Trabuco Oaks Steakhouse 20782 Trabuco Oaks Rd, Trabuco Canyon, CA; ℄ 949 586 0722; www.trabucooakssteakhouse.com. *Open Sun–Thu 5–9pm, Fri and Sat 5–9.30pm.* Directions: on SR-241 northeast of Mission Viejo, take the Santa Margarita Parkway exit and head north, then left onto Trabuco Canyon Rd. Then turn right onto Trabuco Oaks Rd.

One of a dying breed, the **Un-Urban Coffee House** is what a coffee house used to be before Starbucks came along and homogenized the concept. A mix of café and community, this quirky place, with its eclectic mish-mash of furniture and its colorful walls, gives a multitude of artists a chance to showcase their work and their talents at the endless theme nights. Monday offers music or poetry; Wednesday, live jazz. Thursday is for comedy; Friday is open mic night. Saturday is devoted to singers and songwriters and Sunday is for the blues. At other times it a place to hang out, a place the neighborhood calls home. Their motto is 'Death Before Decaf!'.

Un-Urban Coffee House 3301 Pico Blvd, Santa Monica, CA 90405; ℄ 310 315 0056. *Open Mon–Thu 7am–12 midnight, Fri 7am–1am, Sat 8am–1am, Sun 8am–7pm.* Directions: the café is at the corner of Pico Blvd and 34th St. Events are listed at www.casenet.com/coffeehouse/unurbancalendar.html

Smokey Bear is America's icon when it comes to the forest so he fits right in at **Bigfoot Lodge**, guarding the entrance to the Doe and Buck restrooms. Meanwhile, the Welcome to Sasquatch National Forest sign sets the stage for this log cabin, *après-ski* type bar and lounge straight out of the 50s. Dark, comfortable and woodsy, Bigfoot is the opposite of the harsh, noisy bar scene where you have to scream to be heard. Plush animatronic woodland creatures frolic amid the faux walls and faux antlers while the stone fireplace and redwood ceilings complete the look of understated kitsch. First timers will only know they're at the right place by the small rock garden piled with twigs: their address is intentionally unlit.

Bigfoot Lodge 3172 Los Feliz Blvd, Los Angeles, CA 90039; ☎ 323 662 9227; www.bigfootlodge.com. *Open daily 8am–2am*. Directions: on I-5 in Glendale, take the Los Feliz Blvd exit and head east.

What jumps right out at you from the menu at **Typhoon Restaurant** is the variety of insect dishes they serve along with their traditional Asian-Pacific cuisine. On the dinner menu you'll find deep-fried waterbugs stuffed with chicken, stir-fried crickets with raw garlic, Manchurian ants sprinkled on potato strings, and white sea worms (crispy style, of course) served on a spinach leaf. Located at the upscale Santa Monica Airport, the aviation-motif restaurant is noted for the authenticity of its cuisine.

Typhoon Restaurant Santa Monica Airport, 3221 Donald Douglas Loop South, Santa Monica, California 90405; ☎ 310 390 6565; www.typhoon-restaurant.com. *Open Mon–Fri 12 noon–3pm and 5.30–10pm, Sat 5.30–11pm, Sun 5.30–10pm*. Directions: Donald Douglas Loop South at the Santa Monica Airport. On Airport Ave, turn left onto the loop. The restaurant is on the 2nd floor of the building at the end of the road.

Only in LA will you find **Pacific Dining Car**, an upscale restaurant offering an only-in-LA menu option – a hand car wash while you eat. Available from 7am–3pm weekdays during breakfast, lunch and afternoon service, the quality wash is a great convenience for the restaurant's customers, many of whom visit every week knowing their cars will be taken care of at the same time as their appetites. Built in 1921 as a replica of a dining car, the restaurant is open 24 hours, serving mesquite-grilled beef any time day or night.

Pacific Dining Car 1310 West Sixth St, Los Angeles, CA 90017; ☎ 213 483 3030; www.pacificdiningcar.com

You don't dine at **Clifton's Cafeteria** as much for the food as you do to be part of a remarkable 113-year history. They've served millions and millions of people over the years, guided by the Golden Rule: treating customers as 'guests', employees as 'associates' and guaranteeing that you 'Dine Free Unless Delighted'. No-one has ever been turned away hungry because they couldn't pay and founder Clifford Clifton's philosophy was to make a friend of every guest. The largest public cafeteria in the world, its interior, with its waterfalls and brooks, was designed in 1935 to echo California redwood groves. Five generations of the founder's family have continued the legacy, their motto proudly proclaiming, 'We pray our humble service be measured not by gold, but by the golden rule'.

Clifton's Cafeteria 648 South Broadway, Los Angeles, CA 90014; ☎ 213 627 1673; www.cliftonscafeteria.com. *Open daily 6.30am–7.30pm*. Directions: the restaurant is on S Broadway between 6th and 7th St.

Hotel Bel Air offers dining with a behind-the-scenes spin. Table One is a private dining room for diners accustomed to privilege and privacy, with windows and mirrors that look into the adjoining kitchen. Accessible through a semi-private entrance in the back kitchen, the table seats eight where the lucky few can watch the preparation of their meal. You'd best be a celebrity or someone similarly important if you expect to get a reservation.

Hotel Bel Air 701 Stone Canyon Blvd, Los Angeles, CA 90077; ✆ 800 648 4097 or ✆ 310 472 1211; www.hotelbelair.com. Reservations required, $1,000 minimum charge. The hotel is on Stone Canyon Blvd, north of UCLA and the Bel Air country club.

Arranging dinner at the **Magic Castle**, a century-old Gothic Victorian mansion, may seem like pulling a rabbit out of a hat, but your hotel or one of the magic shops on Hollywood Boulevard can possibly help you secure a hard-to-come-by reservation for one of their nightly dinner/magic shows. Headquarters of the 5,000-member Academy of Magical Arts, the shows take place in the 100-seat Palace of Mystery or in the more intimate Parlour of Prestidigitation, a showroom that recreates the Victorian experience of the living room magician. The Close-up Gallery presents magicians expert in the art of close-up magic. In keeping with the elegance of the setting, there's a strict dress code: jackets and ties for the men and cocktail dresses for the ladies. The building itself has a bookshelf that responds to the command to 'Open, Sesame!', a piano-playing ghost who accepts requests, animated paintings à la Harry Potter, Ed Wynn's bicycle piano, W C Fields's trick pool table and loads of magical memorabilia.

Magic Castle 7001 Franklin Ave, Hollywood, CA 90028; ✆ 323 851 3313; www.magiccastle.com. Dinner seatings at 6.30pm, 8pm and 9.30pm. Reservations and invitation required. No-one under 21 except at Sunday brunch. Dress code. Directions: the Castle is on Franklin Ave between La Brea and Highland.

A mushroom, walnut, almond and sunflower-seed 'cheeseburger'? Sushi made from almond paste, spices and powdered seaweed? How about bread and zucchini 'French fries' or noodles made from mango? You must be at **Juliano's RAW,** doyen of the living cuisine and raw food movement. Proponents of the diet believe that any food heated beyond 118 degrees (not much hotter than the water in a nice, hot bath) loses nutrients, so the food is prepared by dehydrating and pulverizing, using equipment like hydraulic juicers, food processors, dehydrators and warming ovens. There's no meat, no rice, no pasta, no dairy, no eggs, and no chocolate at RAW, but you might see stars like Woody Harrelson or Demi Moore eating – or, rather, nibbling – there. "Out of every living thing on the planet,' says Juliano, 'animals, plants, insects, none is overweight or out of shape except for the ones that eat cooked foods.'

Juliano's RAW 609 Broadway, Santa Monica, CA 90401; ✆ 310 587 1552; www.rawrestaurant.com. *Open daily 7am–11pm.* Directions: the restaurant is on Broadway between 6th and 7th St.

ROOMS WITH A SKEW

The **Queen Mary** is a very large place to hang your hat. This most famous of cruise ships is permanently anchored in Long Beach, her final berth after 30 years of sailing. Bigger than the *Titanic*, this retired Cunard ship is a floating museum, hotel and haunted house all rolled into one. Spending the night in one of the restored deco cabins gives you the run of the ship after hours and a chance to experience a slice of the grandeur her passengers enjoyed while criss-crossing the Atlantic. It also gives you time to take the daily Behind the Scenes tour as well as a history-laden self-guided one. Ghost-wise, the ship is notorious for ghost sightings and paranormal activities and you can sign up for the Ghost Encounters tour that takes you to the various haunted areas. Besides passenger service, the ship served as a troop carrier during World War II, once ferrying a record 16,000 military personnel across the Atlantic.

> **Queen Mary** 1126 Queens Hwy, Long Beach, CA 90802; ✆ 562 435 3511; www.queenmary.com. Directions: the ship is at the end of Hwy 710, on the water in Long Beach.

You can also sleep in the shadow of the *Queen Mary* on your choice of six yachts through **Dockside Boat and Breakfast**. Accommodations range from a 38-footer to an authentic 50ft Chinese junk.

> **Dockside Boat and Breakfast** Dock 5 Rainbow Harbor, Long Beach, CA 90802; ✆ 562 436 3111; www.boatandbed.com. Directions: take I-710 south to where it ends near the Aquarium on Shoreline Dr. Take a right on Pine Ave and park in the turnaround circle. Dock 5 is the first dock on the right.

Whacha' 'ya gonna' do with a run-down 60s-era motel utterly lacking in architectural distinction? Pete and Ellen Picataggio knew the boxy, homely Farmer's Daughter motel was desperately in need of a makeover, including a personality transfusion, so they teamed up with an architect and a designer to turn the undistinguished property into a hotel worthy of its name. Now wrapped in bright blue-and-gold gingham squares, the **Farmer's Daughter Hotel** has gone kitsch-hip, from a dumpy hayseed to a gal clearly ready for the big city. In their ads they refer to their look as 'farm fresh frou-frou' and their service as 'It's hard to be pretentious when you don't know what it means.' From the cowskin rugs to the rooster wallpaper and to the overall-clad staff, the Farmer's Daughter exudes homespun warmth, kitschy as that may be in a setting like La-La land. The hotel is directly across the street from the studio where the game show *The Price Is Right* is filmed. On show days the hotel is packed with wanna-be contestants who start standing in line at the farm-like milking hour of 04.15. Every evening before a show day they hold a tip clinic with insider information on how to get picked to play the game on the air.

> **Farmer's Daughter Hotel** 115 South Fairfax Ave, Los Angeles, CA 90036; ✆ 800 334 1658; www.farmersdaughterhotel.com. Directions: the hotel is on South Fairfax between W 1st and W 3rd St.

You have to pretend to know the sign is purposely hung upside down if you want to pass for hip at the **Standard Hotel Hollywood**. You also need to be blasé about what you see in the glass enclosure behind the reception desk that serves as a space for human performance art. During the evening hours, models and actors are hired to 'live' in the glass box for the night and do whatever they want. Always clad in white underwear, some sleep, read, write, do their nails, knit, or watch TV. Some wear additional clothing; others may not. In the daytime the enclosure is filled with an odd assortment of stuff. The on-site barber shop gives you the latest do – or tattoo – so you'll be appropriately styled to join the hip crowd in the bar or on the pool deck. The property used to be a nursing home and has been redone in an over-the-top, retro 50s/Jetsons theme. The lobby ceiling is carpeted and the rooms have silver beanbag chairs.

Standard Hotel Hollywood 8300 Sunset Blvd, Hollywood, CA 90069; ☎ 323 650 9090; fax: 323 650 2820; www.standardhotel.com. Directions: the hotel is on Sunset Blvd between N Olive Dr and N Sweetzer Ave.

The **Standard Hotel Downtown**, housed in the former headquarters of the Superior Oil Building, isn't at all what you'd expect in a downtown hotel. Maintaining the 50s' corporate modernism of the now-historic architectural landmark, the lobby still has a 15 time-zone clock and a wall sculpture above the front doors depicting the drilling and refining of oil. The hotel is most notable for its trendy rooftop sundeck, complete with heated lap pool, pool toys, and private 'pods' with heated vibrating waterbeds. Waitresses are dressed as cheerleaders with an 'S' appliquéd on their panties. Soundless movies are projected on the side of a building across the street. In some rooms a see-thru glass cube serves as a shower, turning the experience into something of a performance. The place is so cheap-chic that they wouldn't dream of vacuuming before noon since they know you probably didn't get to bed until dawn and probably don't need more than a few hours sleep anyway. Both hotels are owned by Andre Balazs, a hotelier known for stylish boutique properties, who is fond of shattering the notion of what is standard. 'When you expect a straight line at this hotel, sometimes you get a curve.'

Standard Hotel Downtown 550 South Flower at 6th St, Los Angeles, CA 90071; ☎ 213 892 8080; www.standardhotel.com.

Taking the kids to a resort doesn't sound like much of a vacation but the **St Regis Monarch Beach Resort & Spa** offers so many Kids Club activities that you'll have plenty of time to relax. Designed for kids from 4–12, the program starts each day at 9am when you drop the kiddies off dressed to play and toting their swimsuits. Depending upon the season, they many learn how to surf or body board. Or they may board a yacht with a marine biologist for a day of dolphin, whale and sea lion watching while playing in the on-board marine lab. They might also take hula and yoga classes, learn etiquette and manners, or learn to build sandcastles. Mother & Daughter Teas and Father & Son Teas let you spend quality time when you reconnect. At Christmas time they bring in nine tons of sand and sculpt a giant holiday-themed sand sculpture right there in the lobby. Past themes included Santa on a lifeguard chair and Santa surfing with reindeer.

St Regis Monarch Beach Resort & Spa One Monarch Beach Resort, Dana Point, CA; ☎ 949 234 3200 or ☎ 800 722 1543. The resort is equidistant from Los Angeles and San Diego. Directions: from the 5 freeway exit at Crown Valley Parkway, turn west. Turn left onto Pacific Coast Hwy; left onto Niguel Rd and left onto Monarch Beach Resort Dr. From the 73 toll road, exit at Greenfield, turn right, then turn right onto Crown Valley and follow directions above.

JUST PLAIN WEIRD

Southern California is known for its amusing mini-landmark buildings. Two of them are donut shops: the **Donut Hole** and **Randy's Donut**. You actually drive through the donut's center at the Donut Hole while the giant donut on top of

Randy's looks as if it's about to roll right off into the street. The **Coca-Cola Building**, built in 1937, resembles an ocean liner complete with catwalk, bridge, cargo doors and portholes for windows. **Tail O' The Pup** is a 17ft stucco hot dog that perfectly captures the kitsch for which LA is famous. Venice sports the **Binocular Building** designed by famous architect Frank Gehry, while Beverly Hills has the **Witch's House**, built by a movie studio in 1921. Looking like something out of a scary fairytale, the house is all askew, with sagging, pointy roof lines, a warped picket fence and bizarre, gnarled landscaping. It's not open to the public but you can drive by and take pictures.

The Donut Hole 15300 E Amar, La Puente, CA; ✆ 626 968 2912. Between E Elliot Ave and N Hacienda Blvd.

Randy's Donuts 805 W Manchester, Inglewood, CA; ✆ 310 645 4707; www.randysdonuts.com. At the junction of W Manchester and S La Cienega Blvd.

Coca-Cola Building 1200–1334 S Central Ave, Los Angeles, CA. Between E 14th and E 12th St.

Tail O' The Pup 329 N San Vicente Blvd, West Hollywood, CA 90048; ✆ 310 652 4517; www.tail-o-the-pup.com. Between Rosewood Ave and S San Vicente Blvd.

Binocular Building 340 Main Street, Venice Beach, CA. Between Rose and Sunset Ave.

The Witch's House 515 N Walden Dr, Beverly Hills, CA; ✆ 310 271 8174. At the northeast corner of Carmelita Ave and Walden Dr 1 block north of Wilshire.

San Diego–Southern Desert

FESTIVALS AND EVENTS

The **Mud Run** at Camp Pendleton is so popular that registration is cut off after the first 3,500 racers sign up. A family affair, the course is 10km-worth of hills, tire and straw obstacles, slippery mud walls, slimy mud pits, and knee-to-waist deep water. There are two 5ft-high mud walls, a tunnel crawl and a 30ft mud pit to negotiate. Competitors race individually or in teams over the rugged terrain, many of them doing so in costume. Make no mistake – while entertaining, this rugged race is no walk in the park.

> **Mud Run** is held annually in June. Contact Race Office, Box 555020, Camp Pendleton, CA 92055-5020; ✆ 760 725 6836; www.camppendletonraces.com. Registration is required, and participants must get to the base by 6.30am. Directions: Camp Pendleton is on I-5, 38 miles north of San Diego.

Since 1975 as many as 100 people have gathered at sunset on the first Saturday of every April to compete in the most unlikely of competitions, the **Pegleg Smith Liars' Contest**. Hoping to win the title of 'Greatest Prevaricator of All', these hardy souls venture to the remote desert location where prospector Pegleg Smith supposedly made a gold strike in the late 1800s. Unfortunately, Pegleg forgot exactly where he'd seen the gold and spent the rest of his days telling increasingly tall tales about his exploits to anyone who would listen. The contest takes place around a campfire, next to a sign erected in 1947 that proclaims: Let him who seeks Pegleg Smith's gold add ten rocks to this monument.' Would-be liars do their best to convince the judges, sometimes county law enforcement officials, of their sincerity, spicing up their five-minute (yea, right!) tales of gold and greed with costumes and props. Anyone can enter; just sign up when you get there.

> **Pegleg Smith Liars' Contest** takes place annually the first Saturday in April at the Pegleg Smith Monument. Directions: from Borrego Springs, take S-22 east for about 7 miles. Turn left onto Pegleg Rd.

Most people will tell you there's really no such thing as an ugly dog (well, maybe just a few), but that doesn't stop hundreds of people from entering their pooches in Del Mar Kiwanis Club's annual **Ugly Dog Contest**. The dogs enter in one of 14 different categories including the dog who looks most like his owner, the dog with the most unusual markings, best costume for an owner, prettiest female dog and, of course, the ugliest dog of all. Proceeds from the event raise money for a therapeutic riding program that uses horses to help those with disabilities.

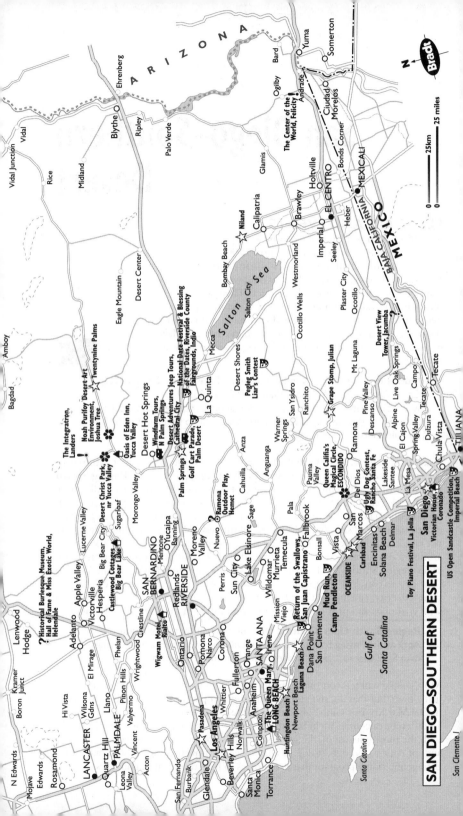

Above The 'Break Out' garden at Cornerstone, a labyrinth of worn screen doors creaking open and clanging shut (MH)

Left A dead tree gets a new lease of life with a covering of 70,000 sky-blue Christmas balls at Cornerstone Gardens in Sonoma (MH)

Below Bathing in mud, a quintessential California quirk (DW)

Above Kinetic sculptures have to be able to race on water as well as on land (BH)

Below The author, dwarfed by the 'Grave Digger' Monster Truck at a rally (JF)

Ugly Dog Contest takes place annually at the Helen Woodward Animal Center, 6461 El Apajo Rd, Rancho Santa Fe, CA 92067; ☎ 858 756 4117; www.animalcenter.org. Directions: on I-5 in Rancho Santa Fe, take the Del Mar Heights Rd/Via De La Valle exit and head east. Turn left onto El Camino Real, then right onto San Dieguito, and left onto El Apajo Rd.

Practically everybody in town seems to enter the **Palm Desert Golf Cart Parade**. The ubiquitous carts, street-legal year around in Palm Desert, abandon the town's 100 golf courses for the day and gather for an event that's been going on for 40 years. Each year's parade has a different theme, such as 'Laughter is the Best Medicine', 'Salute to America' or 'It's Showtime', and the carts are dressed appropriately, transforming into all manner of floats and objects.

Palm Desert Golf Cart Parade held annually in November. Contact the Palm Desert Chamber of Commerce, 73-710 Fred Waring Dr, Ste 114, Palm Desert, CA 92260; ☎ 760 346 6111; www.golfcartparade.com. Directions: the parade runs along El Paso Dr from San Luis Ray to Ocotillo in Palm Desert. It starts at 1pm, with the judging in the morning.

Some people are so fond of toy pianos that they dedicate an entire festival to them. At the **Toy Piano Festival,** held at the UCSD Music Library, they hold the instrument in high esteem, composing music for it and treating the toy as if it were seriously capable of playing actual music. How much do they admire the toy? Instead of ringing a bell for assistance at the library's music-listening desk, you play a toy piano instead. They once hosted a toy piano-themed mail art show, inviting anyone to send in a handmade postcard, poem, or photo paying tribute to a toy piano. The museum itself has quite a collection of the tinkley instruments.

Toy Piano Festival is held annually in August. Contact the UCSD Music Library, 9500 Gilman Dr, 0175Q, La Jolla, CA 92093; ☎ 858 534 8074; www.orpheus.ucsd.edu/music/. Directions: the festival takes place in the Geisel Library on the UCSD campus in La Jolla.

If you wear a turban or dress like an Arabian knight you get into the **National Date Festival** in Riverside County for free. Otherwise, pay the admission, join 250,000 others, and watch jockeys decked out like Ali Baba ride in little chariots hitched to some really big birds during the Ostrich Races. Root for your favorite dromedary during the camel races; cringe during the live alligator wrestling; cheer at the Bull-o-rama Rodeo, and enjoy a Monster Truck making mincemeat out of a car. What does all this have to do with dates? Nothing really, except to celebrate that the region produces 95% of all the dates grown in the United States, and to offer a prayer for date fertility at **The Blessing of the Dates**.

National Date Festival and The Blessing of the Dates is held annually in February at the Riverside County Fairgrounds, CA; ☎ 800 811 FAIR or ☎ 760 863 8247; www.datefest.org. Directions: the fairgrounds are off I-10 in Indio, south of the Joshua Tree National Monument.

Two tons of grapes get stomped in the mountain town of Julian during the annual **Julian Grape Stomp**. First the grapes get blessed, and then they get stomped by teams of kids and adults who compete to see who can stomp the most juice out of their grapes. Finally, the stomped juice is bottled as 'Julian Grape Stomp', not for

Quirk Alert

If you hang out for a few hours on the boardwalk near Oceanfront Walk and Pacific Beach Drive, you may be lucky enough to spot the **Rollerblade Guy**, also known as the **G-String Guy**, who rollerblades up and down the boardwalk most afternoons wearing only a G-String and body paint. He changes the theme every day, sometimes streaking by as Santa Claus, an elephant, a butterfly, or perhaps Spiderman. Uncle Sam is one of his most memorable portrayals. The locals love him and the tourists just gasp and mutter things like, 'Well, what do you expect. This is California.' You can get a cup of coffee at the **World Famous Restaurant** while you wait.

World Famous Restaurant 711 Pacific Beach Dr, San Diego, CA 92109 ☎ 858 272-3100.

drinking but as a souvenir. Strolling musicians are dressed in traditional Italian garb and bocce ball is the favorite game.

Julian Grape Stomp is held annually in September at the Menghini Winery. Contact the Julian Chamber of Commerce, 2129 Main St, Julian, CA 92036; ☎ 760 765 1857; www.julianca.com. Directions: on Hwy 79 in Julian, take Farmers Rd north, then continue on Julian Orchards Dr.

They come from all over the world to participate in the **US Open Sandcastle Competition**, the granddaddy of all sandcastle-building contests. Ten-person and three-person teams, in both master and amateur divisions, compete for the ultimate title as well as for substantial cash prizes. Categories are based on specific themes: the best structural design, the best replica, the best sculpture, real or imaginary sea creatures, and the Executive Sandbox, a category for business-sponsored teams. The rules are simple. Every sculpture has to stay within its 30ft x 30ft building area. Only biodegradable materials like shells or seaweed can be used for decoration and only hand tools can be used for carving. Food coloring and flour are permitted but other adhesives are not. Each team gets one wheelbarrow, one ladder, and four hours to create their giant masterpieces. An average of 40 sculptures end up being judged.

US Open Sandcastle Competition happens annually in July. Contact the Sandcastle Competition, PO Box 476, Imperial Beach, CA 91933; ☎ 619 424 6663; www.usopensandcastle.com. Directions: the competition takes place on the beach along Seacoast Dr in Imperial Beach, south of San Diego.

Fifty acres of flowers is a lot of blooms and from early March to early May the **Flower Fields** attract some 150,000 people eager to roam through ocean-view fields filled with vibrant color and fragrant flowers. Each year the various growers team up with artists who use flowers as art or create unique theme gardens. As part of the decorations the Flag Man of Carlsbad, Alex Kapitanski, displays a portion of his American flag collection. Numbering around 1,400, his collection is one of the biggest in the United States and includes flags from the first Betsy Ross to the current 50-star flag. Now in his eighties, Alex still works with the Camp Pendleton Marine Corp Color Guard.

Flower Fields 5704 Paseo Del Norte, Carlsbad, CA 92008; ☎ 760 431 0352; www.theflowerfields.com. *Open 9am–5pm Mar 13–Apr 3, 9am–6pm Apr 4–May 9.* Directions: located next to Legoland, off I-5.

San Diego Diver's Supply sponsors an **Underwater Pumpkin Carving Contest** that's been going on for almost three decades on the Saturday nearest Halloween. Scuba divers bring their own pumpkin and dive knife, and then carve underwater for exactly 20 minutes. Judging is done on the beach with the audience sometimes breaking a tie vote with applause.

Underwater Pumpkin Carving Contest is held annually at the end of October at Kellog Park/LaJolla Shores, San Diego. Contact San Diego Diver's Supply; ☎ 619 224 3439 or Ocean Enterprises; ☎ 858 565 6054; www.oceanenterprises.com. Directions: between Avenida de la Playa and Vallecitos in LaJolla. Nearby parking is limited.

In the desert community of 29 Palms they celebrate the weed, but not the kind you're probably thinking of. The real thing, knarly, dried up, prickly and all, is the attraction at the **Weed Show**, an annual event that's been going on since 1940. The show got its start when members of a women's club professed embarrassment to their speaker at not being able to provide fresh flowers for her presentation. The speaker reputedly replied, 'Why do you need fresh flowers when you have so many beautiful weeds around here?' (Talk about tact!) Competitors enter their arrangements of indigenous desert plants and found objects in several categories, including compositions relating to cactus, horses, trains, rocks, locks, and broken purple glass. Arrangements can be held together only with clay, sand or sap.

Weed Show takes place in November at the 29 Palms Historical Museum in 29 Palms. Contact the 29 Palms Historical Society, Old School Museum, 6760 National Park Dr, 29 Palms, CA; ☎ 760 367 2366; www.msnusers.com/29palmshistoricalsociety. Directions: on CA-62, take the National Park Dr exit to Inn Ave.

PECULIAR PURSUITS

Some of the most stunning showgirls in Palm Springs collect Social Security retirement income as do most of the men who sing and dance on stage with them at the fabulous **Palm Springs Follies**, a three-hour razzle-dazzle vaudeville-style extravaganza performed by cast members who are all between 58 and 87 years young. To say this production is extraordinary is an understatement. The only one of its kind in the country, it's the brainchild of Riff Markowitz, aka the Follies Man and the driving force behind the show that transformed the historic Plaza Theater into the now-renowned venue for the Follies. Since it's opening in 1990 over 2.5 million people have seen this spectacularly lavish and painstakingly authentic re-creation of the vaudeville variety acts of the 30s and 40s.

Quirk Alert

FLORIDA IN CALIFORNIA?

Working as a model builder at LEGOLAND has to be one of the coolest jobs in America. Miniland Florida, one of six American Minilands the park has created, meant playing with two million LEGO bricks while creating the infield of the Daytona International Speedway. Constructed at 1:20 scale, the infield has fifty 18-wheelers, racecars, boats, and jet skiers moving about, 'watched' by a crowd of 2,000 LEGO mini-figures doing a mini-wave. There's even a real drag strip where you can race cars made of LEGO around a track yourself. The Kennedy Space Center has a launch pad, eight-foot space shuttle, and a rocket garden.

The other Minilands are New York, New England Harbor, New Orleans, Washington, DC, and the California coastline.

Every season – November through May – there's a completely new show and make no mistake about it, this is no geriatric lounge show. It's a vibrant extravaganza with high-kicking Ziegfeld-era production numbers, animal acts, and time-warp comedy shtick. These performers, two dozen of them, shatter stereotypes about old age with astounding vitality and skill and you'll be vowing to head for the gym after watching their limber acts. Their wardrobe alone uses 1,500 individual pieces with costumes as big as ten feet in diameter. Twelve back-stage dressers are needed to facilitate the wardrobe changes, some as short as 75 seconds. (That alone is more exercise than most of us get in a week.) After the show you can meet all the performers and marvel at their age and accomplishments.

Palm Springs Follies 128 South Palm Canyon Dr, Palm Springs, CA 92262; ℡ 760 327 0225; www.palmspringsfollies.com. Follies season runs from Nov–May annually. Directions: the theatre is on South Palm Canyon Dr, between W Arenas Rd and E Tahquitz Canyon Way.

Known far and wide as the **Bridge of Thighs**, the footbridge over the road at Indian Canyon Drive in Palm Springs was built by the Desert Shadow Inn to shield naked pedestrians from gawkers on the road below. The clothing-optional facility had it built so that their members staying in the condos across the road could remain naked during their 'commute'. The resort, one of the first in the country to locate in the midst of an urban area, attracts an upscale clientele including judges, lawyers, doctors, celebrities, and politicians. Sans their usual power suits, these members feel freer to relax and be themselves. There's an artist on site to cast clients' forms and sculpt portions of their bodies, an art practiced by the ancient Greeks and Romans. Lend me your ears?

Desert Shadows Inn 1533 N Chaparral Rd, Palm Springs, CA 92262; ℡ 800 292 9298; www.desertshadows.com. Directions: the inn is on N Chaparral Rd, between East Cottonwood Rd and East Chuckwalla Rd, about 2 blocks from Hwy 111.

A relic dating back to the days of early automobile travel, **Desert View Tower** is a roadside icon, a pit stop that has managed to survive 50 years of roadway changes. Originally built by Bert Vaughn to provide the water that would keep the Model T Fords running over the treacherous Mountain Springs Grade, the tower offers a view of all four versions of today's Interstate 8, the Borrego Desert and the Imperial Valley. But it's climbing around on the boulders that kids find the most fun. During the Depression folk artist W T Ratcliffe carved faces into the boulders, seeing Indians, gargoyles and other mythological creatures in the stone.

Desert View Tower and Boulder Park Caves Jacumba, CA.
Directions: on I-8, just east of Jacumba, take the In-Ko-Pah Rd exit.

California has an official state outdoor theater called the **Ramona Outdoor Play**, a yearly pageant that tells the story of star-crossed lovers caught in the turmoil of the Indian tragedies suffered at the hands of European settlers in the late 1800s. Presented in April of each year, the play is performed in the same natural outdoor theater where it's been held since its origin in 1923, with the scenes taking place in the canyon and on the surrounding hillsides. Only two of the 600 actors and stagehands that put on the pageant (those playing the lead roles of Ramona and Alessandro) are paid; all the rest are volunteers, some of whom have been involved with the production for 40 or 50 years. Whole families get involved, and stay involved, for generations. The show is based on a popular 1884 novel whose author wrote the book in hopes of generating support to end the Indian abuses in the region. While the love story itself is pure fiction, the conditions and locations were true. Sadly the message was lost on readers and instead they flocked to the area as tourists looking for the setting of the compelling love story. Eventually the town got the hint and gave the tourists what they wanted.

Ramona Outdoor Play takes place in April and May at the Ramona Bowl Amphitheatre, 27400 Ramona Bowl Rd, Hemet, CA 92544; ☏ 951 658 3111; www.ramonabowl.com. Directions: on I-10, take the Beaumont Ave/Hwy 79 exit and go south approx 14 miles. Turn left on Stetson; go 3 miles. Turn right on Girard or Columbia to the parking lots.

In 1994 the town of **29 Palms** decided to paint the history of their little community on the walls of their buildings, turning their downtown into an outdoor art gallery showcasing 20 murals painted by a variety of artists. This **Oasis of Murals** tells a most comprehensive history of the area from the effects of flash floods before they constructed flood-control channels to miners using their dirty socks to separate gold from mercury to the colorful characters who settled the town.

Oasis of Murals is located in the town of 29 Palms. Contact the Action Council for 29 Palms, Inc, 455-B Mesquite Ave, PO Box 66, Twenty-nine Palms, CA 92277; ☏ 760 361 2286; www.oasisofmurals.com. Directions: 29 Palms is on Hwy 62, north of the Joshua Tree National Monument.

MUSEUMS AND COLLECTIONS

Lovingly assembled by hundreds of volunteers from various model railroad clubs, the **San Diego Model Railroad Museum** is the largest indoor model railroad in North America. With trains that run in O, HO, and the tiny N scale, the huge 24,000 square foot display is inspiring as each detail closely models the features of the real area it represents. For example, the Tehachapis is a model of the entire 70 miles of line between Bakersfield and Mojave and features the notorious loop where the engine of a 100-car train spirals up to cross directly over its caboose 90ft below, doubling back upon itself in several locations. The Carbillo model has an operating water fountain in the main terminal as well as an electric trolley line that gets its power from an overhead system.

> **San Diego Model Railroad Museum** 1649 El Prado, San Diego, CA
> 92101; ✆ 619 696 0199; www.sdmodelrailroadm.com. *Open Tue–Fri
> 11am–4pm, Sat and Sun 11am–5pm.* Directions: the museum is located on
> the lower level of the Casa De Balboa on the Prado in Balboa Park.

The last place you'd expect to find a comprehensive **Museum of the American Presidency** would be in a high school, but that's exactly where you'll find the only presidential memorabilia collection west of the Mississippi. Housed in the library, and soon to move into the grand foyer of the auditorium, this 40,000-piece collection had its genesis in a program called The Big Idea, a personal entrepreneurship program that encourages kids to develop community service or individual projects. Teacher Jim Fletcher used his own collection of political objects as an example of a personal passion and, quite by accident, the Big Idea was born. Now in its 12th year, Jim considers himself a master beggar, able to wheedle and cajole donations to the burgeoning museum, getting them mainly from members of the American Political Item Collectors association. Their collection displays more presidential memorabilia than the Smithsonian, including the largest collection of Woodrow Wilson material on the west coast, political satire cartoons from 1870–1920, and campaign buttons from McKinley to George W Bush.

> **Museum of the American Presidency** at Clairemont High School,
> 4150 Ute Dr, San Diego, CA 92117. Call Jim Fletcher at ✆ 858 270
> 0694. You can visit any time the school is open, including during
> summer school, or by prior arrangement at other times, including
> weekends.

The **Museum of Making Music** is an interactive experience that takes you through the evolution of instrument design, demonstrating how such innovations have shaped the music we've listened to since the late 1800s. From the invention of the player piano to today's digital instruments, you'll see, hear and interact with a century of musical history.

> **Museum of Making Music** 5790 Armada Dr, Carlsbad, CA 92008;
> ✆ 760 438 5996; www.museumofmakingmusic.org. *Open Tue–Sat
> 10am–5pm, closed Mon and holidays.* Directions: on I-5 in Carlsbad, take
> the Palomar Airport Rd exit and go east. Turn left onto Armada Dr.

If there's one sport endemic to California, that would be surfing, a lifestyle at the epicenter of the state's renowned beach culture. The **California Surf Museum** displays this subculture in all its glory, romanticizing its legends along with its accompanying equipment, music, clothing, art, film, and specialized language – for example, 'Cowabunga, dude', 'Bitchin', and 'Hot Dogger'. You'll see that surfing is far more than just a sport – it's a passion, commitment and obsession that can turn adherents of the sport into lifelong surf bums. From a historical perspective, proximity to the ocean was seen as a source of personal

Quirk Alert

You'll think you've both gone back in time and entered the future when you pull into San Diego's **RTC Fuel** station where uniformed attendants straight out of the 50s offer to service your car as well as fill your tank with alternative fuels made from fish-fry grease or from waste scraped off the floor of a cheese plant. The station offers gas, diesel and six alternative fuels, including natural and liquefied propane gas. While there aren't many takers for the fish or cheese options (yet), the station stands ready to meet the need when California reaches its goal of having one out of every ten new vehicles being sold in the state by 2018 to be non-polluting.

RTC Fuel 4001 El Cajon Blvd, San Diego, CA 92105; ✆ 619 521 2469; www.rtc4afv.com. Directions: the fuel station is on El Cajon between Central Ave and 41st St, just off I-15.

freedom and identity and the surf culture spawned a spiritual community based on surfing over working. A bumper sticker once proclaimed: 'Work is for people who don't know how to surf.'

California Surf Museum 223 North Coast Hwy, Oceanside, CA 92054; ✆ 760 721 6876; www.surfmuseum.org. *Open daily 10am–4pm.* Free admission. Directions: the museum is at the junction of North Coast Hwy and Mission Ave, 6 blocks from I-5.

ECCENTRIC ENVIRONMENTS

'Whatever comes up, comes out.' That was Noah Purifoy's explanation for the art he produced from found objects. **The Noah Purifoy Desert Art Environment**, nearby the windswept town of Joshua Tree, is two acres of sculpture created by the elderly artist from the time he moved to the desert in 1989 until his death in 2004. Always drawn to discarded objects, Noah made a conscious decision as a young man never to buy new materials for his art, finding junk to be evocative and feeling that each piece carried with it the history of its former owners. Dozens of large sculptures, freestanding and suspended, surround his former home, made from materials as varied as bowling balls, Astroturf, newspapers, old windows, foam rubber, bicycle parts, rags, old clothing and burned wood. An educated man with three university degrees, Noah preferred being alone so he could work on his assemblages. Many are whimsical: towering stacks of twisted cafeteria trays; crosses challenging voodoo fetishes; a train made of bicycle wheels, old vacuum cleaners, and beer kegs. Others are more philosophical, inviting contemplation: The White House, open to the sky but with sealed-up windows and The Cathedral, a wooden building with no doors or windows. He enjoyed watching what happened to his work as it aged, exposed as it is to the harsh desert elements. The environment is so large that it attracts tourists viewing it from helicopters.

Noah Purifoy Desert Art Environment located in Joshua Tree, CA; ✆ 213 382 7516; www.noahpurifoy.com. Directions: on Hwy 62 in Joshua Tree, take the Yucca Mesa exit. Turn north onto Yucca Mesa St, then right onto Aberdeen, then left onto Center St. Then curve right onto Blair Lane. The environment is open all hours, and a visitors' center is planned. The site covers 7.5 acres so wear comfortable shoes.

Twenty years ago, Leonard Knight's dream of launching a 300ft-high hot-air balloon, carrying the message 'God is Love', failed him on an impossibly bleak and barren patch of desert near the Salton Sea. It was here, in this inhospitable place, that Leonard had a vision: God wanted him to paint his message instead on the side of a mountain. There was only one problem. He would have to build the mountain first. Today, **Salvation Mountain**, and its message of love and redemption, is a riot of color, three stories high and about as wide as a football field, a brilliant patch of incongruity rising up out of the desolate landscape. Moulded entirely by hand, Leonard, who is in his seventies, made the mountain out of hay bales, adobe, old paint, window putty, and truly astounding tenacity.

You can climb Leonard's mountain, following the yellow pathway to the top and experiencing the enormity of this work of 'outsider' art. The view is constantly changing as you pass through biblical verses, flowers made from cat food cans, and a beach at the bottom representing the nearby Salton Sea. It's all red, yellow, blue, and green, a rainbow of hope in the desert. For all these years, Leonard has lived at the foot of his handmade mountain in a ramshackle truck with no electricity, plumbing or water. To say that Leonard is happy is an understatement. He's a genuinely warm and dedicated man, fully aware of his eccentricity. He doesn't accept any money, asking only for old paint with which he constantly touches up his mountain so it'll stay shiny. He welcomes visitors and delights in telling you about his passion, pressing postcards of his creation into your hands so you can help him spread the word of God's love. A colossal achievement, Leonard's mountain is a monument devoted to peaceful co-existence.

Unfortunately, the government didn't always see it quite that way, declaring the place a toxic nightmare a few years back. They were ready to bulldoze it when a legion of Leonard's fans successfully petitioned the legislature to declare it a work of religious art and therefore immune from destruction. Plus, soil tests eventually proved that the mountain wasn't toxic after all. He and his mountain are now famous all over the world thanks to occasional busloads of international tourists and a host of print and broadcast media stories.

In addition to continually adding more coats of paint to his mountain (so far he estimates 100,000 gallons have gone into its creation), Leonard now spends his days working on a huge 'balloon', again building it out of hay bales, adobe, and paint, and building as a 'hogan', a multi-room structure supported by 'trees' made from old tractor and car tyres, tree branches, telephone poles, and yet more adobe and paint. He's always hard at work but will stop to greet you and share with you his enthusiasm for his creation and for the freedom he enjoys to do as he wishes. If you can, bring old paint (bright colors) when you come to visit. But even if you arrive empty handed, you'll come away with postcards and a memory that won't soon depart.

Salvation Mountain Niland, CA, located south of I-10, 5 miles east of Hwy 111 at Niland. Contact Leonard Knight, PO Box 298, Niland, CA 92257. Directions: on Route 111 in Niland, go east on Main St to the mountain. Visit anytime.

Queen Califia's Magical Circle is the only American sculpture garden created by eccentric French artist Niki de Saint Phalle. Inspired by California's eclectic roots, the garden is graced with nine whimsical, large-scale, brightly colored mosaic sculptures as well as an undulating, 400ft-long mosaic snake circling the garden. You have to negotiate a maze covered in black, white and mirrored tiles to enter the magic circle.

Queen Califia's Magical Circle Iris Sankey Arboretum, Kit Carson Park, Escondido, CA. Contact the Community Services Department, City of Escondido, 201 N Broadway, Escondido, CA; ☎ 760 839 4691; www.queencalifia.org. Directions: on I-15, take the Rancho Parkway exit towards Escondido. This turns into Bear Valley Parkway; the park is at the corner of Bear Valley Parkway and Mary Lane.

Peace, love and concrete all contributed to the creation of the non-denominational **Desert Christ Park**, the remarkable achievement sculpted by Antoine Martin in the mid 1900s. Rising from the desert floor where the artist spent the last 14 years of his life, the four-dozen biblical sculptures are scattered about the park, which itself is in the midst of a long-term renovation by the non-profit foundation responsible for its repair and upkeep. The statues, varying in size from life-size to 13ft in height and weighing up to 16 tons apiece, are crafted from steel-reinforced concrete, a material notoriously difficult to sculpt. That makes the detail on the statues even more impressive than their size. You'll see the apostles, Mary, Jesus, angels, and children, all representing peace, love, and tolerance to Martin who settled in the area after failing to get his first sculpture, a three-ton Christ, placed at the Grand Canyon. You can take your picture at the *Last Supper* by sticking your head through the hole thoughtfully provided by its creator.

Desert Christ Park 6929 Apache Trail, Yucca Valley, CA 92284; www.desertchristpark.org. Directions: on I-10, take Hwy 62 east to Yucca Valley. In Yucca Valley, turn left on Mohawk Trail, and then right on Sunnyslope Dr. The park will be on your left.

QUIRKYVILLE
Slab City is one strange place. You can feel it as you're driving south from Palm Springs, as the roadside changes from opulent luxury to suburban uniformity to the bizarre, surreal landscape of a community of squatters living rent-free in the desert amid tumbleweeds and the hulks of abandoned vehicles. It's the kind of place that makes you want to stop, knock on the door of a trailer and ask, 'What on earth are you doing here?'

The answer would vary depending upon the time of year you come across this city-that's-not-a-city by a sea-that's-not-really-a-sea. In the winter up to 3,000 snowbirds come here, living in an assortment of motley trailers, RVs, campers, pick-ups and tents, and nesting in clusters on the desert or on one of the hundreds of slabs left behind when the US military abandoned their base there after World War II. While the State of California administers this 600-plus acre wasteland, there are no services available, no plumbing or electricity, save in Niland, four miles away where residents can get propane and water and pick up their mail. They communicate by CB radio, with one of their members volunteering to make nightly broadcasts of products and services available for sale or trade. When the snowbirds flee as summer approaches, the population drops to a few hundred diehard loners and misfits, called slabbers, eccentrics with no desire to live among the mainstream.

The **Salton Sea** itself, an inland saline lake, was formed early in the 1900s when the Colorado River burst its irrigation barriers and accidentally flooded the basin for a year and a half, burying entire towns and farms and wiping out the main line of the Southern Pacific Railroad. Today it averages 35 miles in length by 13 miles across although it can be as long as 40 miles in particularly wet years. It still gets water from agricultural runoff and a few other sources, but evaporation is the only means of escape. The sea has become increasingly salty over the years, its salinity now exceeding that of the Pacific Ocean, as well as polluted by pesticides and plagued by algae growth and the accompanying foul smell. The beaches are mainly fish bones. Why anyone would want to squat there, even for free, is a matter for conjecture. There is an organization trying to rally the slabbers and snowbirds to clean up the place, or at least stop illegal dumping, but they're getting lots of resistance from old-timers for whom freedom's just another word for their right to dump.

Slab City is near the town of Niland, CA. Contact the Slab City Organization, PO Box 710152, San Diego, CA 92171; www.slabcity.org. Directions: in Niland, head east on E Beal Rd until you reach the decorated sentry box.

TOURS

Most people think of the San Andreas Fault as a big gaping gorge. But, as you'll find out with **Jurassic Expeditions** on their four-hour eco-tour of the desert area around Palm Springs, the fault contributes more than just heart-stopping, building-toppling moments from time to time. (Without it, most of the southern part of the state would be without water and, thus, without tourist attractions.) On this tour you get to actually walk across the fault, see the world's lowest landmass, and experience the windiest spot on earth. Jurassic Expeditions conducts its tours on luxury motor coaches equipped with plentiful TV monitors. Dubbed 'edutainment', the scientifically accurate expedition is produced just like a movie, complete with scripting, visuals and musical scores to supplement off-coach experiences.

Jurassic Expeditions ☎ 888 528 8133; www.jurassicexpeditions.com. Reservations required.

Desert Adventures offers close-up jeep tours of the fault that take you through the surreal landscape of the Badlands desert. You wind through what is widely considered the most tortuous landscape on earth on your way to the fault, through mazes of steep-walled canyons and ravines. An optional stop adds a visit to a Native American archaeological site that lies directly on the fault.

Desert Adventures Jeep Tours 67555 E Palm Canyon Dr #106, Cathedral City, CA 92234; ☎ 888 440 5337; www.red-jeep.com.

Another way to experience the desert is by covered wagon, this time exploring with **Covered Wagon Tours**. Drawn by a term of mules, the padded-seat wagon, substantially more comfortable than the ones the pioneers had to endure, takes you across the San Andreas Fault with an expert naturalist guide who explains the geological and horticultural facts of life. After the ride you get a chuck wagon cookout and a country music sing-along.

Covered Wagon Tours Contact PO Box 1106, La Quinta, CA 92253; ☎ 800 367 2161; www.coveredwagontours.com. Reservations required.

Three companies offer tours of the windmill farms that dominate the landscape around Palm Springs. **Windmill Tours**, **Windfarm Tours** and the **Best of** the **Best** tours take you through the forests of spinning, towering windmills as their giant blades whoosh overhead. Despite their seeming simplicity, there's a lot of technology involved in harnessing the power of wind and farmers throughout the state are setting up shop on windy passes. San Gorgonio Pass, where these windmills are situated, is one of the most consistently windy places on earth.

> **Windmill Tours** contact Palm Springs Windmill Tours, 15831 La Vida Dr, Palm Springs, CA 92262; ☎ 760 320 1365; www.windmilltours.com. Call for tour times. Directions: on I-10 north of Palm Springs, take the Indian Ave exit and follow the North Frontage Rd (20th Ave) 1.25 miles west.

> **Windfarm Tours** contact Windmill Tours, PO Box 457, N Palm Springs, CA 92258; ☎ 760 251 1997; www.caladventures.com/WindfarmTours.htm. The tours are of the Wintec Windmill farm at 9am, 11am, 1pm, and 3pm. Directions: on I-10 north of Palm Springs.

> **Best of the Best** Contact Best Of the Best Tours; ☎ 760 320 4600; www.bestofthebesttours.com. The tours are on Wed–Sat at 9am, 11am, and 2pm.

Palm Springs became famous in the mid 1900s for a style of architecture uniquely suited to desert living that became known as Desert Modernism. Hollywood celebrities flocked to the city to buy houses notable for their clean lines, open roofs, use of glass and the connectedness of the indoor and outdoor spaces. Architects of the day competed to create the most distinctive buildings of the era. Today, after a period of neglect, these buildings are once again fashionable and **PSModern Tours** will take you on a tour of these architecturally eccentric structures. You can also buy a self-drive map printed by the **Palm Springs Modern** committee to see a sampling of these buildings on your own.

> **PSModern Tours** ☎ 760 318 6118; email: psmoderntours@aol.com

> **Palm Springs Modern** PO Box 4738, Palm Springs, CA 92263; www.psmodcom.org

In San Diego's Old Town they call the **Ghosts and Gravestones** Tour 'frightseeing'. Offered all year long, this lively romp through the city's gravest moments is both entertaining and enlightening. You'll meet the spirit of a long-dead Yankee in one of only two haunted houses officially recognized by the US government, hear about a ghost who does windows, and tour the gravestones in Calvary Pioneer Park.

> **Ghosts and Gravestones** Contact Historic Tours of America; ☎ 800 213 2474; www.historictours.com/sandiego. Directions: tours depart from 4010 Twiggs St in Old Town.

QUIRKY CUISINE

You do all your own cooking at the **Turf Supper Club**, standing around a communal grill and hoping the spatula and tongs are available when you need them. This quirky place has been serving up steaks, kebabs, fish, and chicken this way since the 50s. All the wait staff does is find you a table and bring you your order – raw. The rest of the meal is up to you. Note: the garlic bread goes on the grill too.

Turf Supper Club 1116 25th St, San Diego, CA 92102; ✆ 619 234 6363. Directions: the club is at 25th and C St, 3 blocks from the 25th St exit of Hwy 94.

This diner is the real thing. The **101 Café** has always been a diner, ever since it was built in 1928, and today it sits in its original location alongside Hwy 101, its walls covered with vintage photos and emanating a lived-in feeling that new retro just can't quite manage. The café is a favorite hangout for classic cars and bikes.

101 Café 631 South Coast Hwy, Oceanside, CA 92054; ✆ 760 722 5220; www.101cafe.net. Directions: the café is on the South Coast Hwy between Minnesota and Wisconsin Ave.

No wonder they filmed the sleazy bar scenes from *Top Gun* at **Kansas City Barbeque**. This is guy food eaten in a guy way at a guy place: big, sloppy portions of barbeque served on paper plates at picnic tables. The walls are covered in sports, navy and police memorabilia, the ceiling with bras. What more could a guy want?

Kansas City Barbeque 610 West Market St, San Diego, CA 92101; ✆ 619 231 9680; www.kcbbq.net. Open 7 days a week, 11am–1am. Directions: on I-5 in San Diego, take the Front St exit and head towards the Civic Center. Turn right on W Market St.

ROOMS WITH A SKEW

The newest cottage at **Castlewood Cottages** is 15ft off the ground. Called the Woodland Tree House, this fantasy room features an enormous, realistic-looking apple 'tree', a hot tub carved out of 'rock' and enough silk plants and flowers to make you feel like you're really in a forest. A spiral staircase takes you to the treetop sleeping loft 24ft off the ground. Other cabins are decorated in themes like *King Arthur*, *Anthony and Cleopatra*, and *Gone with the Wind*. The Enchanted Forest is incredibly detailed; you climb the stairs of your oak 'tree' to get to your bed and climb down again to the grotto to enjoy your 'rock' waterfall Jacuzzi and elves house. The Castle Garden cabin has a waterfall, a moat, a spiral staircase to the tower bedroom, and a mural of the English countryside that goes all around the room. The 'knight' in the full-size suit of armor is wired to tell dragon stories. Murals and mood lighting enhance all the themes and every cottage comes with costumes so you can play out the fantasy. These 11 cottages, designed for romantic getaways for couples only, are the work of Dan and Louise Payne who have been fixing up the property, cottage by cottage, for more than a dozen years. They get their inspiration from visits to Disneyland and Las Vegas, excitedly sketching out ideas on napkins during their field trips.

Castlewood Cottages 547 Main St, PO Box 1746, Big Bear Lake, CA 92315; ✆ 909 866 2720; www.castlewoodcottages.com. Directions: Main St is just off Hwy 18 (Big Bear Blvd) in Big Bear Lake, northeast of San Bernardino.

The seventh, and last, of the famous chain of Wigwam Motels built by Frank Redford in the 40s is the **Wigwam Motel** in Rialto, CA. A favorite stop along Route 66 in the mid 1900s, its slogan was 'Do it in a Teepee' and it originally had 12 of them around a kidney-shaped swimming pool. Only three of the original seven motels remain (the other two are in Holbrook, AZ and Cave City, KY) and this one is undergoing a total makeover, including retiring the old slogan and hourly rental rates in honor of the motel's historic significance.

Wigwam Motel 2728 W Foothill Blvd, Rialto, CA 92376; ☎ 909 875
3005; www.wigwammotel.com. Directions: the motel is on US Historic
Route 66 in Rialto, west of San Bernardino.

You get a strange sensation when you get into bed in one of the cottages at the
Crystal Pier Hotel – you'll both feel and hear the waves crash *under* you which is
not surprising since your bed is in a cottage perched 750ft out into the ocean and
75ft above it. The hotel has been drawing visitors since 1927, the only place in the
country where you can sleep on a privately owned pier and be rocked to sleep by
the swaying of the waves and the sound of surf sloshing on the sand.

Crystal Pier Hotel 4500 Ocean Blvd, San Diego, CA 92109; ☎ 800 748
5894; www.crystalpier.com. Directions: on I-5 in San Diego, take the
Grand/Garnet exit and follow Garnet Ave west to the pier entrance.

After Bill Kornbluth retired in 1991, he bought a run-down motel and transformed
the place into a highly personalized theme property. The **Oasis of Eden Inn &
Suites** features 14 theme suites, all created and built by Bill and his friends, one of
whom is an ex-Hollywood prop man. The Cave Room and the Jungle Room are
among his wildest creations although the Rockin' 50s Suite, with its bed in a faux
Cadillac, also deserves a wild rating. The New York, New York comes with
furniture designed as buildings – they even light up. Others, such as the Esther
Williams Suite with its wall mural of synchronized swimmers and ceiling of
clouds, are more sedate, but no less kitschy. Designed as a relaxing getaway, each
suite has its own hot tub.

Oasis of Eden Inn & Suites 56377 29 Palms Hwy, Yucca Valley, CA
92284; ☎ 800 606 6686 or ☎ 760 365 6321; www.oasisofeden.com.
Directions: the inn is on Hwy 62 between Palm Springs and 29 Palms.

Kids bring their sleeping bags and set up in a carpeted classroom for the end of
summer **Zoofari Snooze**s at Moorpark College, also known as America's
Teaching Zoo. Their companions for the evening aren't conventional either as
students learning exotic animal care take the campers on a nocturnal flashlight
safari, introducing them to some of the 200 species represented at the zoo. They
put on an animal show for the kids as well who then get popcorn and a movie
before lights out. The zoofaris are scheduled over several weekends each August.

Zoofari Snooze takes place in August at **America's Teaching Zoo**,
Moorpark College, 7075 Campus Rd, Moorpark, CA 93021; ☎ 808 378
1441; www.moorparkcollege.edu/zoo/. *The zoo is open every weekend
17 11am–5pm.* Directions: on Hwy 118, take the Collins Dr exit in
Moorpark and head north. Continue through two stoplights (freeway and
Campus Rd). Turn right into the 2nd entrance past the stoplights, directly
across from University Dr. (Signs say America's Teaching Zoo and
Communications Building.) Turn to the right in the parking lot and
continue up the short hill to the right.

If you used to love to go backpacking, but your back is no longer enthusiastic about
the prospect, then you'll love the **Wikiup B & B**. Not only do you get luxury, you
get llamas to carry your gear while you go hiking in the Sierras. Linda and Lee
Stanley, owners of both the inn and LeeLin Llama Treks, combined their interests
into a package that lets you get the satisfied feeling that comes with a healthy day

Quirk Alert

Keep an eye out for a character named 'Floomie' whenever you visit a water theme park. Since 1982 Jay Mark Flume has been on a quest to ride every single water ride in America every year, having his picture taken on each and every ride. In California he rides at Six Flags in Valencia.

in the woods with the equally satisfied feeling of soaking in a hot tub and sleeping in cozy guestrooms with names like Shady Lady and Willow Warren.

Wikiup B & B, 1645 Whispering Pines Dr, Julian, CA 92036; ✆ 760 765 1890; www.wikiupbnb.com. Directions: Whispering Pines Dr is just off Hwy 78 in Julian, northeast of San Diego.

Ballantines Hotel in Palm Springs has 50s-style plastic and chrome theme rooms and suites with furniture by the likes of Eames, Miller and Knoll. The place is upscale, fun, and artsy, and they stock classic and B movies that you can watch in rooms dedicated to movie and musical stars. The sun deck is covered with green Astroturf, the rooms sport shag rugs, 50s' music plays in the background, and breakfast is served in your room on 50s-style Melmac (a classic 1950s' tableware collection which gas stations used to give away - it was one of the first plastics put to wide use). Marilyn Monroe actually stayed many times in the very room decorated in her honor. The poolside room has a 1,000-piece Marilyn jigsaw puzzle in case you get tired of just relaxing, retro-style.

Ballantines Hotel 1420 North Indian Canyon Dr, Palm Springs, CA 92262; ✆ 800 780 3464; www.ballantineshotels.com. Directions: the hotel is on North Indian Canyon Dr between East Stevens Rd and East Camino Monte, a block from Hwy 111.

Another retro-hip Palm Springs motel is **Orbit In's Hideaway** with its classic 50s architecture and original mid-century furnishings. They'll even loan you bicycles to get around town.

Orbit In's Hideaway 370 W Arenas Rd, Palm Springs, CA 92262; ✆ 877 996 7248; www.orbitin.com. Directions: the Hideaway is on W Arenas Rd, between South Cahuilla Rd and South Lugo Rd, 2 blocks from Hwy 111.

For Bonnie Marie Kinosian, running the **Coronado Victorian House** B & B is about more than just creating a romantic atmosphere. Bonnie, a professional dancer, offers packages that include dance lessons in everything from tap to belly dancing to Country & Western and ballroom. There's a complete dance and fitness studio right there on the property.

Coronado Victorian House 1000 Eighth St, Coronado, CA 92118; ✆ 888 299 2822; www.coronadovictorianhouse.com. Directions: on I-5 in San Diego, take the CA-75 N (Coronado) exit and go over the Coronado Bridge. Once across the bridge follow 3rd St and turn left onto Orange Ave, then turn right onto 8th St. The Coronado Victorian House is on the corner of 8th St and D Ave.

ATTRACTIONS

You'll be astounded when you see what can be made out of those toy Lego bricks. For instance, how about an entire theme park complete with rides? Named the 'Best theme Park for Kids' in 2004, five-year-old **Legoland** is a big hit with the under-12 set. This place, with its boat and train rides, musical fountain, Lego play town, sports center, and art gallery is a tribute to imagination and skill, with mini-land serving as the heart of the park. Here you'll see seven regions of the USA, replicated in 1:20 scale using 20 million Lego bricks, including unbelievably detailed models of Washington, DC, Florida, California, New York City and New Orleans. But the most amazing part is the model shop where you can see Lego master builders at work in what has to be one of the best jobs on the planet. There are holiday events throughout the year; one of the best is at New Year when they ring in the New Year with a 22ft-high Lego brick drop and fireworks. They hold it at 'midnight' kid-time, 6pm to the rest of us.

Legoland One Legoland Dr, Carlsbad, CA 92008; ☏ 760 918 5346; www.legoland.com. Directions: on I-5, take the Cannon Rd east exit and follow the signs.

JUST PLAIN WEIRD

'I am Knut. I bring you love' intoned **George Van Tassel**, addressing one of his many interplanetary spacecraft conventions back in the 50s. Knut was an entity supposedly stationed on an alien supply ship not far from the **Giant Rock** Mojave Desert site where the UFO's contactees were gathering to hear Van Tassel channeling his alien. The site, containing what is thought to be the world's biggest boulder, was considered by many to be a magnetic vortex of great importance, connected, according to Van Tassel, to the Great Pyramid in Egypt.

You may be finding all this a bit ludicrous, but Van Tassel had thousands of followers who attended his weekly channeling sessions, most of whom believed they had survived physical encounters in spaceships from planets other than earth. They also supported Van Tassel in the construction of the **Integratron**, a device he believed was designed by alien architects and passed through to him to build. The dome-like structure, 38ft high and 55ft in diameter, sits directly in the vortex and was supposed to restore physical youth to humans by rejuvenating living cell tissues. Raising money from the sale of his books, *I Rode a Flying Saucer*, and *Into This World and Out Again,* he spent 18 years building the thing. Sadly, it didn't restore him much youth; he died just before it was completed.

Today his eccentricity is rented out for music recordings and retreats. You can take a tour, inspect the archives, newsletters and photos, and experience the energy and sound properties of the structure. You can also opt for the Sound Bath, a 30-minute sonic healing session that uses quartz crystal bowls played in the resonant, multi-wave sound chamber.

The Integratron 2477 Belfield Blvd, Landers, CA 92285; ☏ 760 364 3126; www.integratron.com. Tours happen in October and November, private tours are available by appointment. Directions: the Integratron is at the junction of Belfield Blvd and Linn Rd in Landers, north of Yucca Valley and Joshua Tree.

Where can you find a 20ft-tall pink marble pyramid, original spiral stairs from the Eiffel Tower, and a sundial featuring a three-dimensional bronze rendering of Michelangelo's *Arm of God*? Why, **The Center of the World**, of course. Located eight miles west of Yuma, Arizona, 15-square-mile **Felicity** has been recognized

Quirk Alert

Californians are always looking for ways to save energy and plans are underway for the $1 billion Harper Lake Energy Park, a project involving 90,000 cows living in cow condos in their very own 2,000 acre gated community. In lieu of rent the cows are expected to contribute 100lb of cow patties each day that will then be converted into methane gas which in turn fuels a jet-turbine generator, providing the park's energy. Excess energy will be sold to Southern California utility companies. That's some cow town!

as the Center of the World by Imperial County, California, the *Institut Geographique National* of France, General Dynamics Corporation, and The People's Republic of China. Taking its name from a town mentioned in a children's book, Felicity was legally established in March of 1986 by Jacques-André Istel, the book's author and internationally recognized father of the sport of skydiving. He first laid eyes on the land that would become Felicity in the 1950s and purchased it shortly thereafter. He returned in 1980 and, with his wife Felicia, began to create Felicity. Istel now serves as mayor and de facto marketing director.

The primary goal of Felicity is 'To engrave in granite highlights of the collective memory of humanity'. This substantial collection of granite walls, each 100ft long, is known as the World Commemorative Center. Dedicated to 'remembering individuals, institutions, and history', the Center is home to intricately engraved granite walls designed to last for 4,000 years. Currently some of the walls feature the history of French aviation, the Foreign Legion, and US Marine Corps Korean War Memorial. For $200 you can have the name of your choice engraved on the Wall of the Ages. The *official* center of the Center of the World is located inside the pyramid, marked by a dot on a bronze plaque. If you take one of the 15-minute tours Felicity offers from Thanksgiving to Easter, it includes a stop inside the pyramid with the opportunity to stand on the brass plaque. Once you do that, you receive a certificate to indicate that you did, in fact, stand at the Center of the World.

The Center of the World One Center Of The World Plaza, Felicity, CA 92283; ☎ 760 572 0100; www.felicityusa.com. *Tours offered daily 10am–5pm, Thanksgiving to Easter.* Monuments open all year round. Directions: on I-8 east of San Diego, take the Sidewinder Rd exit (near the Felicity town sign) and head north.

Central Eastern

FESTIVALS AND EVENTS

Calico, more accurately described as an Old West town than a ghost town, is home to a number of funny events celebrating its heritage as a late-1800s' mining town. They relive their heyday during October's **Calico Days** with a Wild West parade, a national gunfight stunt exhibition, and an old prospectors' burro run where ten people are chosen to each capture a burro, coax it up a hill and through a mud hole, and then set up a sleeping bag and stake a claim. In the spring they hold a hootenanny and a Sing for Your Apple Pie event. Fall brings a Ghost Haunt with haunted ruins, a terror train ride, costume and pumpkin-carving contests and ghost stories in the afternoon and evening.

> **Calico Days** takes place over the Columbus Day weekend in Calico, CA. Contact the Calico Ghost Town, PO Box 638, Yermo, CA 92398; ☎ 760 254 2122; www.calicotown.com. Directions: on I-15 10 miles north of Barstow, take the Ghost Town Rd exit.

Two thousand bullfrogs are recruited for the **Calaveras County Fair and Jumping Frog Jubilee**. There's a lot at stake here as frog jockeys compete for some serious money: $5,000 if the frog breaks a world record; $1,000 if it equals the record and $500 if it just wins without setting any record. The winning jumper in 1928, the first year the Jubilee was held, bounded just 3.5ft. The world record holder today is Rosie the Ribiter who went 21ft 5.75ins. She has her own plaque on the frog hall of fame sidewalk downtown. That's the equivalent of a human jumping the length of a football field.

The contest has come under protest in recent years by animal rights activists (well, this *is* California) who want to make sure the frogs aren't being mistreated. The 'frog welfare policy' has always been to humanely capture the things, jump them, and then put them back where they were found. But, in a peculiar, only-in-California catch 22, it turns out that it's not against the law to catch bullfrogs, it's only illegal to put them *back* – except for an obscure 1957 provision in the Fish and Game Code that specifically exempts frog-jumping contest frogs. It seems that once-captured frogs can alter the ecosystem so fair organizers post signs giving information about safe release zones. After all, it would hardly be PC to serve frogs' legs.

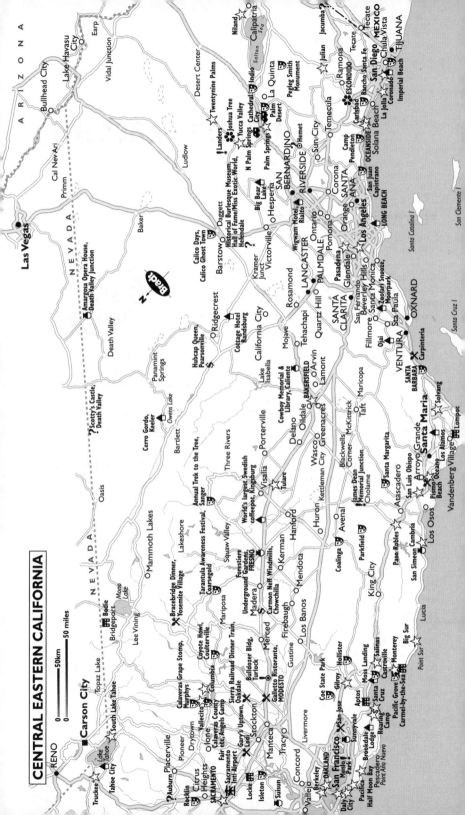

Calaveras County Fair and Jumping Frog Jubilee is held annually the third weekend in May in Calaveras County, CA. Contact Frogtown, PO Box 489, Angels Camp, CA 95222; ✆ 209 736 2580; www.frogtown.org. Directions: Frogtown is located on Hwy 49, about 2 miles south of the town of Angels Camp.

More than 100 teams compete in the **Calaveras Grape Stomp**, a contest based on competitive events dating back to the Greeks. Teams consist of two people, a stomper and a swabby. The hardest work is done by the stomper who pounds away inside the barrel for three very long minutes trying to squeeze the juice out of 25lb of wine grapes. The swabby's job is to collect the juice. Many teams dress in costume and prizes are awarded not just for the most juice stomped, but for the most original costume, the best themed costume, and best effort by a team regardless of the results. The event is part of the Gold Rush Street Faire.

Calaveras Grape Stomp is held annually in October at Murphy's Park in Murphys, CA. Contact the Calaveras Wine Association, c/o Schantz & Associates, PO Box 547, San Andreas, CA 95249; ✆ 209 754 0127; www.calaveraswines.org. Directions: the Grape Stomp takes place in downtown Murphys, but parking in Murphys is very limited so the organizers run a free ferry from the Ironstone vineyards. On Hwy 49, take the Murphys Grade Rd exit towards Murphys, then right onto Algiers St and right onto Six Mile St. Ironstone Vineyards is 1 mile along on the right.

The little town of Coulterville calls itself 'one howl of a town' and for good reason. It's been the home of the annual **Coyote Howl** since 1984, a wacky event involving several dozen adults and kids, all of whom try to duplicate a realistic coyote howl. The adults compete as singles while the kids compete both as individual pups and in packs of four. The Coulterville visitor center maintains a howl of fame – a plaque on the wall.

Coyote Howl takes place on the 3rd weekend in May at 9am in the Coulterville County Park in Coulterville. Contact the Coulterville Visitors Center, PO Box 333, Coulterville, CA 95311; ✆ 209 878 3074. Directions: Coulterville County Park is at the junction of Hwy 49 and 132, 32 miles southwest of the Yosemite gate.

It's the third-largest sequoia tree on the planet, 267ft tall, 40ft across at its base, more than 107 inches around and estimated to be about 1,700 years old. And every year, on the second Sunday in December, the Sanger Chamber of Commerce leads an **Annual Trek to the Tree,** a ritual that got its start in 1925 when the tree, located in Kings Canyon National Park, was designated the **Nation's Christmas Tree**. The trek, now a comfortable bus ride and short walk, can be combined with a festive holiday brunch or dinner. Park rangers place a wreath at the base of the tree to honor servicemen and women who have given their lives in service to their country.

Annual Trek to the Tree takes place annually on the 2nd Sunday in December in Grants Grove in the Sequioa & Kings Canyon National Park. Contact the Sanger District Chamber of Commerce, 1789 Jensen Ave, Sanger, CA 93657; ✆ 559 875 4575; www.sanger.org. Directions: Hwy 180 leads to the park from Fresno. The Sanger Chamber of Commerce runs a tour bus service – call for details.

Ever so carefully is how the contestants in the annual **Poison Oak Show** compete for prizes in categories like best arrangement, most potent-looking leaves, and best poison oak accessory or jewelry item. There's also a prize for the most original poison oak dish (recipe included) and for the best photo of a poison oak victim.

> **Poison Oak Show** is held annually in September outside the St Charles Saloon in Columbia State Historic Park, PO Box 1897, Columbia, CA 95310; ☎ 209 533 4656; www.columbiagazette.com/poison.html. Directions: on Hwy 49 north of Sonora, take the Parrotts Ferry Rd exit heading north.

On the surface it would seem that there's not much to love about tarantulas but, then, that's the whole reason for the **Tarantula Awareness Festival**, an event meant to dispel the bad rap these hairy creatures get. Contrary to popular myth, they're not poisonous. In fact, they're completely beneficial insects, eating real pests like cockroaches, scorpions, baby rattlesnakes and other disease-carrying vermin. Folks (well, kids mainly) even keep them as pets. Held in Coarsegold just before Halloween, the festival includes a scream-off contest, tarantula races and a tarantula derby. The very brave even let the insects crawl on them, claiming they feel just like velvet. The fuzzy spiders, at the height of their breeding season during the festival, are especially active for observers, particularly the males. It's their job to mate with a female and then escape before she can eat him. Bring your own tarantula if possible. You'll see them everywhere in the area from mid October to mid November and they're easy to catch with a can or a box.

> **Tarantula Awareness Festival** happens in October in the Coarsegold Historic Village in Coarsegold. Contact the Coarsegold Chamber of Commerce, PO Box 815, Coarsegold, CA 93614; ☎ 559 642 2262; www.coarsegoldchamber.com. Directions: Coarsegold is 35 miles north of Fresno, and 30 minutes from the southern entrance to Yosemite National Park on Hwy 41.

PECULIAR PURSUITS

If you're going through Death Valley, a visit to **Scotty's Castle** is a must. Sitting virtually in the middle of nowhere and appearing like a mirage in the desert, the castle was built in the 1920s by a wealthy Chicago couple, the Johnsons, who traveled west to check on an investment they'd made with a man named Walter Scott. A rowdy, fast-talking con artist, Scott had been bilking investors by claiming that he was building a castle from the profits from a nearby gold mine. When the Johnsons discovered they'd been defrauded, they befriended 'Scotty' and went along with his scam in the hopes they could recover their money. It was the Johnsons who actually built the castle. During the tour, the guides dress as characters from 1939 and bring the castle's heyday back to life.

> **Scotty's Castle** is located in Death Valley National Park, Death Valley, CA; ☎ 760 786 2392; www.nps.gov/deva/scottys1.htm. *Open daily*

9am–5pm. Directions: I-15 north to US-95, north to SR-267 west (left at Scotty's Junction) to Death Valley National Park and on to Scotty's Castle.

The world of burlesque is still alive at the **Exotic World Movers & Shakers' Burlesque Museum and Striptease Hall of Fame** in Helendale. Lovingly run by seventy-something Dixie Evans, formerly known as the Marilyn Monroe of Burlesque, the museum is crammed to the gills with gowns, feather boas, panties, lingerie and other memorabilia from the golden age of strippers. Located on an isolated, ramshackle ranch in the desert, roughly halfway between Los Angeles and Phoenix, the retired burlesque queen delights in taking you back into her past, smiling coquettishly, chattering enthusiastically and happily posing for pictures amid the stuff of  which fantasies were made. As strippers like Gypsy Rose Lee, Tempest Storm, and Sally Rand passed on, they willed their things to Dixie who somehow makes room for even more breakaway costumes, giant fans, shoes, G-strings, posters, pasties, and cheesecake photos. Wild and wonderful, gaudy and glamorous, Dixie's museum is a memorial to the gone, but not forgotten, days of burlesque. There's no air conditioning, so you may want to visit during the cooler months.

Dixie shares these treasured artefacts with today's strippers who compete once a year at the ranch for the **Miss Exotic World** title. Burlesque dancers come from all over the world to compete for the trophy, teasing, winking and flirting their way to the finals. Considered the Miss America of Burlesque, the pageant draws hundreds of participants ranging in age from their twenties through their seventies, all of whom obey Dixie's strict 'pasties and G-string' dress code.

Historical Burlesque Museum, Hall of Fame and Miss Exotic World 29053 Wild Rd, Helendale, CA 92342; ☎ 760 243 5261; www.exoticworldusa.org. Open Tue–Sun 10am–4pm. Directions: from I-15, head southwest on the National Trails Hwy (Historic Route 66) 15 miles to Vista Rd. Go west on Vista Rd to Helendale Rd. Make a right and proceed 2 miles to Wild Rd. Continue for 2 more miles and the museum will be on your right.

Moaning Cavern and California Caverns have come up with an entirely novel way of matching up singles. They call it **Adventure Dating** and it's a mix of speed dating and cave exploration. It works like this: the group gets together first for an hour of standard speed dating, spending three minutes with each participant of the opposite sex and then completing a questionnaire rating their interest in each person. The next four hours are spent underground, crawling and climbing through tight spaces aided by rappelling equipment and headlamps. Throughout the spelunking experience everyone is presumably sizing up how everyone else performs, looking for signs of courage and co-operative spirit. After an intermission to clean up, the final dating portion begins with a timed seven-minute date with each opposite-sex participant. Names and phone numbers are only provided at the very end after they've had a chance to compare how their initial impressions stood up to the test of time.

Adventure Dating Moaning Cavern, 5350 Moaning Cave Rd, Vallecito, CA 95251 or California Cavern, 9565 Cave City Rd, Mountain Ranch, CA 95246; ☎ 866 762 2837; www.caverntours.com. Costs: $150 per person at Moaning Cavern, $200 at California Cavern. Reservations required.

MUSEUMS AND COLLECTIONS

Paul de Fonville and his wife Virginia are obsessed with keeping the memory of the cowboy alive. At their remote property in Walker Basin they've established the **Cowboy Memorial and Library**, housing their extensive collection of saddles, branding irons (possibly the largest in the country), spurs, ropes, whips, and other cowboy gear in giant tractor-trailer vans until they can afford to build a proper museum. Outside they've set up a corral, chuck wagon, and other tools and trappings of the cowboy trade, hoping to create a permanent memorial to a lifestyle long replaced by freeways and housing tracts. They love to show people around and, if you ask nicely, Paul will let his horse kiss him on the lips, a stunt that got him onto the pages of the *National Enquirer*.

Cowboy Memorial and Library 40371 Cowboy Lane, Caliente, CA 93518; ☎ 661 867 2410; www.tehachapi.com/cowboy. *Open Tue–Sun 10am–5pm.* Free (but donations are requested). Directions: on Hwy 58 east of Bakersfield, take the Caliente exit towards Caliente. Go through Caliente (Caliente Creek Rd). When you reach the 'Y' keep to the right (east) and follow the road to Twin Oaks. Continue on the Walker Basin Rd until you see a sign on the right, which will guide you up the driveway of Cowboy Lane to the memorial.

With 350 agricultural commodities being produced in the state, California is the nation's number one agricultural producer, yet very few people understand what's involved in getting that food from the field to the table. That's where the **Heritage Complex** at the **International Agri-Center** comes in. This museum and learning center exists to familiarize you with agriculture, a subject most Americans never personally experience. The farm equipment museum features antique tractors, including horse-drawn and steam engine equipment, as well as old farming implements while the learning centers offers tours to dairies, farms, feed mills, etc. At Easter they put on a family Easter egg hunt.

Heritage Complex at the International Agri-Center 4500 S Laspina St, Tulare, CA 93274; ☎ 559 688 1030; www.heritagecomplex.org. Directions: the Heritage Center is located on Hwy 99, 45 miles south of Fresno and 60 miles north of Bakersfield.

ECCENTRIC ENVIRONMENTS

Baldasare Forestiere found an unconventional way to beat the central valley's heat – he moved underground, living in a subterranean paradise of his own creation. Using only hand tools on the native hardpan rock, he spent 40 years sculpting

Forestiere Underground Gardens, a network of tunnels, niches, alcoves, passageways, caverns, grottos, and patios well below ground, more than 100 in all. This eccentric visionary, a Sicilian immigrant and vintner, dug a home for himself that included a kitchen, living areas, two bedrooms, a library, a bathroom, and an aquarium viewed from below. An inventive horticulturalist, he strategically placed skylights and airshafts to provide the ideal conditions for growing plants and trees, designing his lair to let in the perfect amount of sunlight and rainwater. From above the treetops look like shrubs. Today relatives keep his spirit alive by maintaining his gardens and giving tours.

Forestiere Underground Gardens 5021 W Shaw Ave, Fresno, CA 93722; ☏ 559 271 0734; www.undergroundgardens.com. *Open September thru mid May, Sat–Sun, with tours at 12 noon and 2pm. Closed Thanksgiving–Jan 1. Mid May thru September Wed–Sun, with tours at 10am, 12 noon, and 2pm. Some evening tours available during this time.* Directions: on Hwy 99, take the W Shaw Ave exit going east.

Death Valley is a pretty good description of the middle of nowhere. It's also the last place you'd expect to find an opera house and the last place you'd expect to find a dancer in her late seventies performing for royalty and nobility, bullfighters and gypsies, monks, nuns, and cats. The **Amargosa Opera House** in Death Valley Junction is the unlikely spot where Marta Becket, an elderly artist and dancer, has spent a good chunk of her reclusive life. Up until the time she and her husband Tom had a flat tyre at the Junction en route to a concert tour, her life was fairly normal, at least as normal as life can be for an artist with a tortured soul. While the tyre was being repaired, Marta came upon the ruins of the Pacific Coast Borax Company, an abandoned hotel and outbuildings rotting in the sun. But Marta had eyes for just one thing: a crumbling theater building formerly used for company events. Marta had found a place for her soul. 'I had to have that theater,' she said, believing she would find new life in it and, in doing so, 'perhaps be giving it life. 'Here,' she continued, 'I would commission myself to do work that no-one else would ever ask me to do.' Renting, then finally buying, the property, she scheduled performances and danced, regardless of whether she had an audience of a few, one, or none.

Mostly, there was none and after a while she imagined a Renaissance audience completely surrounding her. So, acting on her vision, she spent four years painting her audience on the walls of the theater. The King and Queen have the center box, accompanied by nobility. Two of her cats watch from red velvet cushions. Musicians play, ladies dance. Characters from her imagination spilled out on the walls: revelers, ladies of the night, gypsies, children, courting couples and Indians performing for the entertainment of the King and Queen. Now she would never have to dance alone. Word of her accomplishment spread and before long, there were real people sitting in real chairs. Today, after more than 40 years in Death Valley, Marta enjoys packed audiences for most of her cool-season performances.

Amargosa Opera House and Hotel PO Box 8, Death Valley Junction, CA; ☏ 760 852 4441; www.amargosa-opera-house.com. *Performances run Oct–May.* Directions: Llocated on Hwy 160 north to Bell Vista, turn left, 30 miles to Death Valley Junction, at the intersection of Hwy 127 and Hwy 190. The hotel is open all year round.

QUIRKYVILLES
As ghost towns go, **Bodie** is among the best. Impossibly picturesque and perfectly preserved in a state of arrested decay, it sits all by its lonesome off the high desert

Quirk Alert

Keep an eye out – or rather up – when you're at Yosemite. You just might see a rare performance of **Project Bandaloop** (www.projectbandaloop.org), the most unconventional dance troupe you're ever likely to see perform. Known as rock dancers, the troupe performs aerial dances while hanging from the sheer granite walls of the valley. They also perform against high-rise buildings.

highway, lonely, forlorn and irresistibly inviting. In its heyday the 1880s' mining town had 10,000 residents, 65 saloons, a murder a day and a reputation as one of the most sinful places on earth. Most of Bodie was destroyed by fire but the 10% that remains today is more than enough to justify a visit. A California State Historic Park, access and hours are strictly enforced and the area is renowned for its harsh winter climate (elevation 8,375ft).

> **Bodie** is 13 miles east of US Hwy 395; www.bodie.com. Admission $2 per person. *Open 8am–7pm Memorial day through Labor day, 9am–4pm other times.* Directions: on US Hwy 395, take State Hwy 270 and drive 10 miles until the paved road ends, then continue on for the last 3 miles of an unpaved dirt road.

Columbia is (almost) a ghost town that never gave up the ghost. (Or ghosts, as the case may be, as the town is notoriously haunted.) Also part of the state's historic park system, it is operated as an authentic Gold Rush town, its four tree-lined streets lined with wood and brick buildings dating back to the 1800s. Everyone works in period costume, merchants sell 19th-century goods, and you can pan for gold, tour a mine, ride a stagecoach, and watch a blacksmith at work. Once the largest and most prosperous town outside of San Francisco, it fell into decay but was never completely deserted. Lodging is available within the town and every June the docents present a four-day living-history event known as **Columbia Diggin's 1852**. Gold Rush Days are on the second Saturday of each month, adding experiences like authentic period gambling (farm monte, chuck-a-luck and faro) and cooking the foods popular in the late 1800s.

> **Columbia** is 3 miles north of Sonora, off Hwy 49. Contact the Columbia California Chamber of Commerce, PO Box 1824, Columbia, CA 95310; ✆ 209 536 1672; www.columbiacalifornia.com. Directions: on Hwy 49 north of Sonora, take the Parrotts Ferry Rd exit heading north.

ODD SHOPPING

Finding the **Hubcap Capitol of the World** means finding **Pearsonville**, a not-quite-on-the-map blip that's home to Lucy Pearson, the **Hubcap Queen**, and Pearsonville Auto Wrecking and Hubcaps. Hubcaps are Lucy's life and she's been passionately, obsessively collecting them for four decades. Now in her seventies, she reigns over the store in her signature blue bonnet and long dress, looking all the while like a wayward Mother Goose. She probably knows more about hubcaps than any other human being on earth and her inventory is most likely the world's largest.

Hubcap Queen Pearsonville Auto Wrecking, 236 Pearson Rd, Pearsonville, CA 93527; ☎ 760 377 4585; www1.iwvisp.com/hubcaps/. Directions: on US-395, take the Pearson Rd exit and drive south.

Technically, a visit to the **Big Shoe Shoe Repair** isn't really shopping, but it is possible buy some shoelaces in the world's biggest shoe. Built in 1947 by a Chester Deschwanden, a shoe repairman who lived just behind the store, the odd structure became a Bakersfield icon until falling into disrepair after his death. The terms of his will required that any future use had to be shoe related, and it took a while to find someone willing to reopen a shoe-repair business on the site. The shoe is 32ft long, 25ft high with shoelaces of 3in-thick oil-field ropes. It's roughly a size 678. Inside, it feels just like you're in a shoe, arch and all.

Big Shoe Shoe Repair 931 Chester Ave (at 10th), Bakersfield, CA 93301; ☎ 661 864 1002; www.worldslargestthings.com/california/shoe.htm.

QUIRKY CUISINE

Aero Dogs, home of the Famous Flying Wiener, is a most unlikely experience seeing as how the fast food restaurant is located inside a 9ft-wide, 74ft-long airplane fuselage that is parked on the street in downtown Tulare. Mike Schoenau and his partner, Don LeBaron, spent two years converting the former 1951 US Air Force training plane into the 18-seat restaurant. Don't expect gourmet here; they serve strictly hot dogs, Frito boats, chips and root beer floats.

Aero Dogs 240 North L St, Tulare, CA 93274; ☎ 559 685 1230; www.aerodogs.com. *Open Mon–Sat 10.30am–9pm, Sun 11am–4pm.* Directions: on CA-99 at Tulare, take the Tulare (CA-137) exit and head towards Tulare on E Tulare Ave. Turn right onto N L St.

For quirky with class – oodles and oodles of it – you can't beat **Bracebridge**, an elaborate Old English Christmas feast and pageant that's been taking place at the elegant Awhanee Hotel at Yosemite since 1927. Presented just a handful of times each December, the hotel's elegant dining room, with its soaring vistas, is transformed into a 17th-century manor for the three-hour costumed pageant of classic Middle Age music, carols, and rituals. The production is loosely based on a Washington Irving sketch book that described a fictional squire, with his family and servants, entertaining at his manor house.

It takes more than 100 players to put on Bracebridge and the food is every bit as impressive and artistic as their performances. The original seven-course menu dictated a plate of pickled relishes, hot soup, a fish course, peacock pie, baron of beef and boar's head, and a salad. Dessert was always plum pudding and wassail. The meal has evolved over the years to reflect more contemporary tastes, but excellence and elegance have always been retained with dishes like 'roast beef tenderloin rolled in crunchy pistachios with a splash of béarnaise demi-glace infused with tarragon' and 'peacock pie made of veal sweetbreads, pheasant dumplings and seared squab breast with wild mushroom ragout and truffle sauce'. Dessert is still plum pudding. This event is so popular that admission for decades was by lottery. Beginning in 2004 they instituted a new first-come-first-served phone reservation system with bookings being taken on a specific day and time in February.

Bracebridge Dinner takes place in December. Contact the Ahwanee Hotel, 9005 Ahwahnee Dr, Yosemite, CA 95389; ☎ 559 253 5635; www.yosemitepark.com. Reservations are required and are made on a first-come-first-served basis in February.

Buck Owens' **Crystal Palace** is a combination museum, country store, honkey tonk, dinner theater and restaurant all rolled into a glitzy tribute to the country music star. The museum, with its memorabilia and minutiae, some narrated by Buck himself, as well as the gift shop with its dozens of Buck signature items, make this place something like a shrine to the sharecropper-makes-good musical legend. But it's an entertaining enough shrine, especially if you're a fan of country music and show up on the weekends to watch him perform. Otherwise you can just go for the steaks, chilli fries and down-home country ambiance.

> **Crystal Palace** 2800 Buck Owens Blvd, Bakersfield, CA 93308; ☏ 661 328 7560; www.buckowens.com. Buck performs at 7.30pm on Fri and Sat. Directions: on Hwy 99 in Bakersfield, take the Buck Owens Blvd exit and turn east.

Thomas and Karyn Gallo wanted their Italian restaurant, **Galletto Ristorante**, to have an authentic northern Italian feeling so they put in a bocce ball court. The court, lighted at night, is used to play a lawn-bowling type of game popular in Italy.

> **Galletto Ristorante** 1101 J St, Modesto, CA 95354; ☏ 209 523 4500; www.galletto.biz. Directions: on Hwy 99 in Modesto, take the I St exit, then turn northeast onto I St, then left onto 11th St. The restaurant is at the corner of 11th and J St.

Bald guys don't get a lot of respect but this one is a doozy: bald guys (and women) eat free on Wednesdays at **Gary's Uptown Restaurant and Bar**. And this is no dive, either; it's a classy place with white tablecloths, cloth napkins and a 'Bald Guy's' menu that includes steak and snapper fillet. Owner Gary Arnold, himself follicly challenged, picked Wednesdays because they used to be the slowest day of the week. But now, with publicity that's reached worldwide, Wednesday is one of his busiest days. What if you're partially bald? You get that much of a percentage discount. Just showing scalp is worth 10% off. Once in a while a guy will deny that he's balding and refuse the discount.

> **Gary's Uptown Restaurant and Bar** 1800 S Cherokee Lane, Lodi, CA; ☏ 209 369 8698. Directions: on Hwy 99 in Lodi, north of Stockton.

The **Sierra Railroad Dinner Train** plies the rails with an entertaining variety of theme brunches and dinners. The murder-mystery trains are among the most popular as are the special chocolate trains that run during the 60,000-person Chocolate Festival. On Mother's Day they offer 'Throw Momma On the Train' brunch and dinner runs. The Wild West adventure includes a train robbery; the Christmas train features Santa and his elves. Plus they offer numerous theme and holiday excursions. They're also known as the movie railroad, favored by movie producers for their scenery and authenticity. Over 200 films have been made on their trains from *High Noon* to *Back To The Future*.

> **Sierra Railroad Dinner Train** 220 South Sierra, Oakdale, CA 95361; ☏ 209 848 2100; www.sierrarailroad.com. The train runs all year, with dinner trips on Saturday evening and special trips at other times. Reservations required. Directions: the train departs from the Sierra Station, on S Sierra between E G St and E H St.

There's probably no better reason to visit **Twisted Oak Winery** than that they're the most irreverent, least pretentious, least intimidating winery in a state known for the pretentiousness of its wine industry. Rubber chickens are their mascots, scattered about to remind everyone to keep a sense of humor, and a tasting event for wine club members might involve pirate costumes and grog. But it's their labels that really set them apart. Instead of the dry, humorless descriptions pasted on the bottles of their competitors, Twisted Oak might describe a wine thus:

> If we were typical wine note writers, we'd probably blather about the
> beautiful golden straw color, wax insufferably on the winsome aromas of
> lavender and peach, speak oh-so eloquently of the tropical fruit flavors,
> and close with a thunderous ovation to the crisp acid balance and fruity
> finish. Well, forget that noise. Chill it down, curl up on the sofa and suck
> this puppy down with a nice big bowl of real buttered popcorn and an Ed
> Wood movie. Or Dr Strangelove, if you insist.

The winery was started in 2003 by self-proclaimed nerd Jeff Stai, a geek whose other passions include rocket building and ham radios, activities that don't exactly lead to being elected high school homecoming king. Jeff showed them, though, making good during the dot-com days and doing well enough to infuse his winery with a sense of anti-establishment humor.

Twisted Oak Winery 4280 Red Hill Rd, Vallecito, CA 95251; ✆ 209 736 9080; www.twistedoak.com. Directions: on Hwy 4 east of Angels Camp, turn south onto Red Hill Rd. At the very first driveway on the right, turn right again.

ROOMS WITH A SKEW

A common reaction visitors have upon driving up the road to the **Cottage Hotel** is, 'Oh dear, where on earth are we?' or 'Does anyone really *live* here?' The questions make sense once you've seen **Randsburg**, the place where the hotel is located. A strange semi-ghost town, it shares its desert surroundings with Edwards Air Force Base and the China Lake Naval Weapons Center, both of which are located in the middle of nowhere for good reason. This weird little late-1800s town is home to around 80 people on a good day, all of whom either work at the Yellow Aster mine or in the smattering of tourist-related businesses that cling to life by a thread. The hotel itself, with its four rooms and family cottage, caters to anyone with a yen to explore Randsburg as well as those who actually choose it for offbeat weddings and festivals. While the hotel is open all year long, the town itself only wakes up Friday through Sunday.

Cottage Hotel 130 Butte Ave, Randsburg, CA 93554; ✆ 760 374 2285; www.randsberg.com. Directions: Randsburg is just off Hwy 395, northeast of Mojave.

In **Cerro Gordo** you strike it rich when it comes to eccentric places to sleep. You see, Cerro Gordo is an old mining ghost town (pop 3) owned by Mike Patterson whose passion is restoring a few of the town's dozen-and-a-half ramshackle and decayed buildings so folks can enjoy the ambiance as much as he does. Your quarters, rustic but adequate, are either in the bunkhouse or in the Bedshaw House. If all the rooms were to be filled, the population would come to a possible 18. Meals are taken at the renovated American Hotel. Mike also offers day tours and has a small museum on the property. The place is a favorite of off-roaders, motorcyclists, photographers, equestrians and film crews. The season runs from late spring through Halloween. Due to the remote location, Mike needs to know you're coming.

Cerro Gordo, PO Box 221, Keeler, CA 93530; ☎ 760 876 5030; www.geocities.com/Yosemite/1911/cerro2.htm. Reservations required. Directions: on Hwy 136 north of Keeler, turn north onto the dirt road with the Historical Landmark. Follow this steep dirt road 8 miles to the hotel. Warning: a 4WD vehicle is strongly recommended, and there is very limited cell phone coverage in the area.

You can also sleep in the not-quite ghost town of Columbia at one of two hotels that serve as training centers for the local college's hospitality management program: the **City Hotel** and the **Fallon Hotel**. Both are historic Victorians, built in the 1850s and located within Columbia State Historic Park. Both are also notoriously haunted. (See *Quirkyvilles* in this section.)

City Hotel & Fallon Hotel 22768 Main St, Columbia, CA 95310; ☎ 800 532 1479; www.cityhotel.com. Directions: on Hwy 49 north of Sonora, take the Parrotts Ferry Rd exit heading north.

JUST PLAIN WEIRD

If you happen to be in Turlock, look for a **building shaped like a bulldozer**, the office of the United Equipment Company in Turlock. It even has dirt and rocks piled in front of the 'blade'. The president of the company sits where the engine should be.

Bulldozer Building is visible just off Hwy 99, 70 miles north of Fresno in Turlock.

Kingsburg can claim two 'world's largest': the **world's largest Swedish coffeepot** and the **world's largest box of raisins**. Their strange claim to fame begins with the coffee pot, dating back to 1985 when they erected the vintage 1911, 122ft-high, 19ft-diameter pot on a water tower. A plaque at the base reads 'To reflect the heritage and friendliness of its citizens, this water tower is being displayed as a coffee pot.' The raisin box, circa 1992, sits near the parking lot of the Sun Made Raisin Grower's Store, 12ft high and 9ft wide and once filled with 16,500lb of raisins.

World's largest Swedish coffeepot & world's largest box of raisins Kingsburg, CA. Contact Kingsburg Chamber of Commerce, 1475 Draper St, Kingsburg, CA 93631; ☎ 559 897 1111; www.kingsburgcofc.net. Directions: Kingsburg is located on Freeway 99, approximately 20 miles south of Fresno.

Statewide Quirks

SOME ECCENTRIC GROUPS

Some weirdness knows no bounds. From peculiar pursuits to bizarre behaviors, eccentric experiences are taking place all across California, many of them by groups with some mighty strange ideas of how to spend their leisure time.

'Forward into the past' is the motto of the **Society for Creative Anachronism**, people who research and recreate the Middle Ages. Not to be confused with dungeon-and-dragon-type role-playing games, these aficionados take their history very, very seriously. From authentic costumes to faking an authentic death on the battlefield, these knights and warriors are exacting in their practice of medieval culture and customs. Feudal society is a lifestyle for its members, many of whom hail from the diametrically opposite high-tech field. Events take place almost every weekend around the country. California is home to two 'kingdoms' as well as the group's headquarters.

Society for Creative Anachronism www.sca.org

Forty years ago California was the birthplace of the first **Renaissance Faire**, now a network of 152 countrywide medieval festivals celebrating the work, play, music, religion, and superstition of the English Renaissance. Featuring re-enactments and historically based entertainment, foods, and crafts, these fairs have spawned an industry of guilds and clans eager to play at all things medieval. Men in tights and women in coarse cloth roam the faire's streets portraying constables, peasants, cutpurses (pickpockets), gypsies, knights, and barons. There are swordfights, jousting knights on horseback, and plenty of brew masters to keep things lively.

Renaissance Faires www.faires.com

Historical Re-enactors are a zealous bunch, recreating historic war battles with fanatical realism. Some go so far as to live on a soldier's diet so they'll be appropriately gaunt, or practice bloating out their bodies so they appear to have been dead for a day or two. They sleep outside in the rain, subsist on scavenged food, and have trouble explaining to their loved ones why they're compelled to do such things. Passionate imposters like these often join associations such as that of Lincoln Presenters, the Gunfight Re-enactors Association, the American Federation of Old West Re-enactors, and Re-enactors of the American Civil War.

Historical Re-enactors log on to 'Google' re-enactors for specific time periods and wars.

The **Friends of the Society of Primitive Technology** go way back, much further back than any of the groups above. These folks teach primitive skill workshops where you can learn seven ways to make a fire (flicking your Bic lighter isn't one of them), craft primitive tools and weapons, and make shelters out of natural materials (we're not talking cotton and linen here). They conduct workshops in various locations across the country, teaching classes in such subjects as 'Brain-Tanned Buffalo Hides'; 'Deer Hoof Rattle'; 'Four Hour Kayak'; and 'Was Agriculture a Good Idea or an Act of Desperation?'

Society of Primitive Technology www.primitiveways.com

Pretending they're scientists living on Mars, members of the **Mars Society** volunteer for two-week stints in habitats they hope simulate conditions likely to be encountered by explorers to the red planet. One of the 'habs', as they're called, is in the Utah Desert near Hanksville. Looking very much like a giant silo, the structure houses would-be colonists who must act in accordance with strict mission protocols during their simulation. The team keeps meticulous records and ventures outside only while wearing their spacesuits: helmets made from plastic light fixtures and trash-can lids, and canvas suits trimmed with duct tape. The society has around 5,000 members worldwide, all sincerely dedicated to the cause of human Mars exploration. They're no dummies, either; many are NASA employees. Another 'hab' station is in Canada and more are planned for Iceland and the Arctic. There are seven branches in California.

Mars Society www.marssociety.org

The popularity of the **Sweet Potato Queens** is best summed up by their motto: 'Never wear panties to a party.' At least that's what they want you to think. Known far and wide for their audacious, mostly-for-show personas, queens from the country's 1,700 branches don wigs, sleazy dresses, sparkly sunglasses, majorette boots and tacky crowns and give themselves permission to behave outrageously, if only for a few hours. Never mind that most of them are usually normal, well-behaved women of a certain age. To a Sweet Potato Queen, it's the inner harlot that counts. The website is a hoot.

Sweet Potato Queens www.sweetpotatoqueens.com

More sedate than the Sweet Potato Queens are the members of the **Red Hat Society**, a 'disorganization' of women 50 and older that get together for outings wearing red hats and clashing purple clothes. Each of the country's 14,000 branches has a queen mother who enforces 'suggestions' (there aren't any rules), one of which is that members under 50 stick to pink hats and lavender clothing until THAT birthday.

Red Hat Society www.redhatsociety.com

Canine freestyle dancing is actually an athletic sport, healthy for both people and dogs. Instructors help you select music suitable for your dog's style and temperament (they really do perk up when music appeals to them!), and then choreograph your dance routines, planning the steps and movements that make up your 'dance'. Add costumes co-ordinated with the theme of the music you've chosen and you're ready to rock. There are lots of local classes and regional events if you just want to have fun while getting Fido in shape. If you get really good you can go on to the national competitions.

Canine freestyle dancing www.canine-freestyle.org; www.worldcaninefreestyle.org

If you're determined to spend your vacation with your dog, log on to **dog-play.com** for links to all kinds of activities you and your dog can enjoy together. This comprehensive site is an amazing resource for dog lovers, covering, among other things, dog camps, carting and scootering, flygility, performance trick art, and rollerblading. If you need accommodation along the way, check out petswelcome.com. There are dozens of Fido-friendly California accommodations listed.

Dog-Play.com www.dog-play.com; www.petswelcome.com

Tattoo conventions include body art contests along with an exhibit floor where artists sell their merchandise and tattooing skills. Unadorned folks attend for many reasons, but the main one is the opportunity to be immersed in a strange, foreign world while having the freedom to stare at other people's tattoos without being considered rude. You also get a unique chance to ask someone with dozens of body piercings or tattoos why on earth they do it. Tattoo contest categories include the best black and white, most unusual, best tribal, best portrait, and best overall. Binoculars are acceptable: it makes it easier to appreciate the body art up close.

Tattoo conventions www.tattoodirectory.com/calendr2.htm

Murder Mystery events take place at country inns, downtown hotels, on cruise ships and on trains. Carefully crafted and cunningly executed, these dinner and weekend experiences range in complexity from simple audience participation to costumed and role-playing involvement. The food is often linked to the theme of the event, and all mysteries end with prizes being awarded to the most clever and most clueless sleuths.

Murder Mysteries www.murdermystery.com/

If **sleeping with ghosts** and **prowling haunted places** appeals to you, there are several websites to help you find your elusive prey. Prairieghosts.com is all things ghostly, providing information and links to hundreds of ghost tours, cemetery tours, and haunted sites. Around Halloween time, BedandBreakfast.com has links to members offering close encounters of the ghostly kind. Click on the specials button, and then use the drop-down menu to choose the theme.

Ghosts & Hauntings www.prairieghosts.com;
www.BedandBreakfast.com

There's more to the 'sport' of **competitive eating** than cramming in food and letting loose with a few hearty belches. For those who criss-cross the country entering eating contests at food festivals, this is serious business indeed because the prize winnings can be considerable. Except for one ironclad rule – 'if you heave, you leave' – competitors are on their own to devise winning strategies and to train effectively. For example, pickles require more jaw stamina than do hotdogs, especially if you dunk the buns in water to cut chewing time. Some prefer to fast before gorging; others work on expanding their stomachs in the days prior to an event. Referred to as 'athletes' by their brethren, these glutton gladiators compete by eating everything from beef tongue to butter, cow brains to matzo balls. The website has listings of events countrywide.

International Federation of Competitive Eaters (IFOCE)
www.ifoce.com

As accommodations go, it's not the most luxurious way to travel but taking a **Green Tortoise** adventure tour does have its moments. Dubbed the 'hippie bus line', this thirty-something company has been taking travelers around the state, and around the country, in a style best described as communally relaxed. No ordinary busses, the Green Tortoises are equipped with mattresses laid upon elevated platforms, elevated bunks, and booths that convert to sleeping platforms at night. The trips are a combination of camping and hostelling, with riders sharing cooking chores as well as sleeping space with up to three-dozen other trippers. Fast friendships are formed as the buses make their way through a variety of scenic and experiential itineraries, including Northern and Southern California, Yosemite, and Death Valley.

Green Tortoise www.greentortoise.com

Zoos all over California are offering **zoo sleepover** experiences, turning that trip to the zoo into a 24-hour adventure. Bring your pillow and sleeping bag and the zoo will provide the rest: a place to camp within earshot of the big animals, dinner, breakfast, a campfire, and behind-the-scenes animal experiences.

Zoo Sleepovers log on to 'Google' or call your local zoo directly.

KEEP AN EYE OUT. . .

Shoe trees, not the type you put in your shoes, are the kind you throw your shoes up and into. Shoe trees, and sometimes shoe fences, pop up from time to time on back roads where trees still line the highway. No-one really knows how or why a particular tree is selected, but all of a sudden there'll be shoes and boots hanging from it. You won't find them listed in this guide, though, because nature usually has her way with them. So just keep your eyes out or, better yet, start your own.

Street performers work the heavily touristed areas of California's cities, delighting passers-by with their antics while earning a living of sorts. Louis Armstrong, BB King, Bob Dylan, Johnny Carson, and Robin Williams all got their start on the street. From chain-saw juggling to flying house cats to living statues, there's some fine – and wacky – talent to be found out there.

If you see something going on in San Francisco or LA that seems just too weird even for California, it may be the work of the local **Cacophony Society**. Cacophony societies are loosely organized 'lodges', networks of fringe individuals that enjoy playing pranks on society at large. Comprised mainly of eccentrics who already behave outside the norm, their pranks include bizarre performance art, mass visits to weird places, guerrilla theater, and public hoaxes. They may create false flyers, alter billboards, or hold fake protest marches or fundraisers.

Cacophony Society www.cacophony.org

IT'S A GUY THING

Nothing gets the testosterone flowing like a good car crushing, which is exactly what you'll get at **Monster Truck Rallies** and Demolition Derbies. Events like these symbolize America's worship of motorized power and are, not surprisingly,

ART CARS

Art cars are vehicles that have been transformed into mobile, public folk-art, their owners merging their adoration for their car with their need to express themselves in a very public way. Art car events are quite the opposite of the testerone-driven pursuits described above. Steered by highly individualistic and artistic men and women, they slowly cruise the highways on their way to the dozens of art car parades held every year. There are several hundred art cars nationwide, and California is home to many of them. Some artists even dress like their cars (see this book's cover!). Anything on wheels, from unicycles to lawnmowers, can be decked out and join the parades. Log on to the art car websites below to find out about art car parades and events in the state.

Art Cars www.artcarworld.com, www.artcarfest.com, and artcaragency.com

almost exclusively male domains. With names like Bigfoot, Grave Digger, and King Krunch, monster trucks are preposterously modified, 4WD vehicles that compete by driving off an elevated ramp and seeing how many cars they can crush beneath them before grinding to a stop. The truck body sits way, way up on top of tyres 6ft high and almost 4ft wide. They're towed to stadium racetracks where they battle it out for superiority. Between 15 and 25 cars are crushed during the average rally, an event attended by tens of thousands of rabid fans. The resulting auto carnage leaves the stadium looking like a cross between a battlefield and a junkyard, which is where the crushed cars came from in the first place.

Dubbed 'legal road rage', **Demolition Derbies** are carnage of a different kind, the place to smash, crash, wreck, and otherwise destroy, junk cars that no longer have any business being on the road. Dozens of these events are held statewide each year during which drivers bump, ram, and hammer their cars into each other until only one vehicle is left operating. To begin, drivers line up their cars in a circle on a dirt field surrounded by a 4ft-high wall of mud. As the siren sounds, the cars begin crashing into each other and the air is filled with the sound of satisfying crunches. Auto parts fly everywhere as, one by one, the cars bite the dust. Helmets and seat belts are the only safety requirements for these modern-day gladiators. Good sense is optional.

Monster Truck Rallies www.truckworld.com/mtra

Demolition Derbies www.DENTUSA.com

The **Hobby Club of California** website puts you in touch with an amazing number of California clubs devoted to train, plane, car, boat, and rocket hobbyists. For example, the Bay Area Garden Railway Society consists of 450 families proud to boast, 'We play with large-scale trains in the garden'. There are clubs for fans of rocket launchers, radio-controlled jets, barnstormer aircraft, soaring, slot car racing, radio-controlled boats, and 4WD sedan racing.

Hobby Club of California www.rcsource.hobbypeople.net/ link/clb_ca.htm

With five branches in California, the **National Woodie Club** honors those wood-sided wagons, convertibles, sedans and trucks so popular in the 50s. The San Diego branch hosts Wavecrest, the largest woodie meet in the country. Held every September in Encinitas, it brings 300 woodie lovers together for a weekend of car and surf fun.

National Woodie Club www.nationalwoodieclub.com

CORPORATE KUDOS

You wouldn't normally associate 'quirky' with 'corporate' but in the case of **Hampton Inns & Hotels**, you'd have to make an exception. This hotel chain, part of the Hilton family, has made it its mission to renovate and preserve roadside landmarks all across America. Dubbed '**Save-A-Landmark**', the program was launched in 2000 as a way to bring the 1,000 Hampton Hotels together on a single-focused, service-oriented cause. They identified hundreds of beloved American landmarks – historical, fun, and cultural – in need of repair, most of them built in the 30s, 40s, and 50s. A million dollars later, they're making a real difference, fixing up icon after icon. Inn employees and volunteers do the actual work. In 2003 they turned their attention to Route 66, fixing up landmarks in eight states and donating 100 route markers.

The corporation also has a fondness for festivals and events, maintaining a comprehensive website, '**Year of 1,000 Weekends**', of the most unique, entertaining, quirky, educational and enjoyable events happening each weekend in cities and towns across America. Organizing them into ten different categories of interest, the most eccentric events can be found in the 'really different' section of the website.

Save A Landmark Hampton Inn www.hamptoninn.com/landmarks

Hampton's Year of 1,000 Weekends www.hamptoninnnweekends.com

Appendix 1

NUTS & BOLTS
Getting around the state

Getting around the Golden State is easy as long as you do as the natives do – drive. There's really no other choice as public transportation, widely heralded but seldom built, is limited mostly to the core of a few cities. The state was a dream come true for the automobile, coming of age in mid-century as Americans took to the road in their Fords and Chevys. Today the car is even more revered than it was when giant oranges, tepee motels, and dinosaurs defined roadside architecture.

Driving

Driving here is both a sport and a strategy requiring quick reflexes and planning skills. While you won't be dodging livestock or passing overburdened trucks on blind curves, you will be challenged by drivers distracted by kids, phones, and lattes as well as by monumental traffic jams, abrupt lane changes, incomprehensible interchanges, directional signs that require knowledge of the geography ahead, unexpected on-ramps, unmanned toll booths, and gas stations with employees that haven't a clue where they, or you, are. So here are a few tips on driving in this oasis of oddity.

Traffic – timing is everything

California drivers don't measure distance in miles. They measure it in minutes, carefully calculating the time it takes to get where they're going. Three of the country's most congested regions are in California: the San Francisco Bay area, the Los Angeles/Riverside area, and the San Diego/Long Beach region. (Outside of these areas traffic isn't all that horrendous and, in some cases, it's hardly a consideration.) Fortunately, most of the eccentricities in this guide – outside of the cities, that is – are located where they won't bother anybody, namely out in traffic-free boondocks.

In congested regions, however, your best chance for avoiding heavy weekday traffic is from about 9am until 2pm. This is your window of opportunity to transition from one area to another without spending too many hours doing so. Miss this window and your next chance is after 7pm. Or you could try leaving around 5 in the morning. This is not to say you shouldn't drive at peak times; just be prepared with an empty bladder and a full IPod.

Weekends require a different strategy. For example, heading to the beach on a hot day takes some planning. Spontaneously deciding to go at noon will likely mean arriving hours later cranky and irritable, assuming you ever do find a place to park. Getting back that evening will prove equally problematic, so it's best to plan ahead, if not to beat traffic, at least to join it before it becomes gridlocked.

Ditto heading out of the city for a weekend away. Traffic begins early Friday afternoon, with return traffic becoming positively brutal on Sunday evening. If you can, avoid the getaway crush by traveling longer distances at more leisurely times, all the while anticipating congestion at peak times up the road. Ski weekends can turn into traffic jams you'll be telling future generations about if both the weather and the traffic conspire against you, so leave with a plan and be prepared for the unexpected.

Holidays require even more strategizing as America's three-day holidays often morph into five-day excursions. Most major holidays fall on Mondays, meaning that the rush to leave can start as early as Thursday, peaking on Friday. The return crush can extend from Monday afternoon and evening all the way into Tuesday.

If you have a phone in the car, you can call 511, the traffic and weather advisory number. This amazing free service will guide you, using voice prompts, through a menu of options including precise, up-to-the-minute reports on traffic conditions, average speeds, and accident locations for where you are and for where you're going.

Directions/maps/gasoline/tolls

Know where you're going and use good, local maps. A map of the whole state will give you a nice overview, but it's like looking at the earth from space when it comes to helping you navigate busy freeways. In southern California you'll need a Los Angeles/Orange County map and another one of the San Diego area. They refer to freeways down there by name as well as by number so be sure to identify both on the map. Get a separate San Francisco Bay Area map too, although up there they refer to freeways more by number than by name.

Road signs, entrances, and exits often refer simply to a city ahead, sadly neglecting to point out the direction as well. Thus it helps to know, for example, when heading up to the wine country from San Francisco, that you need the freeway toward 'Eureka', a town almost at the Oregon border. You'll actually be on 101 North, but good luck trying to figure that out from the signage. You need to be especially alert navigating the Los Angeles freeways as the interchanges are unforgiving if you've failed to plan ahead and get in the correct lane well in advance.

If you need directions while on surface streets, ask just about anyone except the clerk behind the counter in a gas station. For some inexplicable reason most such employees haven't a clue where they are. Anyone standing in line, however, will likely be able to point you where you need to go. If you don't see a gas station, just look for anyone, anywhere, who looks local. Folks love to help strangers bearing maps. They may even offer to have you follow them. If you need directions on the freeway – and do this *only* if you're bumper to bumper – roll down your window and ask someone who looks friendly. Maybe they'll stop reading their paper or putting on their makeup long enough to give you some advice.

If you're not an American you're probably in shock at how low gas prices are. If you are, you're reeling at how prices have skyrocketed.

Always keep quarters and small bills on hand for tolls. While the majority of roadways and freeways are toll-free, the bridges are not and will cost anywhere from a dollar to five dollars to cross. The Los Angeles area has some private toll roads that will cost you as well. Most toll crossings have manned booths, usually with lines of cars, where you can pay the toll and ask for directions if need be. While you're waiting you can watch those with Fast Pass, an electronic toll device, sail through unmanned booths, their tolls being automatically deducted from pre-paid accounts. But if you go through one of those unmanned lanes without a Fast Pass you'll be liable for fines and penalties. On some of the private toll roads the booths are always unmanned and you'll need a pile of quarters to exit without penalty.

Car rental agencies

Enterprise Rental Car ℓ 1-800-261-7331; www.enterprise.com. Unlike other rental car companies, they'll pick you up and the rates are often cheaper than the big companies.
Alamo ℓ 1-800-462-5266 www.alamo.com
National ℓ 1-800-CAR-RENT; www.nationalcar.com
Avis ℓ 1-800-230-4898; www.avis.com
Hertz ℓ 1800-654-3131; www.hertz.com

Telephones

America runs on cell phone use and the easiest way to have a smooth trip is to have one with you. You can usually rent one along with your car or you can buy pre-paid, disposable cell phones. Public pay phones have practically disappeared as they're simply too expensive for the sponsoring companies to maintain. If you need to phone ahead, and don't have a phone of your own, show someone the number you need to call and ask if they'd be willing to make the call for you. It helps if it's really obvious that you're a tourist, so wear your most trusting face and be sure your maps are sticking out of the back pocket of your Bermuda shorts. You can offer to pay, but with today's calling plans even long-distance usually won't cost the owner anything.

Should you have to dial a number by yourself, all long distance calls, meaning those out of the three-digit area code you're in, require you to first dial a one (1), then the area code (three digits), then the seven digit number.

Accommodation: hotels/motels/B&Bs

If you can't make it to one of the delightfully daft accommodations reviewed in this guide, then you'll likely be relying on roadside stops. You'll get plenty of notice of what's available up ahead as billboards will start alerting you a hundred or more miles in advance. Hotels are mostly around cities and airports; motels more abundant everywhere travelers stop. As soon as you've targeted your stop for the night, call the hotel/motel and reserve your room with a credit card. If you wait too long they may be sold out. Bed and breakfasts in America are more luxurious and pricey than their European counterparts and need to be reserved in advance of your planned stay. You'll need a separate guidebook to find them as they don't advertise along the highways.

Weather

Tourists show up in California wearing the most outlandish clothing. (They must get their weather reports from watching reruns of *Baywatch* or *OC*.) Contrary to popular belief, the state does have seasons and weather ranging from bitter cold to excruciatingly hot, often during a single visit. Basically you can expect mild to hot weather in the southern part of the state; cool, often cloudy weather around the Bay Area; and then a variety ranging from quite hot to quite cold, with snow in the mountains during the winter, in the rest of the state. The rainy season runs from October through April. Dress in layers and bring at least one pair of grownup long pants and a sweater or jacket. At least you won't have to buy a sweatshirt at Fisherman's Wharf that proclaims your ignorance.

Alternate transportation

Besides driving, transitioning from one part of the state to another can best be accomplished by air or, in rare instances, by Amtrak. Air is by far the fastest and most convenient option. Once you land, just rent your car and hit the road once again. If you have the time, Amtrak's Coast Starlight train runs both directions between Oakland (near San Francisco) and Los Angeles, taking a leisurely 12 hours to get you from one place to the next. You can also get from the central coast to San Diego on the Pacific Surfliner in about six hours.

Amtrak ✆ 800 USA-RAIL (800 872-7245); www.amtrak.com

Airlines

Southwest Airlines (✆ 1-800-I-FLY-SWA® (800-435-9792); www.southwest.com) serves the state admirably well between northern and southern California. They're the only airline with a reasonable refund/change policy.

You'll find the best fare comparisons among the other airlines at www.orbitz.com or www.travelocity.com

The Bay area: public transportation/parking

San Francisco proper is the one place in the state where it's best to leave the car at the hotel during your eccentric explorations. Parking is extremely expensive and driving from neighborhood to neighborhood can be nerve-racking, mainly because your travel companion will be slamming on imaginary brakes each time you crest one of the city's very steep hills. Buses and streetcars are plentiful and BART (Bay Area Rapid Transit) runs smoothly both underground and above. You can take taxis as well.

BART can also take you to suburban cities in the South Bay (Silicon Valley) and the East Bay (Alameda and Contra Costa counties). This includes Berkeley where arrival by public transportation will earn you respect to compensate for the scorn they'll heap on you for wearing politically incorrect clothing, eating anything at all besides seeds and berries, and carrying your Telegraph Avenue souvenirs home in anything other than your own cloth bag.

For a summary of all public transportation options, including ferries, Caltrain, BART, Muni, and all bus systems: www.sfgate.com/traveler/guide/transportation/publictrans.shtml

Los Angeles: public transportation

Los Angeles has a surprisingly comprehensive public transportation system of buses and subways, but you'll still need to get from your stop to your destination. In some cases the system will work fine for you. In many others, though, you'll probably prefer to drive yourself. Parking can range from plentiful to scarce depending upon where you are.

Public transportation is quite convenient if you're staying downtown or along the routes to Little Tokyo, Chinatown, Korea Town, Hollywood, Thai Town, Beverly Hills, Santa Monica, and the beach between Venice and Santa Monica Pier.

For maps of the transportation system: www.experiencela.com/GA.html.

Appendix

FURTHER READING
California-specific guides

San Francisco As You Like It: *23 Tailor-Made Tours for Culture Vultures, Shopaholics, Neo-Bohemians, Famished Foodies, Savvy Natives & Everyone Else*, Bonnie Wach, Ulysses Press, 2004. A great companion guide to Eccentric America.

Frommers Irreverent Guide to San Francisco, 5th Edition, Matthew Richard Poole, Frommers, 2004. A classic companion.

The Xenophobe's Guide to the Californians, Anthony Marais, Oval Projects, LTD, 2000. Frank, irreverent, funny and surprisingly useful if you want to understand California quirkiness.

Avant-Guide San Francisco, Dan Levine, Empire Press, 2003. Covers the hip and stylish, including restaurants, nightclubs and hotels.

Southern California Car Culture Landmarks, AAA Western Travel Publications, 2001. Laminated map and guide of sites like diners, drive-ins, motels, and giant-object buildings.

The Mad Monks' Guide to California, James Crotty and Michael Lane (The Monks), Frommers/Macmillan, 2000. These guys tell it like it really is.

Lonely Planet San Francisco, Richard Sterling and Tom Downs, Lonely Planet Publications, 2004.

Lonely Planet California, Andrea Schulte-Peevers, 2003.

Lonely Planet Los Angeles, Andrea Schulte-Peevers, 2001. Good, basic guides with lots of lively anecdotes.

Fun With the Family in Southern California, Laura Kath, Globe Pequot, 2003.

Fun With the Family in Northern California, Karen Misuraca, Globe Pequot, 2003. No more bored kids.

Southern California Off the Beaten Path, Katy Strong, Globe Pequot, 2003.

Northern California Off the Beaten Path, Mark Williams, Globe Pequot, 2004.

San Francisco Off the Beaten Path, Michael Petrocelli, Globe Pequot, 2003. Getting to hidden, unspoiled and out-of-the-way places.

San Francisco Bizarro: *A Guide to Notorious Sights, Lusty Pursuits and Downright Freakiness in the City by the Bay*, Jack Boulware, St Martin's Press, 2000. A look at the very bizarre side of the city.

LA Bizarro: *The Insider's Guide to the Obscure, the Absurd, and the Perverse in Los Angeles*, Anthony R Lovett and Matt Maranian, St Martin's Press, 1997. Another look at the very bizarre.

OffBeat Overnights: *A Guide to the Most Unusual Places to Stay in California*, Lucy Poshek, Rutledge Hill Press, 2000.

The Great San Francisco Trivia and Fact Book, Janet Bailey, Cumberland House, 1999.

California Travelers' Trivia: Historic and Contemporary: *Fabulous Firsts, Fascinating Facts, Legendary Lore, One-of-a-Kind Oddities, Tantalizing Trivia*, Bob Carter, Falcon, 2001.

Guides with California references

Let's Go Buggy! *The Ultimate Family Guide to Insect Zoos and Butterfly Houses,* Troy Corley, Corley Publications, 2002.

Route 66: The Best of the Mother Road, a Greatest Hits Maps by AAA.

OffBeat Food: *Adventures in an Omnivorous World*, Alan Ridenour, Santa Monica Press, 2000.

Roadfood: *The Coast-to-Coast Guide to 500 of the Best Barbeque Joints, Lobster Shacks, Ice-Cream Parlors, Highway Diners, and Much More*, Jane Stern, Broadway, 2002.

Roadtrip, USA: *Cross-Country Adventures on America's Two-Lane Highways*, Jamie Jensen, Avalon Travel Publishing, 2002.

USA by Rail, John Pitt, Bradt Travel Guides, 2003.

Watch it Made in the USA: *A Visitor's Guide to the Companies that Make your Favorite Products*, Karen Axelrod and Bruce Brumbert, Avalon Travel Publications, October, 2002.

America Bizarro: *A Guide to Freaky Festivals, Groovy Gatherings, Kooky Contests and other Strange Happenings Across the USA*, Nelson Taylor, St Martin's Griffen, 2000.

Weird US: *23 23 Guide to America's Local Legends and Best Kept Secrets*, Mark Sceurman, Barnes & Noble Books, 2004.

Eccentric reading

The Banana Sculptor, the Purple Lady, and the All Night Swimmer: *Hobbies, Collecting, and Other Passionate Pursuits*, Susan Sheehan and Howard Means, Simon & Schuster, 2002.

Eccentrics: A study of Sanity and Strangeness, Dr David Weeks, Villard Books, 1996.

The Good, the Bad, and the Mad: *Weird People in American History*, E Randall Floyd, Harbor House, 1999.

Why People Believe Weird Things, Michael Shermer, W H Freeman, 1997.

Holding On: Dreamers, Visionaries, Eccentrics and Other American Heroes, David Isay and Harvey Wang, W W Norton and Company, 1997.

How to Talk American: *A Guide to our Native Tongues*, Jim 'the Mad Monk' Crotty, Houghton Mifflin Company, 1997.

Little Museums: *Over 1,000 Small (and Not-So-Small) American Showplaces*, Lynne Arany and Archie23bson, Henry Holt and Company, 1998.

The Museum of Hoaxes, Alex Boese, E P Dutton, 2002.

Quack! *Tales of Medical Fraud from the Museum of Questionable Medical Devices*, Bob McCoy, Santa Monica Press, 2000.

Wacky Chicks: *Life Lessons from Fearlessly Inappropriate and Fabulously Eccentric Women*, Simon Doonan, Simon & Schuster, 2003.

Bradt Travel Guides

Africa by Road Charlie Shackell/Illya Bracht
Albania Gillian Gloyer
Amazon, The Roger Harris/Peter Hutchison
Antarctica: A Guide to the Wildlife
   Tony Soper/Dafila Scott
Arctic: A Guide to Coastal Wildlife
   Tony Soper/Dan Powell
Armenia with Nagorno Karabagh Nicholas Holding
Azores David Sayers
Baghdad Catherine Arnold
Baltic Capitals: Tallinn, Riga, Vilnius, Kaliningrad
   Neil Taylor et al
Bosnia & Herzegovina Tim Clancy
Botswana: Okavango, Chobe, Northern Kalahari
   Chris McIntyre
British Isles: Wildlife of Coastal Waters
   Tony Soper/Dan Powell
Budapest Adrian Phillips/Jo Scotchmer
Cameroon Ben West
Canada: North – Yukon, Northwest Territories,
   Nunavut Geoffrey Roy
Cape Verde Islands Aisling Irwin/
   Colum Wilson
Cayman Islands Tricia Hayne
Chile Tim Burford
Chile & Argentina: Trekking Guide
   Tim Burford
Cork Linda Fallon
Croatia Piers Letcher
Dubrovnik Piers Letcher
East & Southern Africa: The Backpacker's Manual
   Philip Briggs
Eccentric America Jan Friedman
Eccentric Britain Benedict le Vay
Eccentric California Jan Friedman
Eccentric Edinburgh Benedict le Vay
Eccentric France Piers Letcher
Eccentric London Benedict le Vay
Eccentric Oxford Benedict le Vay
Ecuador: Climbing & Hiking in
   Rob Rachowiecki/Mark Thurber
Eritrea Edward Denison/Edward Paice
Estonia Neil Taylor
Ethiopia Philip Briggs
Falkland Islands Will Wagstaff
Faroe Islands James Proctor
Gabon, São Tome & Príncipe Sophie Warne
Galápagos Wildlife David Horwell/Pete Oxford
Gambia, The Craig Emms/Linda Barnett
Georgia with Armenia Tim Burford
Ghana Philip Briggs
Hungary Adrian Phillips/Jo Scotchmer
Iran Patricia L Baker
Iraq Karen Dabrowska
Kabul Dominic Medley/Jude Barrand

Kenya Claire Foottit
Kiev Andrew Evans
Latvia Stephen Baister/Chris Patrick
Lille Laurence Phillips
Lithuania Gordon McLachlan
Ljubljana Robin & Jenny McKelvie
Macedonia Thammy Evans
Madagascar Hilary Bradt
Madagascar Wildlife Nick Garbutt/
   Hilary Bradt/Derek Schuurman
Malawi Philip Briggs
Maldives Royston Ellis
Mali Ross Velton
Mauritius, Rodrigues & Réunion Royston Ellis/
   Alex Richards/Derek Schuurman
Mongolia Jane Blunden
Montenegro Annalisa Rellie
Mozambique Philip Briggs/Ross Velton
Namibia Chris McIntyre
Nigeria Lizzie Williams
North Cyprus Diana Darke
North Korea Robert Willoughby
Palestine, with Jerusalem Henry Stedman
Panama Sarah Woods
Paris, Lille & Brussels: Eurostar Cities
   Laurence Phillips
Peru & Bolivia: Backpacking and Trekking
   Hilary Bradt/Kathy Jarvis
Riga Stephen Baister/Chris Patrick
River Thames, In the Footsteps of the Famous
   Paul Goldsack
Rwanda Janice Booth/Philip Briggs
St Helena, Ascension, Tristan da Cunha
   Sue Steiner
Serbia Laurence Mitchell
Seychelles Lyn Mair/Lynnath Beckley
Slovenia Robin & Jenny McKelvie
South Africa: Budget Travel Guide Paul Ash
Southern African Wildlife Mike Unwin
Sri Lanka Royston Ellis
Sudan Paul Clammer
Svalbard Andreas Umbreit
Switzerland: Rail, Road, Lake Anthony Lambert
Tallinn Neil Taylor
Tanzania Philip Briggs
Tasmania Matthew Brace
Tibet Michael Buckley
Uganda Philip Briggs
Ukraine Andrew Evans
USA by Rail John Pitt
Venezuela Hilary Dunsterville Branch
Your Child Abroad Dr Jane Wilson-Howarth/
   Dr Matthew Ellis
Zambia Chris McIntyre
Zanzibar David Else

Bradt guides are available from all good bookshops, or by post, phone or internet direct from:
Bradt Travel Guides, 23 High Street, Chalfont St Peter, Bucks SL9 9QE, UK
Tel: +44 (0)1753 893444   Fax: +44 (0)1753 892333
info@bradtguides.com   www.bradtguides.com

Index